THE NORTH AMERICAN SMALL & BIG GAME HUNTING SMART HANDBOOK

By Bob Banfelder

BONUS FEATURE

HUNTING AFRICA'S & AUSTRALIA'S MOST DANGEROUS BIG GAME LAND ANIMALS

Meet big game hunters on safari—employing rifles and handguns—who have dispatched Africa's and Australia's most dangerous big game animals. These adventurous men have generously contributed their stories and photographs for this handbook. Whatever your present level of proficiency, you will benefit from their extensive experiences and vast knowledge of heavy calibers, cartridges, bullet designs, and firearms.

AFRICA

elephant ~ rhinoceros ~ hippopotamus ~ Cape buffalo ~ lion ~ leopard

AUSTRALIA

banteng ~ water buffalo

Broadwater Books
Riverhead, New York

Copyright© 2016 Robert Banfelder

All Rights Reserved
No part of this publication may be reproduced, distributed, or transmitted in any form or by any means, or stored in a database or retrieval system, without prior permission of the publisher.

Broadwater Books
141 Riverside Drive
Riverhead, New York 11901

www.robertbanfelder.com

ISBN: 978-0-9915912-7-5

Printed in the United States of America

Tom Turkey photo compliments of Chris Paparo

DEDICATION

For the past forty-four years, Donna Derasmo has been my soul mate and outdoors partner. The time I have spent enjoying the outdoors with Donna has made those moments most memorable.

ACKNOWLEDGEMENTS

Acknowledgments for a work that covers a span of sixty years can be a daunting endeavor, for I must delve deep into my memory bank to recall all those fabulous folks who have helped me course a winding path through forests and fields in order to bring this handbook to you: authors, ballistic experts, range officers, photographers, columnists, authoritative safari hunters, and marketing folks. Their names would fill several pages. What to do? Well, in order for those acknowledgments not to overwhelm and detract from my intended purpose, I decided to thank all those who have had the *most* impact on the course of my successes.

Of course, there is the fear of forgetting to name a special someone who had contributed in helping this hunting fanatic see this work come to full fruition. Therefore, if you fail to note your name listed below, take solace in realizing that my apology is sincere.

Ron Atkinson, Jason Banfelder, Ken Birmingham, Stephen D. Carpenteri, Roger Casterline, Ron Cormier, Donna Derasmo, David Lee Fulton, Ron Guidice, Iain Harrison, Marshall & Jason Hill, John Mandrafina, Amy Miller, Nick McCabe, Ron & Diane McGee, Wayne W. Nester, Mary Ashley O'Reilly, Chris Paparo, Randy Parks, Angelo Peluso, Rob Pollifrone, Joe Privitera, Jeff Puckett, Ed Scalice, Dan Schmidt, Luce Skrabanek, Dennis Weinand, Rock Wilson.

My deep gratitude goes to those men who have contributed their big game hunting stories and photographs for this publication: Mark Hampton, J.D. Jones, Michael McCourry, Leon Munyan, Larry C. Rogers, M.D.

My special thanks to J.D. Jones for being instrumental in bringing his fellow hunters on board for this publication.

AUTHOR'S NOTE

Except for one quality name-brand product model featured in this book, all others are currently available as cited at the time of printing. Manufacturers continuously improve and update their products, resulting in previous models being discontinued. For example, Bushnell's quality Legend 1200 ARC laser rangefinder for both gun and bow modes has been replaced with Bushnell's comparable Scout DX 1000 ARC rangefinder. If a model is no longer available, prospective purchasers should research newer models of similar quality under the brand-name(s) discussed herein so as to ensure confidence and consumer satisfaction.

CONTENTS

Chapter		Page
1	The Ultimate Shooting Bag Rest Systems	1
2	Boresighting	8
3	Zeroing Iron Sights Made Easy	10
4	Zeroing In Optics Made Easy	13
5	MOA (Minute Of Angle) Clearly Explained	19
6	Everything You Will Need for the Shooting Range	24
7	Gun Cleaning and Care	29
8	Selecting Hunting Clothing, Footwear & Accessories for All Seasons	33
9	Virginia Whitetail Hunting Strategies	42
10	Archery & Gunning Stands	52
11	Wisely Selecting the Proper Compound Bow	56
12	All Broadheads Are Not Created Equal—Not By A Long Shot —>	61
13	Arrow Shafts, Arrow Releases, Arrow Rests, Sight Pins	64
14	Crossbows vs. Traditional Bows	69
15	Manufactured & Natural Ground Blinds	76
16	Processing Your Deer	79
17	Long Island Whitetail Hunting Opportunities	89
18	Shotguns	92
19	Migratory Waterfowl	95
20	Hunting Diminutive Marsh Birds	107
21	Top-Flight Upland Action	110
22	Wild Boar & Other Game	123
23	Elk Hunting	126
24	Moose Hunting the Canadian Northwest Territory	129
25	Explaining Rifle Calibers, Cartridges & Confusion	132
26	Black & Brown Bear (Grizzly)	139
27	Handguns	141
28	Hunting Vermin with an Air Rifle	151
29	Holographic Sights for High-Powered Rifle Cartridges	155
30	Hunting Small Game, Predators, Varmints/Pests	161
31	Gourmet Game Recipes	170
32	Africa's Largest of the Six Most Dangerous Big Game Animals	178
33	Africa's Second Largest of the Six Most Dangerous Big Game Animals	188
34	Africa's Third Largest of the Six Most Dangerous Big Game Animals	195
35	Africa's Fourth Largest of the Six Most Dangerous Big Game Animals	199
36	Africa's Fifth Largest of the Six Most Dangerous Big Game Animals	205
37	Africa's Smallest of the Six Most Dangerous Big Game Animals	212
38	Australia's Bad-To-The-Bone Bovines	219

CHAPTER 1

THE ULTIMATE SHOOTING BAG REST SYSTEMS

The key to consistent bullet placement—meaning perpetually shooting tight groups—is analogous to the prevailing mantra referencing real estate: location, location, location. And where is that location? It is in the black of the bull's-eye. Or is it just anywhere in the black of the bull's-eye? We'll return to that question in a moment.

The key to putting one bullet after another through virtually the same hole (often referred to as a cloverleaf pattern) comes with practice, practice, practice. This is generally attained by using a shooting rest comprised of bags filled with sand, lead, organic media, et cetera, and set upon a flat surface. Sometimes expensive shooting tables coupled with equally expensive metal mechanical devices are employed to lock the firearm in place. But what generally happens is that when the shooter transitions from a firing range to a hunting scenario, although he or she may harvest the animal sought (sometimes only marginally), bullet placement was not precisely executed as when that person had been practicing earlier. Why? There are, of course, a multitude of factors that can throw one's shot off the mark, and sometimes more than just fractionally. What likely happened is that the shooter's point of impact changed because he or she transited from the relatively flat plane at the outdoor shooting range to uneven terrain—be it shooting uphill, downhill, or from a treestand—coupled to the fact that virtually all shooting systems perform differently at the shooting range than in the field when hunting. Not necessarily so with the portable shooting bag rest systems to which you are about to be introduced. Not that you'll *normally* be employing such aids afield; however, in certain instances you might. We'll examine those situations, too. Executing tight groups is all about consistency, both at the range and hunting afield. In short order you will begin to understand that practicing with a shooting rest bag system at the range is more akin to hunting afield than with other types of devices. It is one thing to be in the black of the bull's-eye. It's quite another to be in the bull's-eye's **center ring**, each and every time.

Kind of like counting say a seven-piece cookware set, in which you may receive four pots and three covers (one item being a topless skillet), the X7 Bulls Bag Shooting Rest System is comprised of three to five separate shooting rest bags. Two detachable zippered side sleeves each contain two fully-functional bags; that is, one regular rectangular bag measuring 10 inches long by 3½ inches wide by 5 inches high, and one alier-style (owl/rabbit ear) bag measuring 10 inches long by 3½ inches wide by 5 inches high—with a tapered middle 2-inch depth conforming to the alier design.

The top bag that sits upon the four contained bags is a detachable dual 10-inch long by 3¼-inch diameter log-shaped suede support that forms a channel. This bag securely holds and locks the others firmly together via wide bands of heavy-duty Velcro, which completes the 32-pound package. The bags' outer surfaces are covered with a durable 2 millimeter PVC coating for preeminent moisture resistance. Its double-seam construction promises many years of reliable service. This is by no means a cheap, lightweight shooting rest but rather a solidly constructed shooting system that comes with a lifetime guarantee against manufacturer defects.

X7 Bulls Bag (seven piece) Shooting Bag Rest System

Unlike my quasi seven-piece cookware set analogy, the zippered compartment bags containing the two pairs of bags cited above may serve as one separate fully-functional bag with a cradle height of 7½ inches. Ostensibly, you *do* have seven bags. If you begin to play with the aforementioned dimensions in your mind, you begin to realize that you can configure these bags to fit virtually any shooting situation that suits your fancy. All-in-all, you can configure fifty-plus shooting rest arrangements.

Also, keep in mind that you can accommodate many shooting techniques from practically any type of terrain. Talk about versatility in a shooting- rest system.

The X7 Bulls Bag Shooting Bag Rest System is the ultimate stable shooting platform for *any* action firearm: single and/or double action, bolt, pump, lever, semiautomatic, automatic; anything from zeroing in a pistol or revolver, patterning a shotgun, sighting in a slug gun, delivering deadly long-range shots with a high-powered caliber rifle, an assault rifle with extended magazine, right down to a precision pellet air rifle.

X7 Bulls Bag Shooting Bag Rest System & Thompson/Center .50 caliber Encore 209 x 50 Magnum muzzleloader with EOTech's XPS2-0 holographic sight

The X7 Bulls Bag is an all-in-one system arrangement that delivers unparalleled consistency and accuracy without changing bullet impact between the shooting range and the field. You are not going to be toting a metal shooting table/bench rest into the field. However, you can occasionally transport and configure select sections from X7's transportable arrangement. Example: For hunting from a solidly built unit, such as a shooting tower, you merely position (drape) the saddlebag configuration over the window frame's base then reposition the top dual log-shaped bag perpendicular to the saddlebags. Position your firearm into the suede channel, and you're good to go.

Let's begin to understand how this patented butterfly-grip design works with a long gun. You simply place and gently massage the forearm of your firearm into the top section of the 10-inch long, suede-cradled channel of your X7 Bulls Bag Shooting Rest. Next, separate the base (bottom) bags ever so slightly that they spread outward, thereby gripping and firmly locking the forearm into the vise-like but protected suede channel. It is just that simple. What you are doing is creating a glove-like hinged grip. Depending on the width of the firearm's forearm, you can easily widen the channel to accommodate virtually any weapon save a cannon as artillery pieces are not part of the program. Levity aside, this is one serious shooting-rest bag system for virtually every portable firearm.

Simply put, the physics involved is a weight and balance distribution formula. The engineering formula for matchless accuracy is stability. It is a hinge-design system offering a wide footprint for maximum forearm/barrel support, creating a vise-like gun grip. The high- and low-center-of-gravity profile, 20% above and 80% below, respectively, makes for maximum stability. From a precision pellet air rifle to a high caliber, heavy-duty barrel sniper rifle, you are good to go.

For handguns, you can simply separate then invert one of the side (saddle) bags, unzip the other and remove the rectangular bag, configuring a toe-and-heel arrangement. The handgun barrel is placed within the inverted 7½-inch high alier-style (owl/rabbit ear) bag to form the toe, and the 5½-inch high rectangular bag is placed behind it to form the heel. This literally takes only seconds to set up and start shooting.

Author set up with Thompson/Center .308 caliber Winchester Encore Pro Hunter pistol & X7 Bulls Bag Shooting Rest System

The X7 Bulls Bag Shooting Rest System is available filled or unfilled. I elected to purchase the already filled bags. The filled bags are solidly packed and securely double stitched. You won't have to bother shopping for ancillary tools then fill the bags with the proper recommended material: Tidy Cat Kitty Litter from Purina, play-school sand, and/or other items like polymers, walnut/corncob media, bird seed, rice, et cetera. Different bags take different materials, so rather than concern myself with these issues, I left it to the pros and had the bags properly filled and secured by the company. No fuss, no muss. The difference in price between the unfilled and filled bags is approximately $30 plus shipping. It's worth the extra cost. Models come in Law Enforcement Black as well as other colors and accoutrements such as a Rocky Mountain Elk camo pattern, Olive-Drab Green with webbing for cartridges, and D-rings. View the colors and models of the X7 Bulls Bag Shooting Bag Rest System online at www.bullsbag.com.

Why would anyone in the world purchase several different shooting rests for multiple firearms when a single system does it all? The probable answer is that a person started out with one type of shooting rest for one type of weapon and wound up with several rests over the course of years to accommodate all of his or her toys. Either that or those folks simply lived with the typical sandbag setup—mediocre at best because it cannot accomplish what the X7 Bulls Bag Shooting Rest System achieves. Not by a long shot (pun intended). The X7 butterfly system is patented and unparalleled, locking in your long gun within a protected suede vise-grip channel support for matchless accuracy and consistency.

At this point, you may be asking yourself: What is all this? Is it hyperbole (hype referencing advertising), or harmony (referencing the pleasing arrangement of parts)? We're talking here about the perfect union between a shooting-rest system, you, and your firearms. Let's digest who has bought into Bulls Bag Shooting Rest products over the course of the past twenty-plus years:

Endorsed by the National Tactical Officers Association (NTOA), Department of Defense (DOD), Special Operation troops, as well as many other law enforcement teams across the nation, this sanction speaks volumes as to the reliability and quality of Bulls Bag Shooting Rest products, inclusive of Uncle Bud's Bulls Bag 15-inch long, low-profile camo model with a 2-inch depth channel. Additionally, such firearm manufacturing companies as Browning Arms, Remington Arms, Winchester Repeating Arms Company, and Mossberg & Sons, just to name a few, have long praised Bulls Bag products. Under the CSS ™ guarantee, Bulls Bag makes a 500% promise that its shooting rest products will ". . . outperform all others by improving your group and accuracy every time." I can certainly attest to this, having employed both shooting-type rests in many configurations for all the firearm actions mentioned earlier. In fact, I have never before been as impressed with any firearms related product as I am with the Bulls Bags product line. Both the X7 Bulls Bag Shooting Rest System and Uncle Bud's Bulls Bag 15-inch long, low-profile rest come with detachable padded shoulder straps.

Heel/Toe Combo: Base section of the X7 Bulls Bag Shooting Rest System combined with Uncle Bud's Bulls Bag, exhibiting the author's Remington Arms .30-06 Springfield 742 Woodmaster semiautomatic with Redfield 3x–9x scope

There is no escaping Newton's third law of motion; that is, for every action, there is an opposite and equal reaction. Therefore, no shooting rest can counter that law by reducing recoil. However, some companies claim that their systems can do exactly that. They conveniently leave out the word "felt" from the phrase "felt-recoil." Some shooting rests can reduce felt-recoil. Other shooting rests, such as those made of metal, can magnify vibration. It's all about harmonics. Harmonics? What the heck is that? Let's take a quick look as to how harmonics (in this case vibration) play out in either of the Bulls Bag Shooting Rest System:

Both the X7 Bulls Bag Shooting Bag Rest System and the Uncle Bud's Bulls Bag absorb harmonic vibration into the bags, thereby reducing felt-recoil and muzzle jump. If you were to utilize a sheer metal shooting rest in lieu of an acoustically absorbent material to lock a firearm firmly in place when squeezing the trigger, you would intensify harmonic vibration; that is, felt-recoil, muzzle jump, and the noise (explosion) that goes along with it. In other words, you would be amplifying that sound and movement. In some cases, shooters have experienced cracked stocks and/or damaged optics.

Both the X7 Bulls Bag Shooting Rest System and the Uncle Bud's Bulls Bag are your benchmarks for accuracy and consistency. Bulls Bag products are made in the USA and, interestingly, shipped from Needmore, Pennsylvania. Actually, if you purchase both the Bulls Bag X7 Shooting Rest System and Uncle Bud's Bulls Bag you won't ever *need more*. They will be the last shooting rest bags you need ever buy. I have both products that I often use in a heel-and-toe configuration.

CHAPTER 2

BORESIGHTING

Boresighting is an adjustment method of pre-aligning a firearm barrel and its sights (whether iron [open] sights or optical sights), matching them up with a given target. The process expedites zeroing in for precise bullet strikes and will save you considerable ammunition. Otherwise, you will be homing in on the bull's-eye through a series of trial-and-error shots. There are, of course, tricks of the trade to finesse and fine-tune this achievement, which will be covered here as well as in subsequent chapters.

Recently, with a new (out of the box) precision German-made RWS Diana 34 T06 .22 caliber Classic air rifle, I put three pellets on paper in a cloverleaf pattern. Initially, I shot the group at 25 yards before zeroing in on the very center of the bull's-eye's **x**, then at 35 yards with the awesome aid of the Bulls Bag Shooting Rest System covered in Chapter 1. Boresighting wasn't really necessary for sighting in the gun at that distance. Besides, pellets are cheap as is .22 caliber ammunition. You can shoot all day for very little cost. However, shooting high-powered ammunition for the purpose of zeroing in, especially slug-gun ammo, can quickly add up to a significant dollar amount. Boresighting will save you beaucoup bucks.

Bolt-action firearms easily lend themselves to boresighting, for you simply remove the bolt, fix the firearm upon or within a stable platform, then line up the bore with the target by looking down the barrel, adjusting you sights (open or optical) accordingly. However, with all other firearm actions that impede peering down the barrel's bore, one must use a boresight tool (collimator). Modern laser boresight kits are the key to quick and initial homing-in accuracy. After considerable research, I found the ultimate Laser Boresight Ballistic Targeting System, offering both quality and value for virtually all of your firearms; for example, pistols and rifles for calibers ranging from .22 through .50; .50 caliber muzzleloaders; 20 and 12 gauge shotguns. The SiteLite 100 Mag Laser boresight is your ticket to primary accuracy.

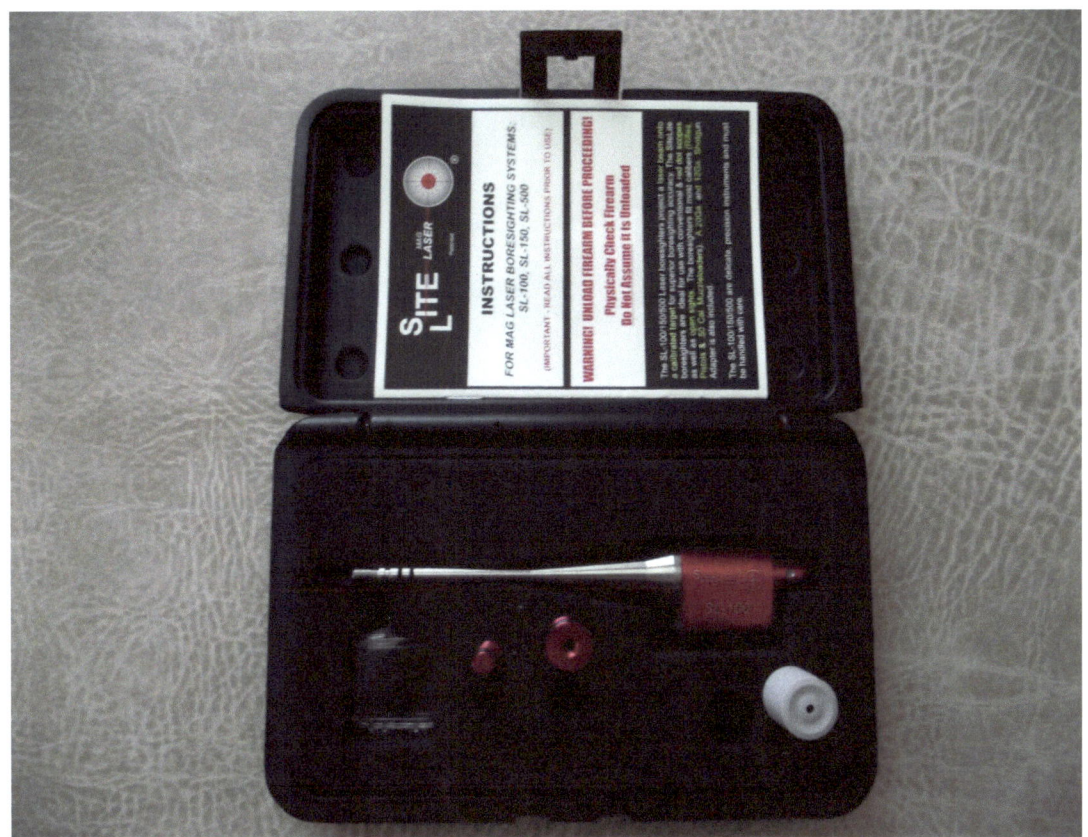

SiteLite Laser Boresighter

The kit contains thirteen (13) different size O-rings to accommodate a wide range of calibers and gauges: [.22 caliber; .243 caliber; 25 caliber to .270 caliber; .284 caliber (7mm) inclusive of .323 caliber (8mm) to .338 caliber; .308 caliber to .50 caliber; .35 caliber & 9mm; .375 caliber; .40 caliber, .44 caliber; .45 caliber; .50 caliber muzzleloader; 20 gauge shotgun; 12 gauge shotgun]. Also included in the kit are adapters, a scope reticle leveler, a calibrated scope alignment verification card, and an instruction booklet, which contains an O-ring matching-chart. Additionally, you will have access to SiteLite's Ballistic Targeting System Software Program to create a custom laser boresighting target for your specific rifle and ammunition, which can be saved on your computer.

The visual red-laser image is good out to a distance of 300 yards in low-light to darkened conditions and operates on two button-cell 303/ 357 batteries for up to one hour. The laser boresight has a lifetime warranty, valid for the original owner. Two other laser kits (the SL 150 and the SL 500) are available and offer increased laser power and battery life. For the average hunter, the SL 100 more than suffices. Good to go for iron, crosshairs, red dot (LED), and holographic (laser) sights. For further information, visit www.sitelite-lasers.com.

CHAPTER 3

ZEROING IRON SIGHTS MADE EASY

Iron sights (also referred to as open sights) are, obviously, less accurate at greater distances than optical aids such as a telescopic sight, a red dot scope, or a holographic sight. Generally, your rifle or handgun has a fixed post, blade, or bead for a front sight and an adjustable rear sight, which may be raised or lowered for elevation [up-and-down movement], as well as left or right adjustments for windage [side-to-side movement]. On some firearms, the front sight may also be adjustable; however, we'll keep things simple by sighting in firearms with stationary front sights and adjustable rear sights for both elevation and windage. Sight alignment is simply a matter of aligning and leveling the top of the front sight between the top edges of the rear sight. That's our sight picture. It's about as simple as things get.

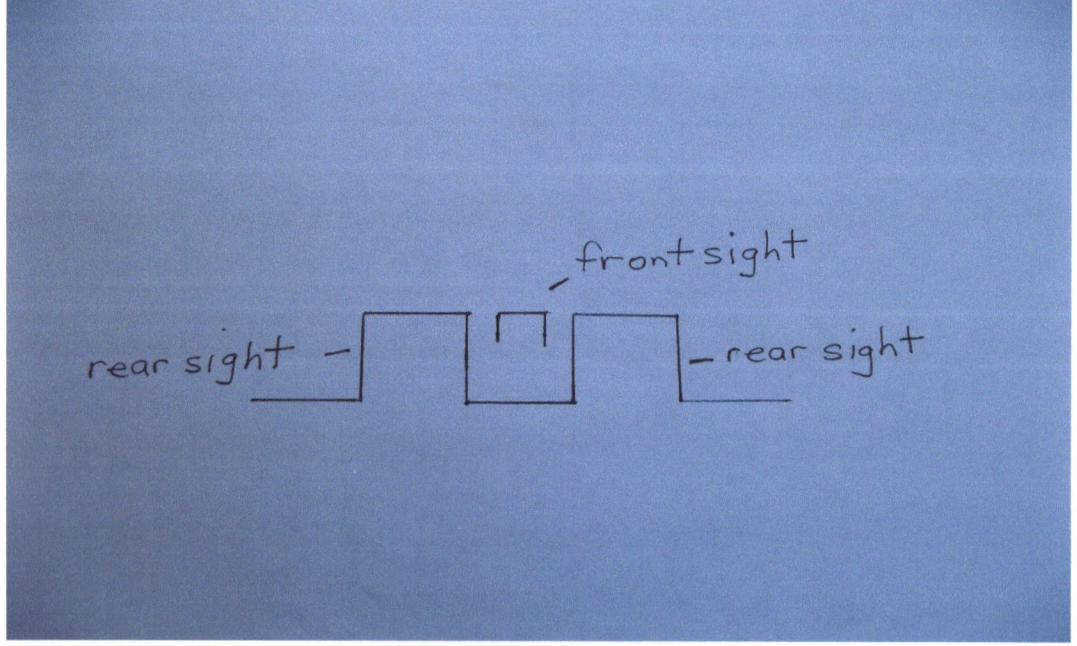

Diagram of Open Sights

Initially, zeroing in may not be as simple as it sounds for the beginner. Actually, sighting in may range from *complicated* to downright *confusing*. Therefore, we'll take this one step at a time.

For example, if your point of aim is the bull's-eye (which of course it should be) but you are hitting low on the target, you obviously need to come up. In order to come up, you must lower [not raise] your rear sight so as to hit higher on the target.

Conversely, if you are hitting high on the target, you obviously need to come down. In order to come down, you must raise [not lower] your rear sight so as to hit lower on the target.

Similarly, if you are hitting to the right of the target, you obviously need to come left. In order to come left, you must move your rear sight to the right [not left] so as to hit to the left of the target.

If you are hitting to the left of the target, you obviously need to come right. In order to come right, you must move your rear sight to the left [not right] so as to hit to the right of the target.

In other words, you are moving your rear sight in the opposite direction that you want the projectile to travel: up or down for elevation; left or right referencing windage. Consult your owner's manual to learn how to adjust your rear sight for elevation and windage.

A single bullet fired from your weapon at a target is not necessarily going to tell you in what direction to move your sights. Several shots at the same point of aim, meaning the bull's-eye, will speak volumes. Are your shots all over the target, or are they grouped closely together? If the former is the case, it is likely the operator's fault and not that of the firearm. If the latter is the case, it is the alignment of the firearm that needs adjustment(s) as explained above.

Ready for a quiz? Good.

You are shooting groups too low. What to do? Move your rear sight in what direction? Answer: downward.

You are shooting groups to the right. What to do? Move your rear sight in what direction? Answer: to the right.

You are shooting groups too high. What to do? Move your rear sight in what direction? Answer: upward.

You are shooting groups to the left. What to do? Move your rear sight in what direction? Answer: to the left.

What you are doing by moving the rear sight accordingly is realigning the front sight so as to bring bullet impact to the bull's-eye.

In the following chapter, once again taking things one step at a time, we'll examine how to achieve *precise* bullet placement via optical aids—namely, crosshairs, which will also apply to the previous discussion referencing iron (open) sights. Therefore, you shall think of crosshairs as the equivalent of rear iron sights because they will function accordingly in terms of adjustments.

CHAPTER 4

ZEROING IN OPTICS MADE EASY

Generally speaking, the desired distance to *initially* sight-in most long guns is 50 yards. Actually, 25 yards might be a better choice for the beginner. However, some shooting ranges may restrict 25-yard distances (and shorter) solely for small caliber handguns, along with a minimum 50-yard distance for shotguns (both smoothbore and rifle-barreled). High-powered handguns shooting rifle cartridges, too, are often restricted to a minimum 50-yard distance at the rifle range, separate and well apart from the aforementioned. Therefore, if you are restricted to sighting in your firearm at a minimum of 50 yards, so be it. But again, as a beginner, if you have the choice of sighting in at 25 yards, start there before making your way out to 50 yards, 75 yards, 100 yards, 200 yards, and beyond.

As our hometown shooting range is set as described above, after boresighting at home, Donna and I usually sight in our firearms at 50 yards before zeroing in at 100 and 200 yards. I record the ammunition used as well as trajectory information for those distances; more on that matter will follow shortly. Depending on where you will be shooting, staying zeroed at 50 yards may be perfectly suitable. If you are hunting the wide-open spaces of say Arizona, you will certainly want to become skilled at far greater distances. Learning a few tricks of the trade will quickly put you on the right path toward your target. After having read Chapter 2 referencing boresighting (which I do at home), you are now ready to head for the shooting range. For openers, safety being your primary concern, your weapon is generally placed in a designated upright position, unloaded, action open, and safety on. A pistol would be placed upon a shooting bench/table and pointed downrange; again, unloaded, action open, safety on. You are about ready to start placing several shots on paper to find your zero at a given distance.

Your shooting table or bench should be a solid, stable platform. Let me clarify. I have seen guys and gals confidently take up a position at a shooting table; however, that platform rocked ever so slightly. Not good. Make sure your shooting platform is rock-solid. Once again, as safety is your first concern, know the rules of the range. If in doubt, ask questions of a range officer before engagement.

Let's assume that you are at the rifle range, sighting in your weapon with a telescopic sight at a minimum distance of 50 yards, which will likely be the case. You have hung an official 50-yard NRA (National Rifle Association) 24 x 14 x 6 inch black bull's-eye paper target. The line has been declared *hot* by the range officer (cleared for firing). You are wearing ear and eye protection. With your weapon pointed downrange, feed a round into the chamber. Get into a comfortable shooting position, butt of the firearm fixed firmly into your shoulder and/or supported by a shooting-rest system as described in detail in Chapter 1. Take the safety off.

The author sighting in his Remington 12 gauge Premier 11-87 semiautomatic slug gun with Redfield 1¾ x–5x scope at 100 yards, employing Uncle Bud's Bulls Bag

Align the crosshairs [or other sight(s)] on the bull's-eye, relax, let your breath out slowly and . . . carefully, steadily *squeeeeze* off a round—without thinking about when that round is going to sound aloud. If you do not adhere to this advice and pull or jerk the trigger instead of *squeeeezing* it, you are probably afraid of the anticipated recoil and will undoubtedly flinch. If all went well, hopefully, you are on paper. If not, we'll deal with that issue later. But let's assume that you are on paper. Do not concern yourself if you are not in the black. If you hit anywhere upon the paper target, you are on your way to zeroing in on the bull's-eye. Take two more shots in order to confirm that you are consistently handling and aiming the firearm correctly.

Ideally, you should have grouped all three shots—regardless of where you hit upon paper.

If you have a *fairly* good grouping (say no more than an inch or two apart for openers), it's time to move your point of impact into the bull's-eye without having you waste time and ammunition by guesstimating where and how to move the crosshairs. Sadly, many beginners continue to do exactly that, foolishly expending boxes and boxes of ammunition in order to finally hit the bull's-eye. They may raise or lower–shift from left to right those crosshairs, moving them through a series of random clicks, trying desperately to home in on the bull's-eye—taking shot after unnecessary shot. A good many shots later, that person still may not be in the bull's-eye because sheer confusion has reared its ugly head. *Why are my shots striking the target higher when, in fact, I lowered those crosshairs?* you may be wondering. *Why are my shots striking the target even further to the right when, in fact, I moved those crosshairs to the left to compensate?* you may be thinking incorrectly and in wonderment. Well, it's no different than the examples given in Chapter 3 under 'Zeroing in Iron Sights Made Easy.' For in essence, your scope is functioning exactly like a rear sight on your firearm with open sights.

In a moment, you'll be given the magic to quickly bring your point(s) of impact into the black if not the very center of bull's-eye itself. But first, keep steadfastly in mind that your crosshairs operate precisely like your iron (open) sights. If you are shooting high and to the right, obviously you want your point of impact to come low and to the left. Therefore, you want to move your crosshairs (reticles) up and to the right. I'll repeat. In order to align your point of impact with the bull's-eye, you want to move your crosshairs up and to the right. Similarly, as explained in the 'Zeroing in Iron Sights Made Easy' chapter, you move your rear sight in the same direction of your point of impact. Referencing crosshairs, you move them in the same direction of your bullet impact.

Another example: Your point of impact is low and to the left of the bull's-eye. What to do? You lower the crosshairs and move them to the left, aligning them with your point of impact. If you are employing a red-dot scope or a holographic sight, you also move the dot or circle to your point of impact. Now, when you place your crosshairs on the bull's-eye, your point of impact should be dead-on or close to it. You can then make finer adjustments. I want you to try and understand this often confusing concept before moving ahead. A humorous approach taken, one person explained it away on an Internet forum as follows: "It's sort of like pouring piss out of a boot with the directions printed on the bottom of the heel. Easy for Texans to understand; just follow the arrows." A variation of *up* is really *down*.

Explained next, as promised, is not only a far faster way to home in on the bull's-eye from that three-shot grouping, but to begin understanding point of aim and point of impact when adjusting elevation and windage.

The Simple Magic

Step 1. Place the crosshairs at the center of your three-group shot—not the bull's-eye.

Step 2. Keeping your firearm steady—crosshairs still firmly aligned on the center of your three-shot group—move the crosshairs to the very center of the bull's-eye by carefully adjusting the elevation and windage knobs. For openers, it would be extremely helpful if someone made those adjustments for you while you peered through the scope and guided that person, holding the firearm steady upon the three-shot group.

Step 3. After these two adjustments have been made (elevation and windage) and the crosshairs are now aligned on the bull's-eye, *squeeeze* off a round. Are you not delighted that the bullet now impacted near or through the bull's-eye? If not, fine-tune by repeating this procedure until you are zeroed in, eventually working your way out to desired distances. If your rifle range has a 75-yard target, shoot at that distance before reaching out to 100 yards. Better to *aim* toward those greater distances gradually. This way, you can record how your firearm shoots at different yardages: 25 yards, 50 yards, 75 yards, 100 yards, and so forth.

3a) You can also invert this procedure by holding your point of aim at the bull's-eye while aligning the crosshairs to the center of your three-group shot. This will also move your point of impact closer or into the bull's-eye. Your choice. However, you have a better reference point with the first procedure because you are aiming and holding on a fine fixed point (the bull's-eye) rather than holding your point of aim upon the *approximate* center of your three-shot grouping.

Note: You may be thinking that a metal vise-type shooting rest is going to be more secure in holding a firearm than a sandbag setup and will not necessarily necessitate a partner making those adjustments for you. You may recall my mentioning harmonics and the negative effects of such shooting-rest systems in general. Unless you are strictly shooting paper targets with an eye toward competitive shooting, demanding tack-driving accuracy, you might find the need to purchase a prohibitively expensive shooting rest specifically designed to handle explosive vibrations. Remember, this is a handbook on hunting, not world-class competitive shooting; two completely different sports. After a time, you will make those elevation and windage adjustments by yourself while holding your firearm rock-steady. Practice makes perfect or darn near close.

I suggest keeping a notepad in your gun bag for recording relevant information. Examples:

Firearms: rifle, muzzleloader, handgun, slug gun, smoothbore shotgun (reference patterning).

Ammunition: manufacturer, caliber/gauge, weight (grain/ounce), bullet type, shell length, velocity (feet per second), energy (foot pounds), lot #, price, zeroed trajectory measured in yards; bullet drop measured in inches.

Open Sights/Optics: iron, telescopic (reticles), red-dot scope, holographic sight —set in specific inches above bore; example ~ scope mounted 1½ inches above center of barrel's muzzle.

Yes, you can make this as involved or as simple as you wish. Keep firmly in mind that certain weapons prefer a certain type of ammunition. Once you find that niche, stick with it. Sight in and shoot ammo from the same box or lot number. Do not mix ammunition when zeroing in and fine-tuning. There is no substitute for consistency—from the time you put the firearm into your shoulder, cheek upon the stock, specific round into the chamber, and so forth.

After you have experimented with different types of ammunition from reputable manufacturers such as Hornady, Remington, Winchester, et cetera, having reached a level of proficiency at the shooting range, it is time to go hunting—and with utmost confidence. To be consistent, shoot the same ammunition while hunting as you did shooting paper targets at the range.

Up to this point, I have purposely held off from addressing zeroing a firearm's sight via a specific number of graduated *clicks*, referencing what each click represents over a given distance. The reason for this is simple. It involves math, an abridged form of the word mathematics, which is perhaps an even more frightening term. Plainly put, a good many folks are intimidated by math. Math and its application is nerve-racking, second only to public speaking. However, in the next chapter titled 'MOA (Minute Of Angle) Clearly Explained,' I am going to do just that—and that is to clearly explain what is seemingly an arcane language. Simply put, math is a higher branch of arithmetic, whereas mathematics puts forth signs, symbols, and theories using, yes, arithmetic, algebra, calculus, geometry, and trigonometry. We'll be using mostly simple arithmetic to examine and understand MOA (Minute Of Angle). The mathematical symbols used will merely be those that most all of us are familiar with: circles, crosses, dots, arcs, and cones lying horizontally.

However, you do not need to understand Minute Of Angle in order to impact bullets into the bull's-eye. All you need to do is follow the three-step procedure put forth in **The Simple Magic** section. So, why am I even about to explain this MOA concept? The answer is simple, too. I'm sure you'll all agree that calculators have a definite place in a child's education, but not to the exclusion of their understanding the concepts of adding, subtracting, multiplying and dividing, thereby using their own brain and not a machine that does these functions for them. Therefore, for the sake of understanding, turn the page in a moment and let's give this a *shot*.

By the same token, if you're remiss to do this and want the easy way out, which you now have via **The Simple Magic**, I'll understand. I'll chalk it up to something along these lines: When I was very young, an older gentleman wanted to *teach* me a lot about fishing. But all I wanted to do is catch fish. He would always out-fish me, and I often wondered why. As I got older, I paid more attention to his lessons and, therefore, caught more fish. I learned certain concepts. Need I say more?

CHAPTER 5

MOA (MINUTE OF ANGLE) CLEARLY EXPLAINED

Please read at least the last three paragraphs in the preceding chapter before beginning this one. If you are ready to digest what is ostensibly a complicated concept [which it is not], it will help you to become a better shooter/hunter. Why? When aiming at a big game animal (for instance, a deer) that is a good distance beyond what you are zeroed in for, you are obviously not going to be able to use the simple three-step procedure explained in 'The Simple Magic' section and reset your sights. You need to know how to readjust your sight for various distances, and rather quickly. Here is where understanding Minute Of Angle will aid you considerably. Ready?

To better understand Minute Of Angle (MOA), picture a pie, a circle, or better yet, the face of a clock—which, of course, is divided into 60 minutes. As a circle or the shape of a clock is comprised of 360 degrees, one Minute Of Angle represents $1/60^{th}$ of that one degree. This translates into capable bullet accuracy of <u>1 MOA equaling approximately 1 inch at 100 yards</u>. I say *approximately* 1 inch because the actual measurement is 1.047 inches at 100 yards. However, rounded off to 1 inch at 100 yards is close enough for our intended purposes, on out to let's say 600 yards. We'll be hunting game, not sniper-shooting considerable distances in Afghanistan. Therefore, the following formula will be quite accurate for our intended purposes. Hence, we'll dispense with the word *approximately*.

As the bullet travels over a distance of 100, 200, 300, 400, 500, and 600 yards, the angle (arc) is going to widen. Picture a cone lying horizontally with you looking through the narrow end.

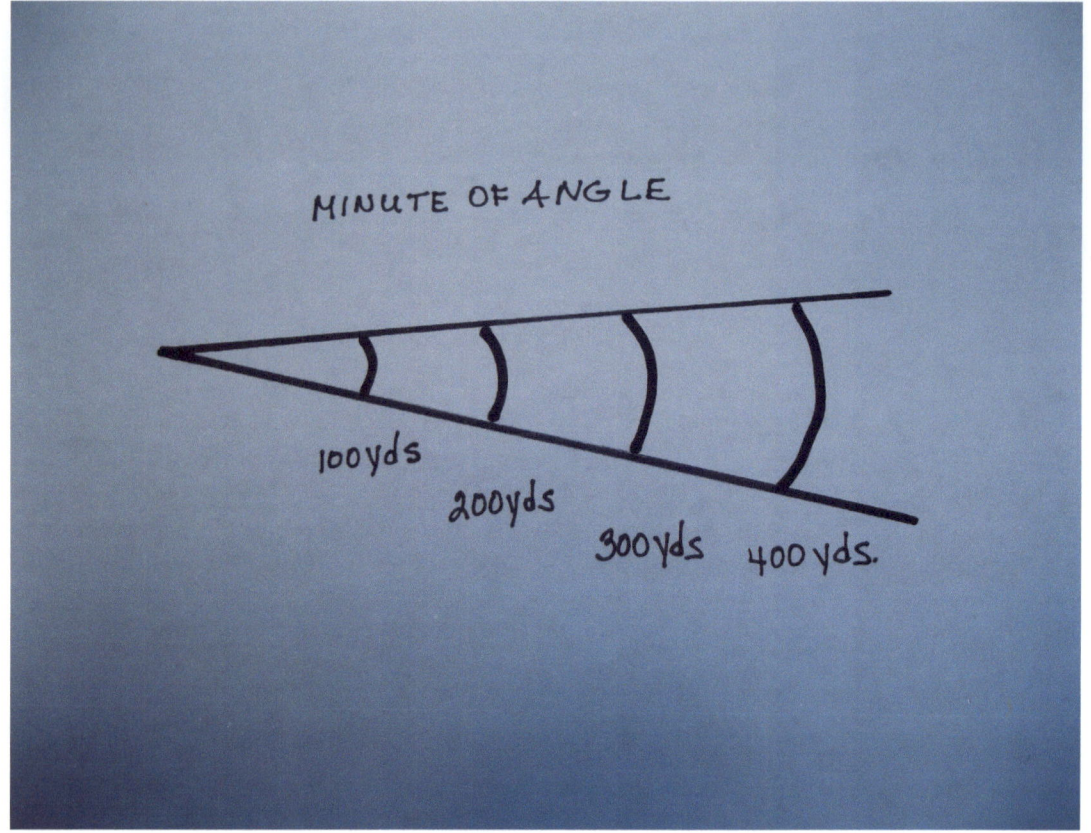

Diagram illustrating widening of the arc as bullet travels

Referencing elevation and windage, *most* firearm optic adjustment knobs or screws for crosshairs, red dots, and holographic sights are calibrated in increments of ¼ inch. Others, such as my EOTech XPS2 holographic sights, may have a ½-inch adjustment. We will stay with the more common calibrated sight adjustment of ¼ inch. This simply means that each graduated *click* of either the elevation or windage adjustment will move your point of impact ¼ of an inch. This is how you will think in terms of moving your crosshairs, red dot, or holographic (circle/dot) sight. [Note: Think of your crosshairs, et cetera, functioning as a rear iron (open) sight covered in the previous two chapters.]

We now understand that bullet accuracy of <u>1 MOA equals 1 inch at 100 yards</u>. If you are shooting at fifty yards, half the 100 yard distance, your MOA will be ½ inch. If you are shooting at 25 yards, your MOA would be ¼ of an inch.

ONE MINUTE OF ANGLE (MOA) AT VARIOUS DISTANCES

25 yards	50 yards	100 yards	200 yards	300 yards	400 yards	500 yards	600 yards
¼ inch	½ inch	1 inch	2 inches	3 inches	4 inches	5 inches	6 inches

Now, let's suppose that we're trying to hit the bull's-eye of a paper target at a distance of 200 yards. Consult the chart, which is a constant and makes this concept easier to follow. <u>One MOA at 200 yards is 2 inches.</u> Therefore, if my point of impact is hitting 2 inches below the target at 200 yards, I need to come up (either scope or iron sights) 2 inches; 3 inches at 300 yards; 4 inches at 400 yards; 5 inches at 500 yards, and so forth.

Note: In order to adjust your sights accordingly, and to avoid confusion, review Chapters 2 and 3.

Let's consider a 400-yard target. <u>Think in increments or blocks of 4 referencing 400 yards.</u> If my point of impact is hitting 8 inches below the bull's-eye at 400 yards, I'd have to come up 8 inches or 2 MOA. In other words, how many blocks of 4 (MOA at 400 yards) are in 8 inches? The answer is 2; that is, 8 ÷ 4 = 2 MOA.

Let's stay with the same 400-yard target. If my point of impact is hitting 6 inches below the bull's-eye at 400 yards, I'd have to come up 1½ inches or 1½ MOA to put myself in the center ring. In other words, how many blocks of 4 (MOA at 400 yards) are in 6 inches? The answer is 1½. 6 ÷ 4 = 1½ MOA.

Once again, let's consider the 400-yard target. <u>Think in increments or blocks of 4 referencing 400 yards.</u> If my point of impact is hitting 4 inches below the bull's-eye at the 400-yard distance, I'd have to come up 4 inches or 1 MOA. In other words, how many blocks of 4 (MOA at 400 yards) are in 4 inches? The answer is 1. 4 ÷ 4 = 1 MOA.

The same procedure holds true for windage adjustments. If you are shooting with iron (open) sights, you will be adjusting your rear sight in lieu of moving crosshairs or dots on your optics.

Let's continue with other examples at different yardages:

Let us say that I'm zeroed in at 100 yards, so obviously I do not have to make any adjustments. However, at 200 yards, I note that I'm hitting 4 inches below the bull's-eye. I record this difference in my notepad. Remember that 1 MOA at 200 yards is 2 inches (refer to MOA chart). How many of those 2-inch blocks fit into that 4-inch difference? Well, 4 ÷ 2 = 2 MOA. Therefore, I'd have to come up 2 MOA.

Let's us go out to 300 yards and assume that my notepad indicates that I'm hitting 15 inches below the bull's-eye. Remember that 1 MOA at 300 yards is 3 inches. How many of those 3-inch blocks fit into that 15-inch difference? Well, 15 ÷ 3 = 5. Therefore, I'd have to come up 5 MOA.

Let's move out to 400 yards and assume that my notepad indicates that I'm hitting 32 inches below the bull's-eye. Remember that 1 MOA at 400 yards is 4 inches. How many of those 4-inch blocks fit into that 32-inch difference? Well, 32 ÷ 4 = 8. Therefore, I'd have to come up 8 MOA.

Let's move out to 500 yards and assume that my notepad indicates that I'm hitting 60 inches below the bull's-eye. Remember that 1 MOA at 500 yards is 5 inches. How many of those 5-inch blocks fit into that 60-inch difference? Well, 60 ÷ 5 = 12. Therefore, I'd have to come up 12 MOA.

Using our knowledge of MOA for sighting in

As already mentioned, different optics employ different calibrations. Again, we'll stay with the most common ¼-inch adjustment, typically measured in and referred to as *clicks*. Always consult your owner's manual to be certain we're on the same page, figuratively speaking. As one turns the adjustment knobs (turrets) for elevation and windage, one can feel the dials click into place. Too, these increments are visible and can be audible as well. Some inexpensive optics offer only a visual determination. Avoid them like the plague.

We will use a 100-yard example employing a rifle scope. I want to sight in at 100 yards. Remember, 1 MOA at 100 yards is one inch. After shooting a three-bullet grouping, I see that my point of impact is 4 inches below my point of aim (the bull's-eye). In order to adjust my sight, I need to know how many inches are in 1 MOA at that 100-yard distance. Consult the chart if you need to. At 100 yards, 1 MOA equals one inch. I ask myself: How many blocks of 1 are there in 4 inches? The answer is 4 MOA. How many clicks do I need to adjust my scope? In other words, how many ¼ inches are in 4 inches? The answer is 16. Therefore, I need to come up 16 clicks.

Using the following 3-step formula for the above scenario may also help:

Step 1. Distance of target ÷ 100 yards = number of inches in 1 MOA; that is, 100 ÷ 100 = 1 inch per MOA

Step 2. Inches of adjustment ÷ inches in 1 MOA = your MOA adjustment.
4 inches ÷ 1 inch = 4 MOA adjustment

Step 3. Number of clicks for 1 MOA on your scope multiplied by your MOA adjustment = number of clicks needed for adjustment.
4 clicks x 4 MOA adjustment = 16 clicks

Other examples:

I'm shooting at 300 yards, and my point of impact is 9 inches high.

Using the above formula, we get:
300 yards ÷ 100 yards = 3 inches for 1 MOA
9 inches ÷ 3 inches = 3 MOA adjustment
4 clicks per 1 MOA x 3 MOA = 12 clicks on scope

I'm shooting at 50 yards, and my point of impact is 5 inches low.
50 yards ÷ 100 yards = ½ inch for 1 MOA
5 inches ÷ ½ inch = 10 MOA adjustment
4 clicks per 1 MOA x 10 MOA adjustment = 40 clicks on scope

Let's stay zeroed in at 100 yards; however, we are going to shoot 25-yard targets. My notepad tells me that I'm shooting 1 inch below the bull's-eye at that distance. Once again, <u>1 MOA at 100 yards is 1 inch.</u> Therefore, 1 MOA would be ½ inch at 50 yards, and ¼ inch at 25 yards. So, 1 MOA at that 25-yard distance equals ¼ of an inch. How many of those ¼ inch blocks fit into 1 inch? Well, 1 inch ÷ ¼ = 4. Hence, I'd need to come up 4 MOA.

Now, let's figure out how many ¼ clicks are needed to come up 4 MOA.
4 MOA x ¼ = 16 clicks.

Are you ready to figure out how many MOA are needed to compensate for an 18-inch bullet drop below the bull's-eye at 600 yards? Sure you are. Remember, if <u>1 MOA at 100 yards is 1 inch</u>, then 6 MOA at 600 yards is 6 inches. Again, <u>think in increments or blocks of 6 referencing 600 yards</u>. How many blocks of 6 fit into that 18-inch difference? Well, 18 ÷ 6 = 3 MOA. And 3 MOA x ¼ = 12 clicks that I'd need to come up to be in the black rings or the bull's-eye.

If I were hunting with a weapon zeroed in at 100 yards, but that trophy buck was out there at 200 yards and definitely not heading my way, a 2 MOA, 8-click adjustment would put me in the kill zone. I'm confident because this information is recorded in my notepad—my point of impact being 4 inches below the bull's-eye. If there was no time for that fine adjustment, a 2-inch *holdover* (that is, raising my point of aim 2 inches) would do the trick. Personally, I wouldn't take the shot at that distance, but that's just me. I limit myself to confident 100-yard clean-kill shots. Other folks, who are quite proficient, know and understand MOA inside and out, can and do take much farther shots and make clean kills. I shoot only paper at 200 yards. To each his own.

In keeping with the theme of this comprehensive yet concise hunting-reference handbook, I'll refrain from complicating matters, veering away from related areas such as ballistic coefficients, muzzle velocities, and other variables that would lead one from basic arithmetic to abstruse mathematics. Extreme long-distance shooting would require said knowledge for a greater understanding and appreciation. However, we have been discussing far shorter shooting distances ranging from 25–600 yards.

CHAPTER 6

EVERYTHING YOU WILL NEED FOR THE SHOOTING RANGE

It is frustrating to go off to the shooting range and then realize that you have forgotten some important item. Actually, every item listed will prove essential at one point or another. The initial item that you should consider (other than your firearm) is a shooting bag in which to carry everything that you will need at the range. It need not be an expensive bag; it needs to be large enough to carry the items shown. My partner in life does not hunt. However, I better not leave for the shooting range without taking Donna along with me. She loves the sport and is a very decent shot, especially with a rifle—scary, in fact. So it is important that I carry 'his and hers' paraphernalia. If you are solo, you obviously do not need such a large bag. However, if you are taking the wife, friend, and/or another member of the family, you will be amazed at how quickly you can fill a range bag.

The shooting bag I tote to the range is a convenient Smith & Wesson 22 x 12 x 12 inches with several external compartments (front, sides, back). Also, there are compartments within—a place for everything and everything in its place. This way, I do not have to hunt through a pile of stuff in order to find what Donna and I need. Her handbag should be so well organized. Shhh.

Noted are several of the basic items that will make your visit to the shooting range complete, comfortable and, therefore, more enjoyable. If pistol shooting, I may also carry handguns in the same bag, ammunition carried separately. Otherwise, I transport firearms in specific gun cases. With the exception of handgun, cartridges, and paper targets (shown for illustrative purpose), I keep all other items permanently stored in the shooting bag. This way, I do not need a checklist, for Donna and I have everything at hand.

Shooting Range Paraphernalia

Sweeping from left to right in some semblance of order: spotting scope and tripod, handgun, ear protection, Band-Aids, permanent markers, official paper pistol targets, notepad, pen, eye protection, hand calculator, ammunition, rags, range finder, shooting gloves, small tape measure, staple gun, staples (9/16 inch-14mm), gun and reel silicone cloth, tool kit (ratchet screwdriver, multi-bits, socket set).

Shown on the following page is a selection of gun cases that Donna and I often take to the outdoor range for a full day of shooting. For a typical outing, we will pack a pair of long guns in the roomy two-gun hard case partially pictured in the background. Next follows a one-gun hard case for any number of weapons one of us decides to employ that day. Perhaps Donna will slip a shotgun into the leather soft-case. For a weapon with a mounted telescopic sight, I prefer a vertical case that sits high enough to comfortably and securely accommodate my Remington 11-87 Premier semiautomatic slug gun with its cantilevered Redfield 1¾ x-5x scope. The case is a 50-inch AirGlide Plano scoped shotgun/rifle case with high-density foam cradles and Velcro hold-down straps for excellent protection. To the left of that gun case is a vintage Orvis Gokeys leather-reinforced canvas ammo tote bag. I carry our ammo plus an assortment of targets. To the extreme right is a Smith & Wesson aluminum foam-padded handgun case with two-latch combination locks. In the foreground, are four handguns and an assortment of paper targets.

Gun Cases

Shown on the next page is a closet shelved with an organized arrangement of ammunition, broken up into shotgun shells (top self); rifled cartridges and pellets (middle shelf); African Game Industries, Inc. Skeet Bag, MTM Case-Guard Ammo Box, and shooting accessories: range finder, boresight kit, binoculars (bottom shelf). Before heading out to the range, I select the ammo and equipment that Donna and I will expressly require for a full day at the shooting range; namely, multiple firearms, applicable ammunition, and paper targets.

Gun Ammo Shelves

Notable Aids: Having shot small to medium caliber handguns ranging from .22 to .45, a recently acquired high-powered .308 rifle-cartridge handgun was, well, initially, a handful. As the day wore on, my trigger finger was getting ripped up and bleeding badly. However, I was there at the shooting range for the day and wasn't about to leave. Donna kept bringing me napkins, and I stubbornly got through the duration. When we got home, I don't know what looked worse . . . my finger or the bloody gun. In short order, I researched and purchased a pair of shooting gloves from Cabela's; item # IK-950139. They run small, so I ordered one size up. Good to go. Next time out, I shot that .308 *caliber* handgun virtually all day without an issue. Too,

I learned to carry Band-Aids merely as a precautionary measure, *measure* being the operative word. I've often seen the result of recoil play havoc upon the foreheads of those who didn't pay careful attention to eye-relief distance (measured distance between the eye and the scope's eyepiece). This is usually part and parcel of folks who bought and brought an improperly mounted scope to the range, having to learn the hard way the importance of a clear sight picture versus vignetting (crescent-shaped shadowy distortions shifting about the periphery of the lens). The tendency is to lean too close to the scope's eyepiece in order to *try* and clear the image. Wham! Proper shooting gloves and/or Band-Aids can save the day.

CHAPTER 7

GUN CLEANING & CARE

Gun cleaning and care is, obviously, quite important to maintaining your firearm in tiptop shape, as the corrosive properties of gunpowder residue can rust and pit a barrel if neglected. It can also cause a firearm to malfunction. Why would anyone not take the proper precautions to protect against such disregard? To protect their investment, many beginners purchase an inexpensive gun cleaning kit that contains a limited number of materials and equipment for their firearm. Before long, it is realized they really need this, that, and another dozen things to make gun cleaning and life easier.

Let's cut to the quick and get virtually everything you need in a single shot. If you have or plan on having more than one gun on hand, which I'm sure will happen if it hasn't already, you may want to consider a cleaning ensemble for multiple firearms —not only existing in those standard rod, brush, mop (swab) combinations, but in the Bore Snake-type cords (ropes) comprised of floss and brass. They make bore cleaning not only exceedingly fast but pretty thorough and will suffice for the moment. However, for a completely thorough job, nothing beats the patch, solvent, brush approach. More on that matter shortly.

Let's say you're away from home on a hunting trip and are not inclined to carry an assortment of gun cleaning paraphernalia. For the barrel, a bore snake is a great field-cleaning tool, made up of 98% cotton and 2% brass. To run it dry through a steel barrel will not cause damage. In a matter of seconds, you are done.

However, some folks will take issue. To put uneasy minds at rest, some folks swear by Breakfree CLP (**C**leaner, **L**ubricant, **P**rotector) from Safariland, first wetting the area before bristle-brushing then pulling the cord (rope) through the barrel. It's your decision. You'll wind up with a messy line—which, to my way of thinking, negates the purpose of a bore snake in the first place.

One-stop-shopping at Walmart for all your gun-cleaning supplies makes perfect sense. Besides the convenience, the store will save you money. Buying gun-cleaning kits instead of individual packages will save you additional dollars. Referencing *complete* cleaning kits for your needs, you may have to shop around. It's important not to overbuy as well. For example, if a kit contains bore snakes for rifles and shotguns but you only own rifles and know you won't have a future need for shotgun paraphernalia, you are probably overspending. If on the other hand you own or know you will own several firearms in various calibers and gauges in the near future, look for packaging and/or universal kits that contain as many items that you can use. This way, you will save a small fortune. You can also find these accessories (and others that I'll be discussing) online at such sites as Cabela's, Dick's Sporting Goods, Amazon, and Midway USA. So, please take the time to shop around for your best pricing.

A convenient place to store and keep these items handy is in a gun-cleaning maintenance center such as those manufactured by MTM. As you will need a fair amount of space to store a good many items, I'd opt for their roomier, deeper (29½ x 9½ x 4½ inches) MTM Gunsmith's Maintenance Center; Model RMC-5. It holds everything I need for cleaning and maintaining many guns that I own. You may also want to consider, the case-guard MTM Gun Vise; Model GV-30. It is considerably shallower (approximately 32 x 8½ x ½ inches deep [tray areas]) and will not hold as many items. However, it may be perfect for those who own but a few firearms. I find the need for both gun-cleaning case-guards essential. To keep the dust off, I simply cover each with a towel when not in use.

Maintenance Center & MTM Gun Vise Case-Gards

I've made a complete list of all items and can assure you that there is not one superfluous article in the kit, which I've put together over time. If you do not have any of these items in your assortment, save yourself time and frustration by filling in what may be missing. You'll thank me later. Referencing cleaning rods, brushes, solvents, et cetera, stick with a gun-care company who has been doing business since 1903: Hoppe's.

Hoppe's Universal three-piece aluminum cleaning rod for all calibers and gauges; Hoppe's cleaning rods have a ball bearing swivel handle, which follows a bore's rifling and cleans thoroughly.

Hoppe's Universal cleaning kit includes the three-piece aluminum cleaning rod for .22 – .30 caliber rifles; .22, 9mm – .38/.357 caliber pistols; 12 and 20 gauge shotguns; 5 phosphor bronze brushes; 5 wool-blend mops (swabs); 3 spear-pointed jags; shotgun slotted patch loop; shotgun adapter; micro-fiber absorbent patches; 2-ounce container of gun bore cleaner; 2-ounce container of gun oil.

Cleaning solvents and accessories: Hoppe's Number 9 powder solvent; Hoppe's Elite gun cleaner—its deep-cleaning action not only removes carbon, copper, and lead fouling, but conditions bores; extra mops (swabs), phosphor bronze brushes, nylon brushes, and Tornado brushes [Hoppe's offers a 3-pack brush and swab kit]. The spiral-wound design of the Tornado bore brush is very efficient for cleaning bores; it is commonly called "The gunsmith's brush." Phosphor bronze brushes make quick work of removing lead deposits from the bore. Soft washable cotton cleaning swabs (mops) are essential for removing fouling and excess solvent.

Hoppe's 13 piece brass jag kit: .17 caliber, .22 caliber, 6mm, 6.5mm, 9mm, .270 caliber, .30 caliber, .33 caliber, .375 caliber, .40 caliber, .44 caliber, .45 caliber, .50 caliber.

Hoppe's larger Bore Snakes for 12 gauge and 20 gauge shotguns are often referred to as ropes whereas the thinner bore snakes for rifles are generally called cords. Two cords from the latter group clean several diameter bores efficiently. The smallest cord cleans .22 caliber, .223 caliber, and 5.56 mm. The next one up in size cleans .308, .30-30, .30-06, .300, and .303 calibers. The smaller of the two ropes is for 20 gauge shotguns, and the larger is for 12 gauge shotguns. You can purchase them individually from Walmart for $15 each. The package labeling explains how the bore snake works:

1. The bore brush embedded in the cord loosens hard deposits.
2. The first floss area removes foreign particles prior to the scrubbing action of the brush.
3. The main floss area, with 160 times more surface area than a patch, cleans the bore.

4. The brass weight slips easily through the barrel until clean. You simply grasp and slowly pull the bore snake through the barrel. The caliber or gauge is conveniently stamped into the brass weight. The bore snake can be washed by hand, air dried, and used repeatedly.

From your local hardware or box store, pick up a set of three toothbrush-shaped and sized mini brushes: nylon for cleaning, brass for burnishing (polishing), and stainless for removing rust.

- chip-brushes in ½ inch, 1 inch, and 1½ inch widths
- plastic slot and crevice pick
- Vaseline/cotton Q-tip swab in film canister [used for lubricating O-rings re SiteLite boresight kit]
- 5½ x 4½ x 2 inch aluminum trays
- Gun & Reel silicone flannel polishing cloth(s)
- toothpicks
- WD-40
- absorbent rags (such as those old-fashioned diapers)
- gun manual(s) [instructions for disassembly and reassembly]
- tools necessary referencing the above
- rubber hammer
- dowels and/or punches for pins
- compact tool kit: ratchet screwdriver ~ multi-bit & socket set

CHAPTER 8

SELECTING HUNTING CLOTHING, FOOTWEAR & ACCESSORIES FOR ALL SEASONS

Outerwear: jackets, pants, jumpsuits

The name of the game in selecting hunting clothing and footwear for all seasons is total comfort. The more time you put into the hunt, the more successful you are going to be. Returning early to your vehicle or lodging because you are cold will limit your time afield. Choosing the right garments for the time of year you will be hunting is not only critical to comfort but for blending in with your environment. Picking the wrong camouflage outfit can be as bad as not wearing camo at all. Convincing yourself that one pattern will suffice for all seasons is one big rationalization, for you want to break up your outline as best as possible, especially when still-hunting deer [explained in the following chapter] and when hunting from a treestand. Unless you are hunting from a gun tower, a ground blind, or some such shelter that conceals your presence, camo is essential. Even then, without the proper backdrop, camo is essential. I have four basic camo patterns that carry me from early fall through the late winter bow and gunning deer seasons, which also takes into account temperature extremes.

For example, this past gun-hunting deer season in Tomkins County, located in the Southern Zone of New York State, had unseasonably warm November/December temperatures ranging from morning lows of 25 degrees Fahrenheit to morning highs of 49 degrees. That's quite a spread. As virtually all the woods were void of leaves at that point, my clothing selection was a two-piece pants and jacket in a Trebark camo pattern, for my surroundings were essentially a bare-timber backdrop lot. The garment's construction is from Cabela's Whitetail Clothing series. While there are a good number of materials used in constructing quality hunting clothing, keep two fabrics predominantly in mind: Gore-Tex and Thinsulate. The former keeps you dry; the latter keeps you warm. Gore-Tex is a 100% waterproof (as opposed to water repellent), windproof, thin, breathable membrane for all-weather use. You do not want water repellent materials; you want waterproof fabrics. Thinsulate is a synthetic fiber that offers warmth. You will pay more for such garments offering truly waterproofing and state-of-the-art insulating properties; however, you will stay dry and warm.

Hence, you will remain comfortable and will, therefore, be able to put in the time needed to give you the added edge in virtually any type of weather.

Pictured upon the chairs from left to right are Cabela's hats, hand-warmer muff, pants, jacket, and shooting gloves in a Trebark camo pattern. Everything else I need for the following day's hunt is laid out the night before as shown.

For extremely cold weather, I don a darker one-piece (jumpsuit-style) Cabela's Mossy Oak camo pattern outfit that is composed of darker shades of browns, grays, taupe [brownish gray], and dark green. I generally plant myself 15-plus feet or higher in a big hemlock tree, hidden well within its shadowy limbs and drooping branches. This dual-purpose pattern (for oaks and evergreens) is a must-have garment. As with the Gore-Tex line of clothing, Cabela's also carries their own line of waterproof, windproof, breathable hunting outfits labeled Dry-Plus, which is likewise comprised of a thin, flexible waterproof, windproof membrane.

For cold, snowy, and/or blizzardy conditions, I opt for Cabela's one-piece (jumpsuit-style) Woodlands Snow-style camo pattern design. Again, look for the trademarks signifying waterproof properties: Gore-Tex or Dry-Plus, along with Thinsulate for added warmth.

For more moderate early-season temperatures, I elect to wear either a camo shirt or an uninsulated light-colored leafy-like brownish-greenish Realtree camo pattern jacket and pants. Hence, there is no need to spring for the added expense of Thinsulate/Gore-Tex garments.

Those are my four basic clothing camo patterns [Trebark, Mossy Oak, Woodlands Snow, and Realtree] that take me through the hunting season. From left to right, covered in clear plastic, are the other three camo patterns.

Realtree shirt, pants, jacket; Mossy Oak jumpsuit, and Woodlands Snow jumpsuit

Still, for safety's sake, I have a three-piece Blaze Orange outfit (jacket, pants, and detachable hood) handy that I wear afield—particularly for hunting upland birds and while still-hunting deer. It, too, is from Cabela's Whitetail Clothing collection. At all other times, I wear an orange vest and hat when walking to and from a hunting location. Although not required in New York State, I strongly suggest adopting this prudent procedure. Some private hunting clubs in the state do make this their rule, requiring a certain percentage of Hunter Orange material to be displayed upon your person via jacket, hat, et cetera. Know the hunting regulations in your state before venturing out.

Additionally, I have two uninsulated hooded outer-shell camo garments to wear over my Blaze Orange jacket, pants, and hood when needed. Pictured from left to right is a 10X (brand- name) Gore-Tex hooded rainwear outfit (dark-colored Realtree camo pattern); Cabela's Blaze Orange outfit; and a long, oversized, inexpensive Cabela's polyester hooded (light-colored Realtree camo pattern) outfit, which can completely cover the Blaze Orange garment in a nanosecond.

Waterproof Apparel in dark Realtree camo, Blaze Orange, light-colored Realtree camo

Too, I carry a green, lightweight hooded rain poncho within a pouch of a seven-pocket Realtree camo pattern RedHead (name-brand) Waist Pack. I have the pack set up strictly for bowhunting, carrying only the essentials I need as pictured.

Bowhunting Waist Pack & Paraphernalia

Sweeping from top left to right then down: camo Mini Maglite (attached to waist pack), field-dressing gloves, ChapStick, small roll orange or red trail-ribbon tape, poncho, archer's Allen wrench set, hand and toe warmers, knife (very sharp), compact binoculars (8 x 12mm), haul strap, camo handkerchief, haul line, gloves, headlamp, compass, bow/pack hook, neck gaiter, and see-thru face mask. Items not shown are bow, arrows, and mechanical release.

For gunning season, I wear Cabela's Mossy Oak camo patterned quality Fanny Pack, carrying only what I need as pictured:

Gunning Fanny Pack & Paraphernalia

Sweeping from top left to right then down: cartridges or shells, 35mm container with reflective thumbtacks, deer-rattling tool (sponges inserted to eliminate sound when walking), headlamp, toilet paper, cotton ball, hand and toe warmers, field dressing gloves, camo handkerchief, ChapStick, gun-hoist strap (Lewis SR Nylon Retriever), Mini Maglite, whistle, haul line, Knives of Alaska Combo Set (skinner/cleaver, caping knife, sheath).

Last but not least, a hunting wardrobe would not be complete without balaclavas (headgear exposing only part of the face) in the aforementioned camo patterns. For cold-weather hunting, I like the hat-type balaclava, which can be quickly converted to cover both head and most of your face. Not only does it protect you from the elements, it breaks up your facial outline. I cannot stress enough the importance of this often-overlooked item. Both the skin of your face and hands can be a dead giveaway to a wary whitetail. Shooting gloves or mittens will take care of the latter; a balaclava will hide your telltale features. Skin will give off a glimmer in certain lighting regardless of ethnicity. Although fully camouflaged, except for my face, I have been made by cautious deer on two occasions. I am convinced in the second encounter that the suspicious animal clearly distinguished my facial features apart from the rest of my melded form. I sat unblinking, staring down from my perch; it stood looking up fixedly. I knew he knew. That was the last time I ever let that happen. Even in uncomfortably warm weather, I wear screen-like, breathable face covering—leaving nothing to chance.

A word about caring for your apparel and accessory items is definitely in order because this is often an overlooked area. You do not want to ruin an outfit that has cost you hundreds of dollars. Instructions are generally noted on the backside of the label; that is, behind the tag that describes the garments construction. Such important instructions as to how to *wash* your outfit are succinct and specific. It may state do's and don'ts such as to Machine Wash in Cold Water–Delicate Cycle; or Hand Wash Only and to Line Dry; or to Air or Tumble Dry Low and Remove Promptly; Powder Detergent Only; No Bleach; Do Not Dry Clean, Steam, Iron, or Press; Zip Zippers and Snap Buttons, et cetera. After several washings, you may not be able to read these *material* instructions. Therefore, I suggest taking a moment to record and file this data. These expensive outfits may be constructed of a combination of shells and linings and insulation comprised of Gore-Tex, cotton, polyester, neoprene (synthetic rubber), nylon, olefin, Thinsulate, ad infinitum. Most of these outfits can be washed with a liquid detergent such as Arm & Hammer, labeled "Free of Perfumes and Dyes." Whether using a powder or liquid detergent, a scent-free washing medium is a must, for a deer's nose is its most powerful defense. Do not delude yourself in this respect, for even in a treestand high above the animal's line of scent, a downdraft could give you away in a heartbeat. Again, give yourself this imperative added edge. Cover-scents to and from your hunting area are covered in the following chapter.

Undergarments

Insulated base-layer clothing is the key to keeping warm in woods, fields, and mountains while hunting. Knowing the ambient temperature in the area you are going to be pursuing game will help you determine the clothing needed for a comfortable hunt. For example, there was an average of a ten degree difference between hunting Long Island and the Southern part of the Finger Lakes Region in New York State this past gunning season. A seven-hour drive north from Suffolk County, Long Island to a cabin in central New York told me beforehand that I needed to pack a heavier set of undergarments than I would need for a Long Island hunt. I have sets in various thicknesses (lightweight, mid-weight, and heavyweight). I have had undergarments comprised of blended materials such as cotton, wool, nylon, silk, poly-fleece, et cetera. The important thing is that the base-layer material next to your skin wicks moisture away via capillary action, not trap moisture, which will make you feel cold.

Undergarments designed with these wicking properties in mind help to evaporate moisture through that base-layer material and retain body heat. Whether you are selecting a one-piece undergarment (union suit); two-piece undergarment ~ top and bottom (long johns); single- or double-layered material(s); thermal or however labeled, the rule of thumb is that synthetic materials accomplish this better than natural fibers. Then again, natural fibers help keep you warm. Hence, the world of blended synthetic fabrics and natural fibers enters the picture. Yes, life is, indeed, a compromise.

To *help* narrow your selection, consider the degree of activity. For instance, while deer hunting, I spend most of my time sitting or standing in a treestand. Therefore, I am not exerting myself to the point of perspiring. Ostensibly, and strictly speaking, I'd be considering wool over polyester. Wool, especially merino wool, is a wise choice because it is an extremely warm natural material—to the exclusion of goose down being bulky and impractical. On the flip side is polyester, undoubtedly one of the wicking-*est* of synthetic properties, but it doesn't breathe. Cotton does. What to do?

One of my cold-weather selections for the above application is a union suit composed of an outer layer blend comprised of 50% cotton, 40% wool, and 10% nylon, and an inner layer of 100% cotton. I love this undergarment for hunting; it is manufactured by Duofold. Additionally, two manufacturers that I would seriously consider for quality top and bottom undergarments are Carhartt and Under Armour. For a comfortable fit, I find that the Under Armour sizing system tends to run small, so I go up one size when ordering. Their base-layer insulating system is offered in ratings ranging from material thicknesses of 1.0–4.0. As there are many variables to consider in selecting undergarments to fit *your* needs, do a bit or research concerning these three companies. Again, always read the manufacturer's Care/Content information label.

A less expensive alternative for base layering is Cabela's 100% polypropylene undergarments. Hunt around and you're sure to find bargain pricing. My Cabela's three-piece top, bottom, and hood (head sock) has been washed many, many times over the course of years. I also have a set of Under Armour 2.0 Base, two-piece long johns, along with my beloved one-piece Duofold union suit.

Footwear: socks, sock liners, and boots

Depending on the weather, terrain, and especially your hunting application, select socks, sock liners, and boots according to their materials and type of construction.

Referencing socks and sock liners, select quality footwear from such manufacturers as Wigwam Mills and REI (Recreational Equipment, Incorporated) such as their fine assortment of merino wool hiker and boot socks. For example, a good blend of materials that go into a pair of Wigwam's Merino wool hiker socks are merino wool (67%), nylon (21%) elastic (7%), acrylic (5%). Interestingly, their Canada model crew sock, Wigwam's thickest and warmest pair, is composed of traditional wool (48%) [not merino wool], acrylic (25%), nylon (17%), olefin (10%). Carefully reading fabric labels gives you a sense of these insulating and ancillary properties. A cushioned sole versus all-around cushioning comfort is another consideration that these two Wigwam models offer.

REI Merino Wool Expedition Socks are constructed from merino lamb's wool, nylon, and Lycra (a brand of spandex) for elasticity. They are a heavyweight, cushioned, cold-weather classic. Coupled with a pair of Silk One Liner Socks, you're good to go in total comfort. Sitting and/or standing in a treestand for hours on end, you will come to appreciate these socks.

Additionally, socks and sock liners from Cabela's have served me well over the years, and you will find some good bargains from time to time. However, I feel that the aforementioned brands are a notch or two up from others. You pretty much get what you pay for when it comes to these items—hunting apparel notwithstanding.

Boots

When it comes to hunting boots, do not hunt around for a bargain. Selections of hunting boots abound, but only two manufacturers satisfy my expectations. Over the years I've narrowed the list down to two companies: Sorel and the Original Muck Boot Company. Both these boots serve different applications.

When it comes to serious cold weather hunting boots, Sorel is a name that stands out among the best of the best. Originating in Kitchener, Ontario in 1962, the company was acquired by Columbia Sportswear Company in 2000, which is now located in Cedar Mill, Oregon. My pair of Sorel Men's model 1964 Premium T-style Boots is a seam-sealed, rubber lower, leather upper, 100% waterproof winner. Within the boot is a removable thick felt liner and insert that helps keep my feet warm and comfortable during those endless hours in a treestand. Combined with a pair of REI-brand Merino Wool Expedition Socks, along with a pair of Silk One Liner Socks mentioned above, you will come to appreciate this trio's warmth and comfort. *Rarely* do I find the need to slip in a pair of toe warmers.

For more ambulatory movement, trekking through muck and mire, I wear The Original Muck Boot Company's over-the-calf Woody Max Cold-Conditions Hunting boot. This 100% waterproof, lighter premium 17¼-inch tall quality boot is constructed with a 9½-inch-high front and rear rubber bottom with scalloped 7¾-inch-high rubber sides. The upper outer section has a nylon Mossy Oak camo pattern; the inner portion is comprised of a fleece lining, nylon jersey material, and 2mm of thermal foam underlay added to the instep for additional warmth.

CHAPTER 9

VIRGINIA WHITETAIL HUNTING STRATEGIES

Reading & Creating Signposts

Treestand hunting is a productive method for hunting white-tailed deer. However, placing your treestand randomly will, most often and at best, net you a nice day in the outdoors. If you do not know how to read deer sign, you are not likely to be a successful whitetail hunter. Deer trails and their proximity are one of the most obvious places to investigate, but do not pass up the opportunity to seek out where these trails converge or where the corner of a field funnels into a woodlot. Look for oak trees and acorns, apple and pear trees, berry bushes and other fruit-yielding plants. A wide variety of vegetables, too, sustain a deer herd's steady diet. A plethora of these plantings fill the bill. Just ask any farmer or gardener.

In a field or woodlot, find where deer are taking a daytime break, bedding down for the evening, or roaming about for food. Rows of corn are like the aisles of a supermarket to deer. In fact, farmers' fields are a whitetail's self-service grocery store. Scout the terrain. Study a tract of land. Once again, think nuts (especially acorns), fruits, flowers, and vegetables. Deer devour them. Many plants are like candy to these hoofed creatures. In a pine barren or woods, search for their bedrooms along the top of a knoll or ridge that offer deer the advantage of smelling, hearing and/or seeing you before you see or hear them. Not only are matted-down grassy areas an indication of a bed, an oval recess upon a snowy blanket where a deer's body heat has melted a white sheet is a dead giveaway. Therefore, do not restrict your pursuit to those days of the actual hunt; scout the area in which you plan to set up well beforehand. That's how I bagged my first deer in twenty minutes while still-hunting (moving slowly and quietly, step-by-step, stopping, standing perfectly still for minutes at a time, listening attentively, then repeating the process), heading toward a field where I knew the deer were bedded down, having stalked them days prior to the hunt. I didn't have a treestand back then. Hunting season or not, take advantage of a snowy day to track deer along travel routes, leading to their bedrooms and favorite supermarkets. You will learn a great deal by keeping your senses alert, seeking out bedding areas to feeding areas and back—that's what it's all about.

Learn to read their **tracks** along with other telltale signs. The depth and size of deer prints can tell you several things. Are we dealing with smaller deer, big bucks, or both? The size of **deer droppings** (scat) can determine other factors as well. Are we talking chocolate-covered raisin-like excrement a size bigger than rabbit poo, or are we talking a serious pile of poop? Deer feces can aid in figuring the animal's size and movement (no pun intended). Contrary to some ridiculous reports, you cannot tell the sex of a deer by its scat. We're discussing deer hunting here, not involved in some sort of forensic exploration coupled to DNA testing.

Scrapes are visual markers, signposts if you will, made when a deer, generally a buck, *scrapes* the ground with its fore-hooves and/or antlers, brushing and raking aside leaves, twigs and other debris, exposing a patch of earth upon which the animal may urinate and/or even defecate. The deer is marking its territory. Too, these creatures may work a ground scrape right below overhanging branches by rubbing and chewing on them, depositing their scent. It's a buck's calling card, serving to advertise its presence and dominance. Paying attention to scrapes is especially important during the *early* phase of the rut (the whitetail's period of sexual excitement). However, this period of hunting deer becomes far less productive as we approach what is often referred to as the middle and later phases of the fall rut. Therefore, you would want to strategically place your treestand near a promising scrape at the *beginning* of the rut, not afterward; otherwise, you are more than likely wasting your time.

There is a good deal of confusion concerning **The Rut** as it pertains to colder and warmer areas of North America. Let's clear up these misconceptions. First off, we must realize that a given property ideally sustains just so many deer, referencing a good buck-to-doe ratio. Does that are not bred during the start of the rut will return to a state of estrus in approximately a month. By this point, many bucks have had their fill so to speak, and their sexual activity is likely on the wane. Hence, as indicated above, your chance of success is diminished proportionately. Therefore, look for scrapes and consider making mock scrapes predominately during the pre-rut and rut period, putting calling, rattling, scents, et cetera in abeyance, for the buck's brain is now not as easily duped. However, this does not exclude aggressive measures when all else fails. A buck decoy along with assertive grunting and rattling may get the better of a territorial buck's ego. This is the time you may see a mature buck enter the scene, snorting before charging and maniacally attacking your decoy. A sight to behold!

Doe Decoy

When does the actual rut begin in the northern area of the United States? Herein lies a good amount of misunderstanding. Veritably, the start date could run quite differently from property to property. Peak breeding periods can vary as much as a month-and-a-half earlier than the norm (which generally begins in late October), depending on several factors, the primary element relating to nutrition. Other considerations are available cover offering protection from predators. According to Jeremy Flinn, biologist for the Cabela's Wildlife and Land Management Division, does can predict favorable conditions to birth fawns more than two hundred days in advance to ensure the best chance of their offspring's survival. Hence, we usually see a much shorter and earlier breeding season than we do in the southern states.

Food Plots

As you continue reading through these sections, you will note the importance of establishing a land-management program that is certain to give you the added edge. It need not be on a grand scale; it need only offer food and shelter that a neighboring property may not provide. Like a magnet, you will draw and hold deer in your desired area. I had permission to seed and hunt a postage-size piece of property on Eastern Long Island. Of late, I have the same opportunity via a thirty-nine acre area in the

Finger Lakes region. Take advantage of such favorable offerings. Both a brook and a pond run through the property. Water is an added bonus; more on that topic later.

To get started seeding, regardless of your level of experience, visit the Whitetail Institute at www.whitetailinstitute.com and search their web pages for any and all information related to Imperial No-Plow Food Plot Seeding, including short videos on the topic. You will be quite impressed to learn that you can get started for very little cost and effort relative to potential gains. Depending on the latitude allowed and available equipment, you can make this project as simple as scratching the surface with hand tools then using a handheld crank-type broadcast seed spreader, to utilizing a tractor for the major work tilling far larger areas. Frost seeding is another way to augment germination, especially if you can't be on top of your game (no pun intended) 24/7. Again, check out Whitetail Institute's recommendations—paying attention to locale and planting dates. Additionally, familiarize yourself with what seeds work well in your area referencing different applications such as initial seeding, overseeding, and frost seeding in relationship to the time of year. However, do not rely *strictly* on packaging information as it may prove generic. Firsthand information from folks in your area will prove invaluable. For example, apply it if a large percentage of a seed mix contains berseem clover. However, you wouldn't use it when frost seeding because berseem clover is a summer annual that wouldn't survive hard frost conditions. Therefore, you would be wasting your money. Ladino clover, red clover, white clover, chicory, alfalfa, and trefoil are perennials that lend themselves well to frost seeding. Moving from a company's formulated mix to your own concoction may be a future decision. In the meantime, stay with a winner—the Whitetail Institute—especially if you are new to planning food plots.

Mock Scrapes are made, of course, by you, the hunter. Much has been written on the subject, and the topic can often be complicated and misleading because individual interpretations are generally advanced as suppositions rather than set forth properly by applying controlled, scientific methodology. That is, tested empirically rather than theoretically; systematically through collective data instead of speculatively. Once again, we'll keep things simple based on what the scientific community knows to be fact rather than what a hunter may assume to be so based on his or her limited observations and experiences.

Fact: Bucks can be made to frequent mock scrapes at a location beneficial to your ambushing them. Fact: An artificial overhead "licking branch/limb" positioned by stapling it to a tree right above a mock scrape will lure bucks and does to visit with a good degree of regularity.

To be assured of success, get started early in the spring and summer months by employing a scrape-dripper bottle such as Wildlife Research Center's Magnum Scrape Dripper or Tink's Scrape Bomb Dripper Combo, which comes with 4 ounces of doe urine. Hang the dripper bottle or bomb approximately 6 feet above an actual or mock scrape. Both scrape drippers are daytime-activated by the rise in temperature and barometric pressure. A 4-ounce bottle of scent will last approximately two to three weeks. During the pre-rut and rut, many hunters use a doe-in-estrus scent.

However, I fill the dripper bottle with buck urine only. This communicates to a mature territorial buck that someone other than he is encroaching upon his realm. A trail camera is sure to capture such events. A definitive procedure is not written in stone, so experiment. After the rut, I put away the dripper bottle and freshen up the scrape scene (actual or artificial) with a trio of scents from Kishel's Mock Scrape Kit. More on those scents in a moment.

The approach to your treestand, ground blind, or other position, be it a morning, noon, or afternoon hunt, is of paramount importance because you do not want to alert deer to your presence. Therefore, you need to know where their bedding and feeding areas are so that you can avoid one or the other while you are getting into position. As an example, for an early morning hunt, you want to be set up far enough away from a bedding area (say a field in which they've bedded down for the evening or along a wooded ridge) before they start traveling toward a known feeding area, close to where you will have prepared a mock scrape. For bowhunting, I'll be positioned fifteen to twenty yards away from the scrape, always cognizant of wind direction. During gunning season, I'll be situated thrice the distance, taking advantage of greater concealment.

The equipment and materials needed to create a mock scrape from scratch are rubber boots, clean latex gloves, foldable handsaw, "licking branch/limb" (freshly cut and preferably from the same tree), $9/16^{th}$ cable/wood heavy-duty metal staples, hammer, short three- or four-pronged hand rake, scent for the overhanging "licking branch/limb" along with scents for the scrape itself. Scents such as Kishel's Mock Scrape Kit work extremely well.

Having donned the pair of gloves, staple a freshly cut branch or limb approximately 4½ feet above where you will create a mock scrape by clearing a 12-inch V-shape, raking the area clean of debris and undergrowth. The "licking branch/limb" above the scrape receives a few generous pumps of Pre-Orbital Gland scent. Next, I use (not overuse) the Tarsal Gland and Interdigital Gland scents, spraying sparingly upon the scrape. Once a mock scrape has been established and visited by does and/or bucks, I do not disturb it. I let the deer do their thing; that is, pawing at the ground naturally.

Shown together from top to bottom for demonstration purposes: Realtree camo pattern Magnum Scrape Dripper (discernible above green branches), stapled "licking branch/limb," mock scrape, crude but effective treestand in background.

Note: Although not considered the norm, deer, when hungry, will eat virtually anything—holly leaves being no exception. Just for giggles, we hung a holly "licking/leaf branch" 4½ feet above a mock scrape, pumped a generous spray of Pre-Orbital Scent upon the leaves [no scents were added to the mock scrape], then returned to the site several hours later. Leaves and branches were chewed, and deer prints were clearly visible in the scape. That was Christmas day, 2015. The temperature reached a record-breaking 70 degrees Fahrenheit. Needless to say, the deer were not starving.

Rubs (marks made by a deer's antlers) found on bushes, saplings and mature trees are signposts that tell you a buck is or has been in the area. Keep your eyes peeled for rubs where the bark from cedar and pine has been recently stripped away, fresh-looking, and fragrant—not the rubs of yesteryear. Rub markings might simply mean that a deer is getting rid of the excess velvet (hairy matter) on its newly-formed antlers. A more serious rub probably means that the buck is marking its territory and communicating to other bucks that "I am the king of this patch of wooded jungle. Keep out."

Fresh Rub

Look for a **rub line** (a series of rubs) that runs approximately fifty yards parallel to either side off a main trail. A smart buck, one that lives to the ripe old age of about ten to twenty years, has survived because it does not travel down the primrose path taken by younger bucks and does. Search for a rub line and set up your stand accordingly during the pre-rut. During the rut, you can set up along a main trail; it's easier pickings because that horny old buck behaves rather stupidly. Its guard is down; therefore, you have a good chance of scoring a wall-hanger trophy at this time than during any other part of the deer hunting season. As the season continues and hunting pressure increases, deer become quite wary, forcing those magnificent creatures to become nocturnal. They tend to take to deeper cover during the day, such as thickets of briars and brambles where you would think only a rabbit could navigate. That's when you'll have your work cut out for you.

Mock Rubs are easily made by using an ice scraper to rough up the bark of an established tree or the skin of a sapling. Scraping away vertically, work an area approximately the width of the blade, starting approximately a foot above the base of the tree to a point somewhere between the height of your waste and shoulders. Do this carefully so as not to break the blade of the tool. Again, always wear clean latex gloves. A mock rub made adjacent to a mock scrape will increase your odds, especially when applying a shot of Pre-Orbital Gland scent along the scraped bark or stripped away skin.

Finding **Funnels** is a sure-fire way to ambush deer. Simply put, a funnel begins as a wide opening that ultimately narrows. On the hunting front, a funnel finishes as a channel or conduit, a confined passageway along which deer travel to avoid daytime detection in open areas. Most of us are familiar with vehicular congestion as a major thoroughfare suddenly bottlenecks, forcing traffic into a single lane. Search for funnels off of fields, forests, woodlots, streams, marshes, and along ridges. Setting up along such travel routes leading from deer bedding areas to their feeding areas (or vice versa) will greatly increase your chances of scoring instead of just randomly selecting a spot. Common sense dictates that you should scout an area well beforehand then set up so as not to put deer on full alert.

Understanding **Feeding Areas**, **Core Areas**, **Bedding Areas**, and **Staging Areas** are your keys to success. Keep in mind that during the fall/winter hunting season, deer head to their **feeding areas** during the early morning hours (approximately 4 to 10 a.m.), and again when the sun is going down (about 4 to 10 p.m.) before returning to the safety of their **core areas**. Some hunters are under the misconception that deer only eat during breakfast and dinner hours, when in fact they browse throughout the day in neighboring areas. Here, they wander about, snacking on grasses and other plants, acorns, et cetera, stopping to rest in one of several **bedding areas** that are easily visible when it snows. Take note and record these areas, ideally using GPS coordinates. Deer beds are oval-shaped, approximately 1½ feet wide by 3½ feet long.

Just as artificial rubs and scrapes can be created, so too can bedding areas be established through what is referred to as hinge-cutting. Hinge-cutting is an involved process that is best left to such professionals as forest/land managers because it is a rather dangerous procedure to partially cut (hinge) a number of trees at head height in order to create a canopy to shelter deer. A forester would know how to strategically fell trees upon one another in order to build buck bedrooms or staging areas that would prove inviting. A hinged tree typically continues to live on for a period, providing nutrients and shelter.

Just prior to entering their primary early morning and late afternoon feeding areas, deer hang out on the fringes of these tracts, scoping out the territory for any sign of danger. I have seen them standing in one spot for as long as thirty minutes before venturing out. A good fifteen minutes seems to be the norm. These are their **staging areas**. Patience will indeed be a virtue while waiting-out a cautious, cagey buck, for within that period of time, its senses are surely at work. Its nose, ears, and eyes will likely reveal your presence in a heartbeat if you are downwind, make a sudden sound, or make a movement. Even while perched high in a treestand, eddying thermal winds can play havoc by giving away your position. Always try and remain upwind from your trophy. Having multiple treestands offers you that possibility.

Taking a Read on Whitetails

The following is excerpted from the sports section of *The Citizen*, a New Jersey community's local newspaper. The year is 1957. The captioned photograph is titled **First Blood**, followed by the reporter's piece.

First Blood: The deer hunting season wasn't twenty minutes old on Monday when Robert Banfelder, 14, Parsippany High School student, brought down his first 6-point buck. The Lake Hiawatha youngster felled the 200-lb. creature in a wooded area of his community. It was his first time out with a shotgun . . . .

Got His First Deer Within 20 Minutes

Bob Banfelder of Lake Hiawatha completed his first deer hunting season in 20 minutes. The Parsippany High School sophomore had scared up a couple of deer in some woods at the far side of a lot off Knoll Rd., not far from Glen Ridge last week. So, with the opening of the hunting season on Monday at 7 a. m., he headed in that direction. Twenty minutes later he had a six-point buck . . . .
 —***THE CITIZEN***
That was fifty-nine years ago. I've learned a lot since then.

CHAPTER 10

ARCHERY & GUNNING STANDS: A BIRD'S-EYE VIEW

With reference to shot placement, switching gears from gunning to bow and arrow hunting for Virginia whitetails—or any related deer of that genus—is not too different. The main distinction is distance. When archery hunting, we all look for that broadside, heart/lung kill-zone shot—occasionally, a spine shot if the animal is directly beneath us and there is little chance that it is going to quarter to the left or right.

Although I practice archery out to 40 yards, I do not take shots over 25 yards. Most of my deer are felled between 15 and 20 yards. This way, I am confident that I am going to hit the mark (its vitals). When hunting, my focus of concentration is not on the deer, per se, but upon a rectangular or square box, whereby I draw a vertical line up the animal's foreleg and *slightly* rearward, holding along a horizontal plane perceived halfway between spine and brisket (lower chest). Once the arrow is released and hopefully hits its mark (the vitals), I wait a good half hour before descending the treestand (from where virtually all of my deer hunting is conducted), having noted precisely the last spot the animal was seen before disappearing from view. Unless I can physically see that the deer is definitely down and positively motionless, I wait for the animal to bleed out (hemorrhage) and die. Otherwise, the deer may find the strength and stamina to run great distances, and you may lose your prize if you pursue too early.

Treestands, as opposed to ground blinds and other types of ground concealment, offer the deer hunter two distinct advantages. You are above the animal's line of sight. You are generally above the animal's scent line (a downdraft notwithstanding). The latter is of paramount importance, for a deer's keen sense of smell is many times greater than a human's. A deer's hearing is acute, and its eyesight is good. Weighing these facts carefully, your first consideration is to get yourself above the animal's line of scent, and a treestand is the ticket. There are many types of stands on the market from which to choose: climbing, tower, fixed, permanent, ladder, and pole stands cover the gamut.

Climbing stands are generally lighter and more portable than other stands. They are manipulated much like an inchworm moving up or down a tree branch; only the hunter is the inchworm, and the vertical branch is the tree. The hunter ascends and descends by raising or lowering two platforms (feet and seat) in increments, controlling the upper platform with his hands, the lower platform with his feet, alternating between sitting and standing, raising or lowering both sections (fashioned about the tree by a chain or cable) until he or she reaches a desired position: a perch perhaps 20 feet off the ground then back to the base of the tree.

Tower stands are a breed unto their own. When there are no suitable trees to be found in the area you wish to hunt, tower stands are your limited choice. They are freestanding platforms supported by legs, generally configured like a tripod with a platform atop. They are cumbersome to carry because of their weight and bulkiness.

Fixed stands are platforms attached to a tree by using any number of materials such as straps or chains. Once erected, strap-on or screw-in type steps are used to ascend and descend.

Permanent stands are a form of fixed stand that can range from a simple platform nestled in the forks of tree limbs to an elaborate, enclosed construction.

Ladder stands, as the name indicates, are ladder-type stands of varying lengths that support a solid platform. The stand is secured to a tree by restraints such as straps or rope. Ladder stands offer ease of climbing and descending.

Pole stands, which are a form of ladder stand, are a favorite of mine. As the name implies, a pole stand is a single leg with its rungs placed and spaced alternately (left and right) to facilitate the hunter's ascent to its attached platform. As ladder stands tend to be a bit bulkier and heavier, pole stands are generally lighter and less cumbersome to carry. Sectioned pieces, with foldable seat and footrest, make the stand quite portable.

I have an Ambusher pole-type treestand that has served me well for many years. I can sit comfortably for several hours. They are a bit difficult to come by because the company is defunct. If you find one, grab it. They pop up now and then on eBay.

Also, I have a climber cleverly named the Tree Lounge, which I use strictly for gunning. It is heavy and bulky; however, once set up, the stand is extremely comfortable. I have sat in it from sunrise to sunset without a complaint in the world. It is literally a reclining lounge in the sky. The company, Tree Lounge, offered an optional bowhunting adaptor, a platform on which to rise from a reclining to a standing position, but I elect to *lounge* about, waiting for a trophy to appear. The Tree Lounge allows the gunner the ability to shoot in any direction; a godsend when taking aim from the rear or your off-shooting side. Like the Ambusher, the company is out of business. Again, they pop up now and then on eBay.

To give you some idea of the comfort factor relating to other more portable types of climbing stands, I also own a Grand Slam Model GS 2500 Magnum from API Outdoors, Inc., a typical style of climber that I can spend a few hours in before feeling any discomfort. With my Ambusher, I am good for several hours. In my Tree Lounge, the sky's the limit.

Hang-on stands are a type of treestand that require a separate series of metal climbing steps in order to ascend. Hang-on stands versus climbing stands create a good deal of confusion when it comes to selection. With a climbing stand, one must pick a relatively straight tree with a minimum of branches that would need to be cut away as you climb upward. With a hang-on type stand, a person first locks in place a climbing stick (step) by wrapping the attached strap around the tree. One of the advantages of the hanging stand/climbing-stick combo is that you can position the strap above and beyond branches and limbs that would otherwise impede progress, whereas with a climbing stand and its encompassing chain or cable (supporting feet and seat platforms), branches and limbs would otherwise thwart movement until removed. When literally weighing the pros and cons of hang-on stands versus climbing stands, be sure to factor in their total weight. Hang-on type stands are generally lighter than climbing stands; however, the additional but necessary four to six stick-steps may exceed the total weight of a climbing stand. No, it's not a perfect world. Always do your due diligence; meaning, do the necessary homework with safety first in mind. Each type of treestand has its own application. Inasmuch as a hang-on stand is versatile—to a degree—a climbing stand is safer. "A man's got to know his limitations," said Clint Eastwood portraying maverick cop (Dirty) Harry Callahan in *Magnum Force*.

Once again, with a hang-on stand, four climbing sticks are required to put the hunter approximately 10 to 12 feet above the ground. Placing the first strap and step-stick around the tree is, of course, easy since you are on terra firma. As you ascend, the task becomes a bit more challenging because you have the hanging stand's seat and footrest platform strapped to your back, along with a safety harness, and a minimum of three more steps to set in place, which weigh approximately 2½ pounds apiece. I really do not recommend this type of treestand unless you are agile and in good physical shape. Personally, I'd choose a climbing stand over a hang-on stand. If, however, you decide on a hanging-stand type, climbing steps are the all-important accoutrement. For a step in the right direction, check out both Muddy (www.gomuddy.com) and Lone Wolf (www.lonewolfhuntingproducts.com).

From left to right, three-type of treestands from which I hunt: Grand Slam climber, Ambusher pole, Tree Lounge (climber), which converts to a deer hauler cart.

Homemade Tower

Although not a treestand, last but not least, is a photo of a homemade unit constructed of sheathing panels, lumber, shingles, and galvanized angle structural supports from which I also hunt, especially when the weather is horrendous.

CHAPTER 11

WISELY SELECTING THE PROPER COMPOUND BOW

In selecting a bow for the purpose of deer hunting, it's wise to buy from a pro shop as opposed to ordering blindly through a catalog or buying haphazardly at a box store, for there are several areas of concern that must first be addressed. This advice is especially sound if you are new to the game (no pun intended) or even an old-timer who is set in his or her ways. Together, we'll cover important considerations—at which point, you'll be in a better position to purchase wisely. Therefore, do not buy a bow willy-nilly. Visit your pro shop, ask questions encompassing the information presented here then politely leave the premises. Before you return home, you'll probably have several more questions. Call the shop and make your inquiries. When you are fully satisfied that your questions have been answered, try before you buy. At this point, no one can accuse you of impulse buying. You should be pretty well-informed.

I dislike when sales people ask, "How much do you want to spend?" This is especially true when considering a bow. I guess an immediate and candid yet inane reply to that rather silly question would be, "As little money as possible to put me afield in order to get the job done efficiently." Be forewarned that the amount of money that you would *want* or *wish* to spend, even when weighed against what you can honestly afford, should have little to do with what you *will* spend in order to successfully and humanely hunt white-tailed deer. In short, you want one of the best bows money can buy. Forget about budgets. I realize that is a bold and presumptuous statement to make. Regardless, I do not want you to make a serious mistake at the onset, or at all. If you buy impulsively, failing to do your necessary homework, what you believe to be a bargain in the beginning will more than likely prove to be a more costly proposition in the long run, coupled to the fact that you will probably wound rather than arrow animals cleanly for a humane kill. That's my sage advice, having hunted whitetails for many years.

Cutting to the quick, you want a compound bow for hunting big game. For example, a compound bow with a draw weight of 50 pounds, boasting 80 percent let-off, is the equivalent of holding back 10 pounds at full draw. The advantage of a compound bow over a traditional straight-limbed or recurve bow is enormous. Picture yourself in a treestand with a trophy buck steadily approaching, offering a perfect broadside shot. You draw down on him, but he momentarily disappears behind a piece of cover. You can comfortably hold that position, whereas with a traditional bow you cannot—having to withdraw the shot. You must now draw back anew, quite likely spooking your prize because your quarry has caught your movement. The buck disappears in an instant. There are two adjectives concerning both man and animal to bear in mind when deer hunting. There are the *quick* and the *dead*. Select a compound bow that you can comfortably handle in the sitting position, boasting 80 percent let-off—preferably a single-cam bow in lieu of twin cams. More on that in a moment.

The power of a bow is determined by its peak draw weight and arrow draw length, measured in pounds and inches, respectively. Folks often make the big mistake of purchasing a bow with a *maximum* draw weight that they can pull back while *standing* in the box store. The prospective customer generally fails to realize that unless he or she is in a standing position while practicing at a target range, come time of the hunt, sitting in a treestand on an especially cold day, bundled up in bulky clothing, that hunter, most probably, will not be able to smoothly pull back the bow—for two reasons. One: It is harder to come to full draw in the sitting position than in the standing position. Two: Even in a standing position, your muscles do not work as well in cold weather.

For openers, the proprietor or salesperson of a good pro shop should sit you on the floor of the store and hand you a bow in perhaps the 50-pound draw-weight range, having you work your way up or down the scale from there. If you strain in handling a 60-pound draw weight in the sitting position, especially when employing a mechanical arrow release, that bow is definitely *not* for you. It is necessary to back down to a comfortable draw weight while still in the sitting position. Don't be a macho man or, conversely, act out a tough tomboyish role, ladies. I've seen over-the-counter sales personnel sell bows to folks that were far beyond a customer's capability to handle that tool at an archery range, let alone a weapon to be carried into the field for the purpose of hunting. Note that you can effectively harvest deer with a 40-pound draw weight bow. As a rule of thumb, 40 pounds of kinetic energy efficiently dispatches whitetails—50 pounds or greater for larger game such as elk, moose, and bear.

By way of confession regarding my first Mathews bow, which I absolutely loved, I was one of those macho men who didn't know any better and was sold a compound bow with a 70-pound draw weight. Oh, I had no trouble pulling the bowstring back with the aid of a release—*standing* in the store. Standing in shirtsleeves in the backyard or my club's shooting range, I experienced no problem whatsoever. I could shoot that bow all day and have. Too, as the start of the bowhunting season on Long Island is generally warm, I had no trouble coming to full draw in either the standing or sitting position from my treestand. However, when the cold weather finally arrived, my muscles did not work the same. I could not come to full draw smoothly. Not good. However, all was not lost. I simply backed off the recommended five turns referencing the bow's limbs with a T-tool, which reduced the draw weight by 10 pounds. Good to go. Or was it?

As the years progressed, as well as the age of my body, I noticed that I was gradually experiencing some difficulty, especially during cold weather, coming to full draw in the sitting position while hunting, so I stood. No big deal, for I stand a good part of the time anyhow. When I grew tired, I sat. Then one *warm* afternoon while hunting with a friend, I found difficulty in coming to full draw in the sitting position. That was in 2011. What to do?

It is important to keep in mind that most compound bows' maximum draw weights can be backed down approximately 10 pounds. However, there are some serious issues to consider with older bows. At a point where you can comfortably handle the maximum draw weight of a newer bow from a seated position, with the capability to back off 10 pounds when a situation might call for it, well, that *could* be the proper bow for you. However, this depends on an important factor. Keep in mind that older model compound bows (such as my first Mathews Solocam purchased back in the mid-nineties) when cranked down 10 pounds from their maximum draw weights are not going to perform nearly as well as newer models because the technology has improved dramatically since that time. Today's bows are far more forgiving. Therefore, if you purchase a new 70-pound pull bow today, then have trouble coming to full draw in the future, you can simply decrease the draw weight by approximately 10 to 12 pounds and expect solid performance. Therefore, do not try and economize by purchasing a used bow dating back several years. Let's take a closer look.

After thorough research, my new Mathews bow, purchased for the 2012 deer season, was a Z7 Magnum compound with a 50-pound maximum draw weight. To give you some idea of how far the technology had advanced over those years (mid-nineties to 2012), my old Mathews Solocam, maxed out at 70 pounds, would only be 64–65% efficient when compared to the newer Mathews Z7 Magnum model bow. When backed off 10 pounds with the older model Mathews bow, the efficiency rate drops to 55%. However, if I were to back off from 50 to 40 pounds with the newer Z7 Magnum, the bow's efficiency rate would drop but 1%. As I get older and may need to reduce the new bow's draw weight by 10–12 pounds, the loss of efficiency is going to be negligible. I won't be running out to buy a new bow anytime soon.

Mathews Z7 Magnum Bow

As I am, admittedly, a dinosaur, having shot aluminum arrows and fixed-blade broadheads for over a decade-and-a-half, having recently graduated to far lighter and faster carbon arrows and mechanical blades when I purchased the new Mathews bow, the overall performance actually came close to that of the 70-pound pull bow as recorded by a chronograph (a device that measures the speed of the arrow in feet per second). Yes, archery is a numbers game.

Keep in mind, too, that a bow with a maximum draw weight of 70 and even 60 pounds is a lot to pull back smoothly for the average person, especially when hunting in cold weather, particularly when sitting. Again, you do not want to find yourself in a treestand with a trophy buck beneath you—or any decent size deer for that matter—and be unable to pull your bow back smoothly, or at all.

Now that we've got our draw weight narrowed down, understanding how both you and your bow should function while standing and sitting in weather ranging from downright cold to often freezing temperatures, it's time to examine another factor regarding compound bows mentioned earlier. Do you want a double or single cam bow? No contest there. I prefer single cam design over dual cams because single cam bows do not nearly require the often necessary tuning of twin cams. Unless you really know what you're doing, tuning a bow is best left to the pros at a reliable bow shop. Bear in mind that regular tuning can become expensive. Mathews, Inc. is the innovator of single cam technology. That should tell you something. Although twin cam bows are also available through Mathews, choose single cam technology. There are several *good* bows on the market. There are a few *great* bows available today. Mathews, in my opinion, is among the *finest*—if not *the finest*.

Let's come full circle, back to the issue of money. When it comes to a fine bow, forget about what you would *want* or *wish* to spend; forget about what you can afford; forget about your budget. You owe it to yourself and, above all, you owe it to the animal. If you feel an ounce of respect toward your quarry, you do not want to settle for anything less than a clean kill. You do not want that animal wounded and suffering for hours or even days. Be prepared to spend in the neighborhood of eight hundred to a thousand dollars, plus tax, for a quality bow. Note that I didn't say anything about arrows or other equipment. That's the reality of the situation.

For a final word on bow selection, I've listed in alphabetical order six companies that manufacture fine compound bows: Bear, BowTech, Browning, Hoyt, Mathews, and PSE. I suggest that you research each, then go out and buy a Mathews.

CHAPTER 12

ALL BROADHEADS ARE NOT CREATED EQUAL — NOT BY A LONG SHOT—>

Fixed Blades vs. Mechanical Blades

For approximately sixteen years, I'd been hunting with both three-bladed and four-bladed "Bad To The Bone" Muzzy broadheads. I've shot these fixed-blade versions in different grain weights: 75, 90, 100, 115, and 125. It's a given that fixed-blade broadheads do not consistently fly as true as field points (wingless projectiles). By attaching fixed blades (wings), aerodynamics has the potential to play havoc upon arrow flight. Wind-planing becomes an issue. Therefore, I experimented with mechanical types of broadheads that were available at the time.

A mechanical broadhead is a projectile with its blades housed within the missile's head. The blades expand outward upon impact. These seemed to be the ticket in overcoming occasional erratic flight experienced with fixed broadheads. There was one mechanical broadhead manufacturer that seemed promising. The year was 1997. Both in practice and while hunting, those mechanical broadheads flew true to their targets, foam and flesh, respectively. However, on more than one occasion while hunting, I was disappointed concerning entry wounds and returned to my fixed-blade Muzzys. They were the rage at the time. Although I would have preferred the wider cutting diameter of the 125-grain Muzzy broadhead, the lighter 100-grain Muzzy performed the best in flight, especially with shots taken beyond 20 yards.

And then came Tuesday, November 2nd, 2010. That afternoon, I went bowhunting with a friend, Chris Paparo. Chris is a true outdoorsman. We headed for Hubbard County Park in Hampton Bays, one of Suffolk County Park's archery access hunting areas. We parked in a designated spot and headed east into a corner woodlot. Approximately 200 yards in, we split up; Chris heading south, roughly 150 yards. I went north, about the same distance. We were set up by 1:30 p.m., Chris in a climber, I in my favored Ambusher pole stand. It was a still afternoon with hardly the whisper of a breeze. Apart from a scurrying skinny squirrel and a gray-white creeper probing while pecking its way steadily upward along the creviced bark of a tall pine tree, there was no other activity.

In the distance, at 4:45 p.m., I heard a headlong crash and sudden thrashing coming from Chris' direction. I raised him on a walkie-talkie.

"Either you fell out of your nest, or you whacked something," I called quietly.

"I think I got a doe," Chris whispered excitedly. "I saw her go down about sixty yards from me."

"Are you going to wait?"

There was a long pause before the reply. "I don't think so. It was a good shot; I saw the hit." There was another long pause. "I think I see her. I'm coming down."

"All right, then. See you in a few minutes."

Several minutes later, I met Chris at the base of his tree. He pointed and we walked together in a southwesterly direction, recovering his perfectly intact blood-strewn carbon arrow and 100-grain mechanical broadhead that had passed completely through the animal. Immediately, we picked up a substantial blood trail. A moment later, I spotted the downed, dead deer. It was, indeed, a doe. Chris had shot the creature at 30 yards. It was clearly a well-placed shot. What impressed me was the size of the entry-exit holes; a 2-inch diameter. The doe hadn't run more than 30 yards from the point of impact, the mechanical broadhead clear through the animal's rib cage. She had practically bled out. Absolutely awesome!

By comparison, my 100-grain Muzzys made $5/8^{th}$-inch diameter holes, occasionally coagulating and allowing a deer to forge ahead a good distance before recovering it. This was not the norm, but it did happen from time to time. The larger and heavier 125-grain Muzzys made 15/16th-inch diameter holes, but, as mentioned, did not fly as well. I'd rather make a well-placed shot (hitting the vitals) than a poor one that struck elsewhere (wounding the creature) for the sake of creating a larger opening.

After Chris and I gutted the animal and gathered our gear, I asked him about those mechanical broadheads he was using and had talked about earlier as we were heading toward Hubbard County Park for the start of the hunt. I hadn't paid too much attention when he mentioned that they were mechanical blades—and only two blades to boot—not three or four blades.

"What did you say was the name of those broadheads?" I questioned in earnest.

Chris smiled, knowing he now had my full attention.

"Rage."

"What?"

"Rage," he repeated. "They're called Rage."

"That's some hole it made."

"Yep."

When I got home, I researched Rage broadheads and learned that they were the *rage* of the moment. My thoughts kept returning to Chris' clean kill, made possible by that lethal broadhead. I was sold. My Muzzys have served me well, but it is time to move on when someone builds a better mousetrap. I looked over my equipment. I knew I was considered a dinosaur by some, for I was still shooting aluminum arrows when lighter and faster carbon arrows are . . . the rage, too. My array of metallic Easton arrows, Gamegetter 2216 and XX 78 Super Slam 2413, had served me well, also. However, it was now time to upgrade. Besides, the mechanical missiles would fly true to their target as would practice field points because there is no wind resistance acting upon exposed, fixed blades. My research told me that the rear-deploying expandable Rage blades opened immediately upon impact, not afterward as what is referred to as over-the-top designs, which open after entry. As mentioned, I had experienced problems with other mechanical broadheads during those early years, finding the flimsy blades not fully deployed, or broken, or having failed to open at all. A quote from the folks at Rage states, "An angled hit with an over-the-top expandable can result in the leading blade grabbing first and throwing the head off line. Rage's rear deploying blades follow the cut-on-impact tip and will not grab or deflect, and give you a full cutting diameter on impact." Was this hype? I know what I witnessed that afternoon with Chris. I know what I heard from other hunters after relating that experience. I believe the unbiased reports that I had been reading from hunters who use Rage broadheads. A sturdy expandable broadhead that flies like a field point and truly opens on impact. Wow! And 2-inch diameter entry-exit holes to boot.

It was on that *warm weather* hunt with Chris when I finally realized that I had a serious issue when coming to full draw in the sitting position. What was I going to do when cold weather arrived, which was right around the corner? For the following fall deer season, I had all new equipment, inclusive of my new Mathews Z7 Magnum compound with a 50-pound draw weight.

CHAPTER 13

ARROW SHAFTS ~ ARCHERY RELEASES ~ ARROW RESTS ~ SIGHT PINS

Arrow Shafts That Will Not Shaft You

As with bow selection, arrow selection is based on several variables; that is, the overall weight (measured in grains), spine weight (stiffness), whether you'll be shooting with an overdraw (an apparatus that allows for a shorter arrow to be propelled, which translates into a lighter shaft, thereby increasing speed), et cetera. Consulting archery charts will help narrow your arrow choices. I'd definitely have you consider carbon arrows over aluminum; also, I'd advise against an overdraw. Keep things simple. Only if you were shooting aluminum arrows would I even have you consider an overdraw.

Keep in mind that (all things being relatively equal) carbon shafts are lighter and therefore faster than aluminum shafts. Without getting too technical, a carbon-shaft pultrusion process is comprised of impregnating fiberglass roving and mat material with resin, resulting in precision spines of a thinner diameter. This translates to increased accuracy and velocity. Too, carbon arrows stabilize faster than aluminum after launch, providing powerful impact and penetration upon game.

As the years fly by, a bowhunter may be tempted to stick with one arrow brand and model that has served him or her well. However, as those years quickly add up, quantum leaps in arrow technology have already been made, and you will be missing out on advancements that are sure to give you an added edge. What to do? I buy a dozen arrows at a time, and when they're almost used up, I research what's 'new and improved' on the market referencing the area in which I may find myself. For example, I would want a lighter, faster arrow/broadhead combination that shoots flatter at longer distances as I may be hunting in open terrain as opposed to heavy cover. In closer quarters such as thick cover, I would want a heavier arrow when employing a merciless mechanical broadhead with a cutting diameter of 2 inches so as to ensure maximum penetration.

My concerns in selecting arrow shafts are their matched weights, spine consistency (measured in grains per inch), and straightness—and in no particular order, for one is as important to me as the other two. Hunters new to the game may not realize that you get what you pay for when purchasing arrow shafts. Once again, without getting too technical, I'll briefly explain these considerations. When a manufacturer specifies their shaft straightness tolerances are an "Average" of .003 (that is, 3/1000 of an inch), the word average means that a box of a dozen arrows could deviate plus or minus .003 inch. In other words, they could run the gamut of .001 inch straightness to .006 inch not as straight. On the other hand, the word "Maximum" means that out of a box of a dozen arrows, no shaft will exceed a .003 maximum tolerance. Not all manufacturers indicate these average or maximum tolerances.

Referencing matched weights, a manufacturer's pultrusion process can result in shaft weights varying from a ½ grain to a 5-plus grain difference. This is the result of differences in carbon fiber roving and mat material application, resin curing, followed by sanding. Close, but no cigar.

Spine consistency, or the way a shaft flexes, is not a given, and there is no industry standard. What to do? The best you can by following these guidelines and purchasing arrow shafts manufactured by leaders in the field. Here is a handful that you can count on: Carbon Express, Easton, Beman, and GoldTip.

Archery Releases
Wrist-Strap vs. Handle-Style Releases

Just as continual innovations are being made concerning bows and arrow shafts and broadheads, so, too, are new designs created by manufacturers of releases for both the bowhunter as well as the competitive 3-D and target archery crowd. As a matter of fact, if your release is more than a decade old, it *may* be considered outdated. Does that mean you should run out and purchase a new one? Not necessarily. But what you should do is compare what you are presently using to what might improve your score whether at the archery range shooting paper targets, bags, and foam blocks, or launching broadheads while playing for keeps in forests and fields.

Many moons ago, I started hunting with a Winn Hook Loop release from Free Flight Archery Equipment Company, South Haven, Michigan. It is an 8-ounce leather glove-style design, covered with reinforced Cordura material. Its trigger and rockers are constructed from file-hardened steel fastened within a stainless steel case. Decades later when I purchased my new Mathews Z7 Magnum and related equipment in 2012, I opted for a new type of wrist-strap release for three reasons. One, it gave me hands-free movement when necessary (which the glove-style did not). Two, it buckled around the wrist in lieu of being wrapped and secured in place by a noisy Velcro strap. Three, it employed a superior two caliper (dual-jaw design) instead of the single-hook loop lock. The new release is from Tru-Fire, called their Hurricane model.

One of the most important features of a release is a close and comfortable feel between the trigger and the bowstring. The glove-style type release certainly affords that attribute a bit more than the hands-free, narrow wrist-strap type style—even with its adjustable threaded bolt design. Well, it's not a perfect world. Therefore, I always carry the two types, especially if one should fail.

Also, there are the T-handle-style releases such as the older thumb-activated types, which grab onto a bowstring; but not all grab a D-loop (rope loop) well. The single- or two-caliper types mentioned will, of course, accommodate either a bowstring or a bowstring's D-loop.

Another T-handle release style is referred to as the "hinge" or "true back tension release," which does not have a trigger but releases the arrow by the archer drawing the bow, anchoring, contracting the muscles in his or her back (that is, tensioning both shoulders rearward), releasing one's thumb from the device's thumb peg while naturally relaxing and rotating the release hand. It is the pivoting action of the apparatus that releases the shot and is generally used as a training aid to teach 3-D and target shooters proper form. This also deters what might otherwise cause trigger panic, for one does not know precisely when the arrow is going to be launched. Most hunters do not use this style of release; serious 3-D and target shooters do. However, more and more hunters do practice with this true back-tension type of release aid. Therefore, it deserves mention. Scott manufactures fine back tension release aids such as the model Long Horn Hunter. Once again, I'd keep things simple and select one of the glove-type or strap-style, hands-free releases.

Arrow Rests

The Trophy Ridge Whisker Biscuit is by far the best arrow rest I have ever used. It does not affect arrow flight as I have shot deer out to 30 yards without an issue. I practice in increments of 10 yards out to 30 yards and can attest to its continued accuracy. Trophy Ridge Whisker Biscuit Arrow Rest manufactures a good many models. I practice and hunt annually, and its synthetic bristles have shown no sign of wear. However, I would neither push a fixed-blade broadhead through the bristles nor backload fletchings through them when loading an arrow, although stated that it is okay to do so on the website's Frequently Asked Questions. Rather ridiculous. Common sense would dictate that you select only those models that provide the custom cushioned rubber entry slot—such as the Trophy Ridge Quick Shot Whisker Biscuit Arrow Rest ($30–$54) for effortless loading. The biscuit's center diameter hole through which the arrow passes comes in three sizes: small (.300 inch), medium (.320 inch), and large (.385 inch).

As for noise from arrow shafts and fletchings (plastic or feathers) passing through the biscuit's bristles, the arrow rest could be aptly renamed the Whisper Biscuit. I have witnessed competitors' arrow rests damage plastic vanes and consequently cause erratic arrow flight. A Trophy Ridge Whisker Biscuit Arrow Rest will allow for consistency. I have seen professional archery hunters consistently hit the bull's-eye out to 100 yards while shooting arrows through a Trophy Ridge Whisker Biscuit. Awesome!

Sight Pins

I started shooting a bow with a simple 3-pin Cobra archery sight. When I purchased my new Mathews Z7, I bought the same Cobra sight. It has never failed me, so why argue with success? A longtime bowhunter, who eats, sleeps, and breathes hunting for deer, elk, moose, and bear, broke me into the sport. He suggested that I do what he now does, and that is to sight in and use only a single pin. Neither of us are what you would call long-distance shooters, as some archers have taken game at 100-plus yards. I have seen my friend consistently shoot tight groups out to 60 yards. He'll shoot game comfortably and responsibly up to 50 yards. Like a good many hunters, he has had as many as five pins on his bow sight, but now employs a single pin set for 35 yards.

"I know how much to aim beneath my single pin to hit the mark at ten to twenty yards. My sight pin is zeroed in for thirty-five yards. I know how much holdover I need to make clean kills out to fifty yards. Why complicate matters with multiple pins?"

I like my friend's reasoning and certainly know his proficiency at those yardages. I listened and took his suggestion, employing a single pin set for 20 yards. I'm proficient out to thirty yards. Both he and I utilize laser rangefinders and use reference points when settled in our treestands, et cetera. Unless you are a long-distance shooter, launching arrows well beyond 60 yards, why confound matters with multiple pins, especially when shooting in close quarters such as a 20- to 30-yard range? Try practicing at 15–35 yardages with a single pin and see if you do or do not agree.

Admittedly, at one time I had in my excitement used the wrong sight pin and shot beneath the brisket of a nice buck at 35 yards. I was, of course, furious with myself. The top pin was set for 20 yards, middle pin for 30 yards, and the bottom pin for 40 yards. I had placed the top pin instead of the bottom pin just to the rear of the buck's shoulder blade (and yes, it was a clear broadside shot). I was mistakenly thinking *high pin for a higher shot*. Had I but placed a single pin zeroed in for 20 yards higher near the animal's spine, allowing for trajectory, I would have arrowed that deer nicely. I have harvested as many as seven deer with a bow in a single season, so it wasn't buck fever that blew the shot. It was sheer stupidity.

For long-distance shooters, however, multiple pins are, indeed, necessary. I am, however, a minimalist and a short-distance shooter (35 yards and less). The prudent Keep It Simple System has been my creed for decades.

In sighting in your bow, start out at 15 yards with a single pin. You first have to establish a consistent grouping of several arrows so as to determine in which direction to move your pin in order to zero in toward the bull's-eye.

If you are shooting too high, raise your sight pin.
If you are shooting too low, lower your sight pin.
If you are shooting to the right, move your sight pin to the right.

If you are shooting to the left, move your sight pin to the left.

In other words, move your sight pin in the same direction that your arrows are grouping away from the bull's-eye in order for them to travel in the opposite direction toward the bull's-eye. Got it? Good.

Still confused? Simply move your sight pin in the direction of misalignment. This will compensate for and correct the error.

These essentially alike set of instructions and/or explanations will eventually become crystal clear, but perhaps confounded anew when employing additional pins above and below a central pin, only one of which is correctly aimed at the trophy buck at 35 yards. There is no confusion when utilizing a single sight pin, for you would instinctively raise not lower the pin to account for trajectory. Of course, you would have to know how much holdover is needed to hit the mark. As there are several variables to consider, such as draw weight, bow speed, wind velocity, et cetera, only target practice, practice, practice will make you proficient. The simpler the pin sight setup, for me, the better. We can make things extremely difficult and costly when it comes to our hunting tools. Keep in mind that you have half the radius of a pie plate as a margin of error (referencing the kill zone) when it comes to proficiently felling an adult-sized deer.

CHAPTER 14

CROSSBOWS VS. TRADITIONAL BOWS

Misconceptions and Realities

Placed smack between the Stone Age and the Iron Age was the Bronze Age. It is believed that the Chinese invented the crossbow during that period, as bronze crossbow bolts and bronze triggers had been discovered in burial sites and tombs during the fifth and six centuries B.C., respectively. Scripted documentation dates crossbows back to the fourth and third centuries B.C. Remember, we're counting backwards in time to before the **B**irth of **C**hrist; B.C. The fifth century is older than the fourth century is older than the third century until we reach the first century B.C., where we begin counting forward. The years that immediately follow B.C. are designated A.D., **A**nno **D**omini, meaning, in the year of the Lord; that is, the birth of Christ. One A.D. immediately follows 1 B.C., followed by 2 B.C., et cetera. By circa 200 B.C., the crossbow had been radically refined and extensively used in China. Repeating-type crossbows and large crossbows of the catapult class used in warfare are the offshoot of the original crossbow, whether invented by the Chinese, Romans, Greeks, or whomever.

In reviewing this applied science, referencing warfare, I sometimes wonder how a medieval crossbowman might react today upon examining a modern day crossbow or compound bow with its wheels and oblong-shaped cams, realizing, of course, that the wheel-and-axle technology concept was already in play by 3,500 B.C., but that we somehow regressed by employing the cam configuration design. I mean, after all, didn't Mathews, Inc., innovators of the single cam bow, revert back to their N**0** CAM™ technology for 2014-15? Silliness aside, to say that crossbows were the implements of antiquity used for hunting and warfare is certainly an understatement. Since the mid-1970s in this country, crossbows slowly appeared on the scene. But there are still several misconceptions when comparing vertical bows to horizontal bows. I'd like to clear away the cobwebs.

In one form or another, crossbow hunting has become legally permitted in every state except Oregon (at this writing). Whether exclusively set aside for the handicapped or senior citizen hunter, or offering hunters their own crossbow season, or having them participate in the regular archery season, New York and Wisconsin have recently joined the majority by creating new and generous regulations. Legions of folks immediately view the crossbow as a *great* advantage over traditional bows. Like any number of things in life, crossbows certainly have their advantages as well as disadvantages. It all boils down to the type of hunting you are accustomed to, along with changes you are willing to make to move from say a longbow, recurve, or the quintessential compound bow. Believe me, there will be a few adjustments that you will have to make, changes that you may not even be aware of. Let's explore these aspects.

First off, you will be handling a horizontal bow (transversely fixed on a stock) as opposed to a traditional vertical bow. This means that you will need a wider space to fire, for many of these bows' limbs measure 22-inches wide (axle-to-axle), 18-inches wide on average when cocked and ready for deployment. Keep in mind that you'll be carrying this implement from point A to point B.

Crossbows are generally two to three times heavier than compound bows. From stock to stirrup and topped with a telescopic sight, the weight of a crossbow can quickly take its toll. You are not aiming through a virtually weightless peep sight, keeping in mind that a crossbow's advertised weight generally does not include the scope. Holding and aiming a crossbow in the offhand position while standing in a treestand is nowhere as easy as holding and aiming a vertical bow, or for that matter, a rifle or slug gun. There are, however, aids such as the aluminum two-section Steady Eddy telescoping monopod system offered by TenPoint Crossbows Technologies to help support an offhand stance. However, the attachment does add additional weight to the package and can be cumbersome when ready to line up a shot. Crossbows fitted with monopods or bipods shine when deployed from a ground blind since your movement is unlikely to be detected.

If you are going to tote a treestand and a crossbow any appreciable distance, a crossbow sling is an important piece of gear in which to travel from point A to point B—and back. Heavy Hauler Outdoor Gear offers the perfect crossbow sling to make travel easier. With fully adjustable swivels and wide nonslip neoprene straps that fit over your shoulders like a backpack, the sling easily and safely carries your weapon of choice: crossbow, conventional bow, rifle, or shotgun. The sling is a must for a crossbow, allowing for balanced transportation and hands-free maneuverability. For $39.99, it is a bargain and comes with a free quiver-hip holster. Can't be beat. Visit www.heavyhauleroutdoorgear.com for front, back, and side view pictures. Also, it would be extremely wise to carry a bow holder (with an extended arm) to screw into the tree alongside your treestand. It need not be fancy and specifically designated for crossbows; it needs to be functional. I have a simple screw-in type that I've used for many years while either bow or gun hunting. Keeping it simple has been my theme for decades. But how simple is this shift from a conventional compound bow to a crossbow going to be?

Hunters unfamiliar with crossbows immediately assume that they are going to straightaway double their shooting distance. They instinctively believe that if one can shoot accurately and consistently out to 25 and 30 yards with a compound bow, 50 and 60 yards is going to be a walk in the park (so to speak) with a crossbow. After all, this coveted tool is going to be equipped with optics. Faulty reasoning, folks. It's the bow's draw weight, coupled to the speed of the arrow (commonly referred to as a bolt), akin to kinetic energy, in conjunction with the quality of the scope, compounded by practice, practice, practice, that are the combined elements necessary to put you in the paper bull's-eye or the whitetail's vitals at greater distances. There are no shortcuts.

For the average Joe or Jane, think of a crossbow as a consistently accurate 20- to 50-yard killing implement—in the right hands. Only when you are accomplished, through continued practice, should you allow that weapon to incrementally deliver bolts out to 40 or 50 yards. To believe that you are going to effectively fell deer out to 90 or 100 yards is delusional. It's analogous to a hunter accurately and consistently making kill-shots out to 20 yards with his or her compound bow but one day decides to take a 40-yard shot, which that person has no business doing, lest you wound the animal. The hunter is foolishly pushing the envelope way beyond his or her ability.

Another misconception some folks are under is that crossbows are many, many times more powerful than a compound bow and arrow. The fact is that crossbow bolts fly at speeds and along trajectory paths not too much greater than conventional arrows. On average (and this is such a loaded term), manufacturers of compound bows deliver arrow speeds of 285 feet per second, striving to reach the 300 feet per second mark. Only a handful of crossbows, such as the Mission MXB400, are capable of producing bolt speeds of 400 feet per second, with the average speed being 327 feet per second. There are so many variables that come into play when determining these so-called averages that it is mind boggling: draw weights, grain weights of the arrows (bolts), power stroke lengths, et cetera.

One of the big advantages that crossbows have over conventional bows, within the parameters cited above, is their given accuracy over a specific range, resulting in cleaner kills. Also, hunters who have physical handicaps that prevent them from coming to full draw with a traditional bow can likely take advantage of crossbows, which allow pre-cocking the bow prior to aiming and firing the weapon, similar to a firearm with a round in its chamber. This can be accomplished in one of two ways: with the help of a manually assisted rope-cocking aid that one physically employs to load a crossbow, or with an integral cranking device utilizing approximately five pounds of effort. The latter not only loads the crossbow effortlessly for bows advancing mighty draw weights, it also self-centers the string to ensure a precision, balanced draw each and every time. This latter cranking device is a no-brainer for young adults, women who lack upper body strength and, in general, older folks with impairments. Obviously, these advantages open up a whole new world for those who would otherwise be excluded from this wonderful sport of target shooting and/or hunting—not only for whitetails but for small game.

However, the cranking-type device is not without issues, for its cord and internal components will eventually need to be repaired or replaced. Too, a crossbow's strings and cables wear more often than one might imagine due to heavy draw weights. I searched high and low for some kind of comparison between a compound bow's and a crossbow's string and cable longevity. The consensus is that a compound bow's components will generally last for a couple thousand shots before needing service, whereas crossbows will likely need service after only a couple hundred shots, especially those bows employing cranking systems. Therefore, if you truly do not need the cranking aid, do not opt for one. If you have to, well, so be it. Considering average use, a crossbow's strings and cables should be replaced every three years.

The draw weight of a crossbow is halved by using a rope-cocking aid. For example, if you are cocking a crossbow of a 150-pound draw weight, you will be exerting a 75-pound upward pull over the length of the power stroke, meaning the distance the bowstring will travel before engaging its locking mechanism. Of course, you will be loading the crossbow on the ground, vertically, by pulling upward with both arms and assisted by the rope-cocking aid that hooks onto the bowstring. Leverage and a foot stirrup make this operation relatively easy for most folks. Interestingly, Mission crossbows by Mathews make use of foot holds set to either side that are fashioned into the bow's limbs in lieu of a stirrup for cocking the weapon. The plus side is that you gain pulling power because the foot holder (either left or right) is further off the ground than a stirrup, resulting in a shorter power stroke. However, you are now cocking the crossbow slightly off its vertical axis as opposed to loading it dead center with an in-line stirrup. Therefore, you must be very careful to pull the rope-cocking aid up *evenly* and along the rail or your shooting accuracy is going to be impaired. So long as you hold this concept in mind, it shouldn't pose a problem. As a matter of fact, the same care should be taken when cocking a crossbow with a stirrup. I like Mission/Mathews' innovative design that eliminates the stirrup altogether, reducing front-end weight.

Here's a thought or two to keep firmly in mind for those with aging issues or serious handicaps. I recently went from a compound bow with a draw weight of 70 pounds down to one of 50 pounds. Good to go; a piece of cake with 80% let-off. However, if I ever reach the point where I'd have to turn that compound down to just a shy less than 40 pounds (which is illegal, 40 pounds being the legal limit) in order to comfortably come to full draw, I'd have to hang it up and shoot a crossbow. If you practice, practice, practice, a crossbow becomes a 50-yard killing tool in the hands of the accomplished. In the hands of a beginner, 30 yards is the ticket as compared to 15 to 20 yards when shooting a compound bow. Practice and hunt with the arrows (bolts and broadheads) that the manufacturer recommends, and you'll be way ahead of the game. Too, read, understand, and follow the bow manufacturer's manual.

Uncocking your crossbow at the end of each day's hunt is a sure way to add to its longevity. To do otherwise is to put unnecessary stress on the bow's limbs, strings, cables, and trigger mechanism. It is a simple procedure to reserve and fire a field point bolt into the ground at the end of the hunt. Then again, there are crossbows that you can safely uncock without having to fire them.

Buying a crossbow straight from a catalog would be a big mistake, for there are bows that feel and fit like a glove when brought to your shoulder, and there are bows that feel cumbersome, their weight being of major concern. A bargain-priced bow that proves unwieldy is truly no bargain at all. You'd be better off sticking with your compound bow. Those who know me well-understand that I only promote high-end (flagship) equipment. Be prepared to pay big bucks for a quality crossbow with a quality scope. If you look to take a shortcut, you'll be disappointed. You get what you pay for. Yes, an inexpensive scope will lower the overall price of the crossbow; however, you'll be shortchanged short-term. If your rationalization is that you'll upgrade down the pike, referencing either scope or bow or both, so be it. However, I'm a firm believer in getting it right the first time.

Do you need a crossbow that approaches speeds of 400 feet per second? Do you need a crossbow that costs $2,000 plus? A quality light crossbow hurling bolts at 350 fps is going to get the job done nicely, comfortably, accurately and, therefore, cleanly. Expect to pay in the neighborhood of at least a grand for a top-quality crossbow; you can even shell out more, but I'll draw a line in the sand at the $1,720 mark. A short list of crossbows that I'd take a serious look at is the Stryker Solution ($899), Stryker LS ($1,049), Barnett Razr ($1,600), Barnett Ghost 410 ($1,199), Mathews Mission MBX400 ($1,200), TenPoint Venom ($1,720), and the Wicket Ridge CLS (TenPoint's entry-level crossbow ~ $820).

Yes, a $1,720 price tag for the TenPoint Venom crossbow package is justified in that you get what you pay for. Let's see what you'll receive for your hard-earned money: First off, you won't find it necessary to upgrade the telescopic sight, as the Venom package comes with a precision RangeMaster Pro Scope, variable speed and arrow-drop compensation, etched glass reticle calibrated out to 60 yards, and fully-coated optics from 1½ to 5X power. That's a $300 scope included in the package. When cocked, the Venom's limbs measure a mere 13.25 inches axle-to-axle. With a 185-pound draw weight, the Venom launches its 370-grain Pro Lite bolt at 372 feet per second, striking with 114 foot pounds of kinetic energy. The crossbow weighs in at only 6.5 pounds. Compare these stats to other crossbows when shopping. The Venom, apart from its sticker-shock effect, would be a serious consideration for the perfect crossbow in terms of axle-to-axle compactness, speed, weight, and optics package. Can you pay even more for a TenPoint crossbow? Yes. Would you believe $2,719 for their Carbon Xtra CLS package? Is it necessarily better? No, because you're paying for heirloom-quality aesthetics while actually losing the benefits of speed, weight, and axle-to-axle compactness when compared to TenPoint's Venom crossbow. *Caveat emptor*; Latin for "Let the buyer beware." Do your homework. Look and listen for crossbows that may be too slow or too noisy. The best way to accomplish this is to find an archery pro shop that will allow you try before you buy. Can you shell out a shy less than a grand for a quality crossbow? Yes. I've listed two that won't disappoint.

Noting New <u>Reverse-Draw</u> Technology

Most interestingly, because crossbows are becoming quite popular, manufacturers are competing to produce faster, lighter, and more compact designs. Referencing the latter, new technology has radically taken a quantum leap forward. The bow's configuration is still, of course, set on a vertical plane. However, its riser and limbs are reversed; hence the term "reverse-draw technology." This evolutionary advancement places the crossbow's center of gravity closer to the archer's body, eliminating the top-heavy, front-end design found in traditional-style crossbows.

I'd suggest taking a look at a few reverse-draw crossbow companies and models if only for a comparison in extremes. One is the Velocity RTD 165, shooting a 400-grain bolt at a staggering speed of 425 feet per second. It's currently the world's fastest production crossbow on the market. It is also the heaviest at 11 pounds. Jim Kemph of Scorpyd is the innovator of reverse-draw technology. There are other excellent reverse-draw crossbows that are more compact and lighter than the Scorpyd Velocity RTD 165.

For example, check out the Barnett Crossbow Vengeance model with its light carbon riser: 365 feet per second, draw weight 140 pounds, mass weight 7.9 pounds. Also, the Horton Crossbow Fury model gets high marks: 360 feet per second, draw weight 160 pounds, weighing in at 7.6 pounds.

What I'd like to see crossbow companies do is to offer its customers the option of either accepting or not accepting the telescopic sight that usually comes with the bow and then price the package accordingly. Invariably, you are at the mercy of what the company chooses to offer regarding optics. Rarely does the crossbow company provide thorough information referencing the quality of the scope that comes as a package. I know the optics I want for a crossbow, and it is not a telescopic sight. I prefer a holographic sight. After touching base with several crossbow manufacturers, their attitude is to have the customer accept the package as is, meaning bow and scope, then have you replace the scope with your preference after the fact. I can't see spending good money for a scope I won't be using. This is analogous to my having shopped for a new boat and motor a few years back. The boat and motor came as a package that included a trailer. As I already had a boat trailer, I asked if the dealer if he would discount the price of the trailer. I was told to purchase the package and put the trailer on my front yard with a For-Sale sign. No dealer in my area would accommodate me, so I went out of area. No problem. The dealer gladly discounted the full value of the trailer from the package price because he wanted my business.

The optics I would choose for a crossbow is the high-quality Model 512 XBOW holographic (laser) sight manufactured by the EOTech, designed specifically for crossbows. More on those fantastic EOTech laser sights [referencing firearms] in chapters 28 and 29. When I find a quality crossbow company that will work with me, giving me the option as described above, I'll be ready to make a purchase . . . probably a reverse-draw-style crossbow. I'm not an impulse buyer, so I won't settle and be at the mercy of what a company wants to sell me. I'll purchase once; I'll do it right. Until such time, I'll stay with my vertical bow. That's just me.

Also, I believe consumers would like to know the specific weights of both crossbow and scope (be it a conventional-style or reverse-draw type) as well as the optics manufacturer and model. I want to know what I'm buying. Most crossbow companies only give you the scope's magnification. You do not have the option of upgrading to a better scope or purchasing the bow separately, requesting the company to discount the full value of the optics from the price of the package. That's when I part *company*.

If you do settle for a package *deal*, do your due diligence; hit those archery pro shops and shoulder those weapons. Ask many questions and compare, compare, compare. Once again, don't look for a bargain bow—not if you're at all serious about hunting. You may find that a pro shop will work with you, providing, of course, that you purchase the upgrade from the shop. If you're getting a RangeMaster Pro Scope telescopic sight as part of a crossbow package, as you would with TenPoint's high-end crossbows, you're getting quality. If you're getting a Hawke scope, which are good optics, keep in mind that they come in several models, ranging from entry level to their flagship model. Will you be happy with something in between, or will you be upgrading in months to come? If you knew what you were getting, instead of buying blindly, you could do a bit of research and determine what's right for you from the start. Enough said on that subject.

Admittedly, I'm a fair-weather hunter, meaning that I don't choose to subject my tools to the elements whether they're firearms or bows. Of course, there are times that I've been caught is both rain and snowstorms. Upon return, I'll turn to the weapon's maintenance.

Crossbows are to be wiped clean and dried from stock to stirrup: risers and limbs, rail, rail fletching groove, trigger and trigger housing to be lightly lubed, all bolts and screws inspected, strings and cables waxed, cams and wheels cared for with a drop of oil and silicone cloth, and the telescopic sights given special attention with lens cleaner and lens tissue if needed. Protect your investment(s). Again, there are no shortcuts.

Presently, perhaps like you, because of new rules permitting crossbow hunting, I am narrowing my choice of a crossbow to the limited selection already cited. My research has been exhaustive, but I still haven't made a definitive decision. I trust this chapter will be of considerable help to you whether deciding on your first or next crossbow. Two positive and indisputable facts remain: Crossbows are far easier to master than conventional bows, and hunting with a crossbow will certainly extend one's season as it did in Wisconsin and New York.

Note: I will be addressing a definitive decision regarding my choice of crossbow. It will be thoroughly covered in my next handbook titled THE COMPLETE BOWHUNTER: *CROSSBOW ~ COMPOUND BOW ~ BOWFISHING*, scheduled for the spring of 2018.

CHAPTER 15

MANUFACTURED & NATURAL GROUND BLINDS

Manufactured Archery & Gunning Gems

Basically, a hunter has two ways to go referencing ground blinds for archery and gunning. You can buy a manufactured model, or you could construct your own. The obvious benefit of buying a ground blind is that it is portable and offers optimum shelter from the elements, whereas a natural blind may not. Depending on size, manufactured blinds are relatively light, and the pop-up type can be set up quickly. You would want to, of course, consider the blind's length, width, and height with regard to your height and whether you'll be hunting solo or with a partner. Keep in mind that once set up, a blind still needs to be brushed in (camouflaged) for maximum effectiveness, especially when deer hunting. Firstly, you want to concern yourself with breaking up the uniform shape of the blind; its sides as well as its top. This can be accomplished with a minimal amount of materials such as tree branches, sticks, leaves, and surrounding vegetation. You need not build a blind around a blind. However, you want to distort the fact that a strange object has been starkly introduced into the area. For deer hunting, it would be beneficial to have the blind set up and left alone for several weeks. Having perhaps noted a somewhat different addition to its territory, it is essential that deer get used to the new structure and feel that it presents no threat. But if deer happened to come across the blind initially, they are going to be cautious if not on full alert. Better that they should have discovered something different in their neighborhood and have time to absorb what the unfamiliar structure is; that is, something ostensibly benign. This will give you the added edge.

For turkey hunting, this approach is not necessary. You can set up your portable blind and hunt out of it immediately. But again, take the trouble to break up its outline as explained. Utilizing either set-up for deer or turkey, it is imperative to clear out the interior floor of any debris that will alert the animal to your presence. Noise from stepping on a stick or rustling dry leaves will send your quarry hightailing or flying out of there.

Primos Ground Blind

Building a Natural Ground Blind

In addition to buying a ground blind, you may also want to build your own blind. It's easier than you think. First, find a suitable area to construct your blind where deer cross; for example, near trails that converge, especially one that funnels narrowly as deer travel to and from their bedding and feeding areas. Ideally, locate an area that provides a backdrop of available cover, such as a good size uprooted tree. Already, you've eliminated camouflaging the rear section of the blind; it's already provided for you. That leaves three sides to cover. You'll collect these natural materials around you: stout sticks, branches, limbs, boughs. No need to carry in paraphernalia, save a fresh pair of latex gloves, folding handsaw, ball of green or tan twine, and a small hand pruner.

To form the front section of the blind, don those gloves and start by firmly sticking two sturdy sticks vertically into the ground, chest high, forked in a V, placed wide enough apart to accommodate one or two hunters sitting side by side, leaving enough width for ample elbow room to comfortably draw a bow or raise a firearm. Lay a limb horizontally across the sticks and within the V.

Using another forked stick to frame the side of the blind from where you figure a deer will approach, similarly position the stick at a rear corner then lay a connecting limb between the front and rear corner. Leave the other side open for easy entrance and egress. Tie the ends of the horizontal limbs to the vertical forked sticks. You have just completed the foundation of your ground blind.

Gather up the necessary lengths of sticks, bare branches, limbs, and boughs to lean against and to form a chest-high structural base. Next, crisscross and lay these materials in a helter-skelter fashion. Freshly cut beech leaf branches, grasses, and other nearby vegetation will put the finishing touches upon your natural deer and/or turkey blind. Complete this step just before the hunt because cut beech leaf branches, grasses and green vegetation will wilt very quickly. You're almost finished building your natural ground blind. Lastly, clean out the floor area of your natural ground blind as you did for the manufactured type.

You will not have the protection from the elements provided by a manufactured shelter should it rain or snow, but you will have adequate cover and comfort, having created a camouflaged ground blind to your specifications, and at a fraction of the cost, meaning next to nothing.

CHAPTER 16

PROCESSING YOUR DEER

Tools and Equipment for Field Dressing ~ Skinning ~ Butchering Packaging & Preserving

Field Dressing

Time is your enemy from the moment you dispatch your deer. Therefore, having the proper tools and equipment beforehand—not as an afterthought—is the proper way to proceed from field dressing, skinning, and on to butchering your prize. Four hands are better than two after dispatching your deer. My hunting buddy and I have a prearranged agreement that when one or the other fells a deer, we communicate via walkie-talkies. The hunt is over, and we help one another immediately. This is the most expeditious way to ensure that the animal will be properly handled from field to table. Let's take these elements one step at a time, beginning with tools and equipment:

1. A top-of-the-line zipper-style (gut-hook) knife—such as the legendary Alaskan Zipper Guide Buck Knife with its 4 1/8-inch blade, rubberized handle, and Cordura nylon sheath—is the perfect tool for field dressing big game; $100 through Cabela's Outfitters. For the more budget minded, note items **1a** & **4a.**

    a) You do not want or need a longer-bladed knife for field dressing. I often use a *sharp* pocket knife, being careful to cut with the blade of the knife and not its point so as to avoid puncturing the membrane holding entrails (intestines).

2. Not essential *but* handy, the Butt Out tool makes quick work of removing a section of the anal alimentary canal from the animal; tie off the membrane, and you have eliminated an unpleasant step in field dressing. Cabela's Outfitters offers the plastic tool for $12.

3. A self-locking gambrel and pulley hoist for suspending, cooling, skinning, and butchering big game such as deer and elk. Cabela's Outfitters offers these items ranging from $20 to $40 dollars. This piece of equipment makes the job so much easier.

4. For camp or home, a game processing kit, such as the high-carbon 420 stainless steel Outdoor Edge set, which includes a 3-inch caping knife, 4¼-inch skinner (zipper-style) knife, 5½-inch boning/fillet knife, 8-inch Bowie-style butcher knife, 10-inch double-ground wood/bone saw, 5¼-inch carving fork, game shears, 10 x 14-inch cutting board, three pairs of surgical gloves, tungsten carbide V-style knife sharpener, steel chest spreader (for cooling cavity); $75 through Cabela's Outfitters.

    a) If you're on a tight budget, find yourself a sheath for the 4¼-inch zipper-style skinner knife noted in this kit in lieu of the high-quality Buck knife mentioned as item **1**.

5. In order to make quick work of cutting through meat and bone, I'd suggest the Wyoming Saw II; a 23-ounce, stainless steel/die-cast aluminum frame with 18½-inch bone and wood blades. Comes with black Cordura nylon case; $43. Perfect for camp or home. It will serve to augment the 10-inch wood/bone saw as noted in item #4.

    a) Extra bone blades are packaged 2 for $8.
    b) Extra wood blades are packaged 2 for $8

Field Dressing in Detail

1. After dispatching your deer, place the animal on its back with the head and chest positioned on higher ground if possible. This will facilitate the removal of the animal's organs as well as draining blood and other fluids away from the carcass.

2. One of you will spread the animal's rear legs wide apart while the other person begins a most shallow two-inch-long abdominal cut starting at the sternum (breastbone) by first grasping and lifting a clump of hide—being extremely careful not to puncture the membrane holding its entrails (intestines).

    a) Insert the forefinger and index finger of the opposite hand within this incision, guiding the blade of the knife from sternum down to the reproductive organs (penis of a buck or the udder of a doe), opening and exposing the stomach cavity.

    b) A zipper-style (gut-hook) knife will make quick work of this first important cut, enabling you to slice only the hide, skin and thin layer of flesh, thereby avoiding the messy/smelly act of inadvertently cutting or puncturing the stomach and/or intestines. Just like the name of the knife implies, that hook-shaped part of the blade opens the carcass like a zipper.

    c) Being careful not to cut or puncture the urinary sac (bladder), cut around the scrotum (pouch that surrounds the testicles) and penis of a buck, or around the vagina (sheath-like organ of a doe); remove those reproductive organs. We'll deal with the bladder in a moment.

    d) If you are going to use the Butt Out tool, now is the time. Easy instructions come with the packaging; otherwise, in a circular motion, cut deeply around the anus of a buck or doe. The cuts should be approximately two inches in diameter and four inches deep.

3. Remove the pear-shaped bladder and urethra (canal duct) from the lower abdomen, being very careful not to rupture the sac, which may be filled with urine. Approximately an inch below the base of the bladder, either pinch off or tie the duct with a piece of cotton string before cutting and removing the sac.

a) Within my hunting license holder, I always keep several short lengths of cotton cord that I use to attach a deer tag to the ear of the carcass.

4. If you are not dealing with a trophy and therefore unconcerned with cutting and ruining the cape for a head mount, you have the option of cutting through the ribs, skin and hide, following along each *side* of the breastbone, right on up to the neck.

a) Attempting to cut through the center of the breastbone will only dull the blade.

5. You will now have a wide enough opening to facilitate cutting the diaphragm loose, which is the sheet of muscle that separates the abdominal cavity (containing stomach, intestines, liver, and such) from the chest cavity (containing heart and lungs). Also, you can now easily cut and remove the windpipe and esophagus (two tube-like ducts). But before cutting the esophagus, pinch and tie it off as high up as possible to prevent any stomach contents from entering and tainting the body cavity.

6. If you have decided not to cut the breastbone, you need to reach well up into the chest cavity in order to cut, pull, and remove the windpipe and esophagus. Once again, before cutting the esophagus, it is suggested to tie off the tube as high up as possible to prevent any stomach contents from entering and tainting the body cavity.

7. Roll the deer back on its side (cavity facing downgrade), allowing the organs to fall freely.

a) Carefully cut away where still attached to the wall of the abdominal/chest cavity.

b) Drain blood and other bodily fluids away from the body cavity.

c) If you are taking the heart and liver, be sure to have gallon-size Ziploc bags, along with a suitable leak-proof container in which to place those organs.

d) Leave the bags open to air and cool the contents.

8. As best you can, remove and wipe away all matter from the body cavity; that is, dirt, debris, hair, foreign substances, et cetera.

a) Remove and properly dispose of these remains as quickly as possible.

Note: When field dressing deer, there are two words to keep firmly in mind about cutting off the tarsal glands (two scent glands located on the inside of a buck's and doe's hind legs). Do not.

If you are going to use the glands as an attractant in a subsequent hunt, they are best left alone until you finish skinning and butchering the carcass. Otherwise, you run the risk of tainting the meat. How so? Because you will undoubtedly forget and use the same knife blade for field dressing the animal as well as for the removal of those glands. And that's a no-no. Additionally, you are sure to have that tainted mess on your hands and clothing.

Skinning Your Deer

Keep in mind that skinning your deer is considerably easier soon after the kill, as its hide is still fresh and warm. As the hide cools and dries, skinning will prove to be a bit of a chore.

1. Hanging a deer from either its neck or hind legs is to be given serious consideration.
 a) As cooling the meat and draining the chest cavity of residual blood, lymph (coagulable fluid), and other body fluids is of paramount importance, it's a no-brainer to hang the deer from its hindquarters. Heat rises, and body fluids drain downward, avoiding contact with the choice sections of meat.
 b) Also, if you are going to have the head mounted, you don't want to damage the cape with a noose around the animal's neck.
 c) If the two above considerations are moot because the cooling and draining issues have already been taken care of at a base camp and ambient temperatures are suitable at home, coupled to the fact that you're not dealing with a trophy wall hanger, you can certainly hang the animal by its head. The choice is yours.

2. Let's assume that you decided to skin the animal while hanging it by its hindquarters.
 a) With your caping knife, make a one-inch slit in the thin skin found within the Achilles tendon (lower rear leg joint). Make the same incision on the other hind leg then pass the ends of the gambrel through these two slits.

3. Connect the pulley hoist to the gambrel and raise the deer to a comfortable level to begin skinning, working from the top of the legs downward.
 a) We'll start by making a shallow circular cut through the hide, just below the first joint of the upper leg, being careful not to cut the Achilles tendon. Otherwise, that side of the deer will fall. Continue cutting to complete the circular cut.
 b) From the top of the circular cut, draw the point of the knife blade downward along the length of the leg, extending a long, shallow diagonal slice through the hide and down toward the pelvic area. Work both sides of the leg until you can start peeling and pulling the hide away from the carcass, right on down and around the hind quarter.
 c) Work the other leg in the same fashion. Try and do more peeling and pulling than cutting.
 d) Work the blade around the tail area, cutting clear down to the bone. Your partner can assist in this step by peeling and pulling while you're cutting away any

sections of thick fat. Using the tail as a handle, the two of you can work the hide right down to the front shoulders.

e) If you haven't already cut through the breastbone, do so at this point so as to facilitate peeling, pulling and cutting the hide away from the carcass.

f) Slice the hide on each side of the front shoulders.

g) Make circular cuts just above the front leg joints as you did the hind legs. Run the point of the blade upward along the length of each leg so as to join the slices made on each side of the front shoulders, working your way around and toward the back of the neck. Take your time; cut, peel and pull the hide until you work its way down the neck. You can now cut completely around the neck, clear down to the bone. Use your bone saw (such as the 10-inch double-ground wood/bone saw described earlier) to sever the head.

Butchering Your Deer

Important Notes: Within the thick-layered tallow (fat), there are glands that will taint your meat if you are not careful. They are the prescapula and popliteal glands that are located beneath the shoulder blades and hind legs, respectively. Rather than worry and hunt for these bean-size glands, simply cut away this thick fat from the carcass and you're good to go.

Keep in mind that the glands and fat, inclusive of the marrow found when cutting through bone, will impart a gamey taste if allowed to come in contact with the meat when cooking. Even if initially freezing the meat, the fat will turn rancid after a couple of months. Boning out your meat as opposed to sawing through sections, except as instructed, will save you frustration and heartache. Properly caring for your prize is the name of the game. Know-how is crucial.

1. With the carcass still hanging by its hindquarters, take your bone saw (such as the Wyoming Saw II, described earlier) and remove the front legs at the knee joint. Discard. Some folks use loppers; others use a reciprocating bladed electric Sawzall.

a) Your partner can start trimming the meat from one foreleg while you trim the other. Set aside these pieces for stews, hamburgers, chili, sausages, soups, et cetera.

2. With your caping knife, cut and separate the upper front leg from a shoulder.

a) To separate the shoulder from the carcass, use a long-bladed butcher knife (such as the 8-inch Bowie described earlier) for this operation.

b) This two-part section is easy to cut and remove because it is attached by thin muscle and skin.

c) With one hand, lay the blade flat and firmly against the rib cage as you cut, while you lift and pull the shoulder section with your other hand, continuing the cut until the shoulder is removed.

3. As you proceed with butchering your deer, cut away the thick-layered fat, along with any gristly, stringy, silvery-white sinewy fascia (tissue/cartilage), serving to connect a muscle to a bone. Conversely, leave whatever marbling fat there is; in other words, those long, thin striations and specks found within the meat itself.

a) Use a warm damp rag to wipe any hair or messy matter from the meat.

4. Proceed with the other leg and shoulder section.

a) It is now a matter of cutting the meat into roasts, steaks, slices, chunks, and/or one-inch cubes, reserving the trimmings for stews, soups, ground hamburgers, chili, sausages, and so forth.

b) There are certainly fancier cuts that we could fashion; for example, blade and bone-in arm roasts. But in keeping with the motif of this handbook, we are going to follow the **K**eep **I**t **S**imple **S**ystem: KISS—at least for the moment.

5. Raise the carcass to a comfortable level and proceed with the hind legs. This is a bit more involved because they are attached to the pelvic plate by ball and socket joints. There are a couple of ways to approach this operation. Again, I am going to offer the easiest for the reason stated above. Why make more work for yourself than necessary?

a) Employing the boning/fillet knife, insert the point of the blade at the base of the tail and cut along one side of the spine to begin removing the hindquarter, keeping the blade flat against the bone while following the irregular contour of the pelvic plate.

b) A good part of this operation is accomplished by Braille; that is, *reading* the anomalous shape by running the tip of the blade down and along the plate, pulling the haunch away from the body, cutting, feeling, and pulling until you reach the ball and socket appendage. Simply slip the tip of the knife between the ball and socket, cutting the cartilage, and the shoulder will begin to release itself from the leg/pelvic bone area. Several more cuts, and you can remove this section.

c) Don't worry about having missed chunks of flesh from that pelvic area. Merely trim away the meat and set it aside for hamburgers, chili, sausages, soups, and other treats.

6. Before butchering the other hindquarter, trim away the fat and sinew as you did with the front legs.

7. You are now ready to start tackling steaks and boneless roasts anew. However, this time around, we'll begin with a sirloin tip. Cut out, carry, and place the upper part of the leg on its side; face the lower section away from you. Just below the ball joint/femur bone (knuckle and thigh bone), cut into the meat beginning on the inside of the leg, running the blade flat and in a circular motion, separating the top section from the bottom section.

a) Remove the sirloin tip.

b) Next, run the knife blade along the length of the femur, both sides, then around the entire bone and remove it.

c) You are left with what appears to be a single slab of meat; however, there is a seam that separates the two sections. Find it with your fingers, cut and pull the halves apart then trim.

d) These three choice sections—sirloin tip, top round, bottom round—may be cooked whole as roasts or cut into one-inch thick steaks.

e) Sirloin tip should be tied with cotton cord to hold it together when roasting.

8. The <u>backstraps</u> are located atop each side of the spine. The <u>tenderloins</u> are located along the inside of the backbone, just beneath the spine.

a) Use the flexible tip of the boning/fillet knife to remove the backstraps, guiding the point up and down and in and out over the bumpy inner surface of the vertebrae (backbone), along both sides of the spinal track. Remove the single long strip of boneless meat. Repeat the process to remove the other backstrap.

b) Use your shorter bladed caping knife (three-inch) to first cut each end of the tenderloin from the backbone; use your longer-bladed boning/fillet knife to work out and remove the tenderloin from its track as you did the backstraps. Repeat the process to remove the other tenderloin.

9. The remainder of the skeletal frame will reap neck, rib, and brisket meat. Hoist the carcass to a comfortable height.

a) Starting at the back of the neck, make a horizontal cut right below the ears. Make a second horizontal cut right above the shoulder. Now make two deep vertical cuts along each side of the neck bone and cut out the meat by working the blade along the periphery of the neck.

b) Ribs must be given TLC; that is, **T**ender **L**oving **C**are. Because they are very fatty, I simply don't care to use them. That's just me.

c) The brisket slabs (lower chest area) are easily removed with the blade of your knife placed flat against the rib cage. Trim and cut away any fat.

d) Both the neck and brisket lend themselves quite well to stew meat. They are to be cooked slowly for hours until tender, for they are rather tough, unlike our other cuts of meat.

Packaging & Preserving
Four Essential Kitchen Aids

Four indispensable pieces of equipment that positively belong in your kitchen for packaging and preserving your finished product are a food slicer, meat tenderizer, meat grinder, and vacuum sealer. Through the years, I have prepared many fine meals (fish and fowl included) by utilizing these essential machines. I could not have done nearly as neat or as efficient a job without them. They go hand in hand to not only help produce gourmet-quality fare, but to also aid in eye-appealing presentations upon the finished plate. But to merely mention these four items rather than specifically elaborate on the important elements to be considered before selecting such equipment for home use would be foolish of me because you'd likely be wasting your hard-earned money in the long run. So let's home in on what's important before purchasing these items.

Pictured are three Cabela's machines that are employed in our kitchen: an electric food slicer with tilted stand for easy cleanup, and stainless steel blade (left); an all-important commercial-grade vacuum sealer, which is a godsend for preserving foods for extended periods (middle); a heavy-duty electric meat grinder (right). As you pretty much get what you pay for in this world of ours, of the three Cabela's machines shown, I'd strongly suggest purchasing the best model of the commercial-grade vacuum sealer that you can afford because of its importance. If you are an angler as well as a hunter, planning to put up fish, fowl, and game through the four seasons, you want a top-quality machine that will last many years. Keep in mind, too, that you can take advantage of fish, poultry, and weekly meat sales offered at your local supermarkets and specialty shops throughout the year. Simply seal, freeze, and savor for a later date. A top-quality vacuum sealer is of paramount importance. You can easily store venison for up to two years without the threat of freezer burn.

From left to right: Cabela's Food Slicer, Vacuum Sealer, Meat Grinder

Next is the Cabela's meat grinder, which I not only use for making venison sausage and burgers in fall and winter, but I also operate the machine to produce fresh, flavorful fishcakes throughout spring and summer. With that kind of a four-season workout, you would not want to purchase just any meat grinder; you'd want to purchase a *heavy-duty electric* meat grinder for all occasions. This will facilitate matters and ensure the unit's longevity. With an eye on heavy-duty quality equipment for home use, do not envision machinery that is going to break the bank and send you to the poorhouse, for companies such as Cabela's offer different grades of heavy-duty/commercial equipment.

Cabela's heavy-duty meat grinder includes a 3mm (fine), 4.5mm (medium), and an 8mm (coarse) stainless steel grinding plate to allow for desired consistency. The unit also includes other accoutrements for additional uses. You can now start grinding your own meats for burgers and sausages whether they be venison, beef, or pork. Simply follow the step-by-step grinding and stuffing instructions in the owner's manual. When it comes to selecting sausage casings, choose collagen casings over "natural" (intestinal) casings. Collagen casings require far less preparation and are uniform in size and texture. They are not artificially made as some folks believe but are produced from beef skin and other tissues.

Last but not necessarily least in the Cabela's kitchen-trio lineup is a stainless steel electric food slicer. Apart from slicing desired thicknesses of venison for perfect cutlets to suit your palate, the machine comes in quite handy for preparing and presenting perfect arrangements of fruits, vegetables, cheeses, and hard breads—even sushi and/or sashimi. Whatever creative ideas you may have in mind, your prep time is *cut* [key word] dramatically.

In concluding, I would like to introduce you to a marvelous tool that is worth its weight in venison backstraps. The Jaccard. It is a must-have implement for the kitchen. Billed as a meat tenderizing machine, it is an invaluable piece of equipment with which to brine or marinate red meat, poultry, and fish for the smoker. It will cut your brining and marinating time by forty percent; cooking time by half. For expediency, I wouldn't be caught preparing fare without this handy-dandy tool. The Jaccard is available in two models: a mini Jaccard with one row of sixteen blades; the larger model has three rows of sixteen blades; that is, forty-eight blades. Donna and I elected to purchase the larger model and are certainly glad we did.

Jaccard Meat Tenderizer Tool

Check out Cabela's Outfitters at www.cabelas.com for the aforementioned machines as well as www.jaccard.com for this handy tenderizing tool. Enjoy some of the best products from the wild that nature has to offer—meats, fish, and poultry. See my gourmet recipes in Chapter 31: GOURMET GAME RECIPES

CHAPTER 17

LONG ISLAND WHITETAIL HUNTING OPPORTUNITIES: BOW SLUG GUN ~ MUZZLELOADER

Many folks find it surprising to learn that there are deer on Long Island. Mark Lowry, a wildlife biologist with the New York State Department of Environmental Conservation (NYSDEC) at Stony Brook says, "Opportunities for harvesting deer in Suffolk County have increased since 1969. Although the deer tend to be smaller compared to other areas of the state, the herd is nonetheless healthy, with many bucks boasting respectable racks."

Although land to hunt is at a premium, a polite request early on (well before the season) to a farmer or other property owner may realize a favorable response. The fact that more than a few Long Island farmers obtain nuisance permits for deer gives a good indication that you might just hit upon a receptive individual. After gaining permission to hunt private property, a Landowner's Endorsement form must be filled out and filed at a town clerk's office (for a fee of $1), and a permit will then be issued.

Even if you have no luck in securing permission, there are other options for taking advantage of New York's Long Island whitetail opportunities.

Suffolk County Managed Lands

Public lands in Suffolk County offer excellent whitetail hunting through cooperative agreements with the New York State Department of Environmental Conservation (NYSDEC). Long Island's public land deer hunting opportunities are available to any hunter holding a valid New York State big game license.

Most hunting options for whitetails lie in the eastern section of Suffolk County. Take Route 495 East (Long Island Expressway) to Exit 71, then Route 24 east to Riverhead. This will put you in proximity of all of the public areas managed by the NYSDEC.

Barcelona Neck offers seasonal scenic hunting opportunities featuring coastal and pine barren habitats. Take Route 27 (Montauk Highway) to East Hampton, then Route 114 north for four miles to Sag Harbor. Access is free by permit only.

East Hampton's cooperative areas also provide hunting opportunities in Napeague, Hither Hills, and Montauk Point State Parks, all located off Route 27, east of Amagansett in East Hampton. Access is by free permit only.

The David A. Sarnoff Pine Barrens Preserve has picturesque hunting trails that wind through classic pine barren habitat. Take Route 495 to Exit 71, then Route 24 east to Riverhead. Travel one mile south of the traffic circle on Route 104. Access is by free permit only.

The Navy Cooperative Area offers excellent hunting opportunities featuring mixed oak, pine barrens, and open habitat. Take Route 495 to Exit 69 North. The area is located two miles north of Schultz Road.

The permit station for the Navy property is located at the Randall Pond Nature Trail. Take Route 495 to Exit 68. Go north on William Floyd Parkway to Route 25 West, then continue a quarter-mile to Randall Road on the right. The entrance is 300 feet ahead on the left. Access is by daily permit. Call the Ridge Check Station (631-924-3156) for additional permit information.

The Rocky Point Natural Resources Management Area, featuring 5100 acres of oak woodland and pine barrens, also offers excellent hunting opportunities. Take Route 495 to Exit 67 North, then go north on Route 21. Continue six miles, taking a right on Whiskey Road. The main entrance to the property is on the left. The permit station is located at the Randall Pond Nature Trail. Access is by daily permit.

Consider Riverhead as your hub, spearheading the North and South Forks of Long Island. The Rocky Point Natural Resources Management and Navy cooperative areas of Brookhaven lie to the west. The David Sarnoff Pine Barrens Preserve is on the North Fork. The Barcelona Neck and East Hampton cooperative areas are on the South Fork.

Eligibility to hunt these managed areas is determined by random drawings held in early December, and daily permits are required for the January deer season. For specifics on the deer season and how to enter the drawing, send a self-addressed stamped envelope to: Deer Info, Bldg. 40, SUNY, Stony Brook, NY 11790-2356. This should be mailed in early November. A designated parking area location will be assigned when a permit is issued and/or a reservation is taken.

If you plan on hunting NYSDEC-managed lands, contact the NYSDEC and ask them to send you information sheets on the special deer season (either-sex hunting) in Suffolk County, referencing the public hunting opportunities on Long Island, and on firearms deer hunting referencing NYSDEC-managed lands in Suffolk County. Also, ask them to send you the Public Use Map and Information Sheet for each area that you plan to hunt. Ask for information on all such areas and keep them on file for future reference.

For regulations and permit information concerning NYSDEC-managed hunting areas, contact the New York State Department of Environmental conservation Region 1 Office, Loop Road, Building 40, Stony Brook, NY 11790-2356. Phone: (631) 444-0273 or (631) 444-0310.

Suffolk County Parks

Suffolk County residents may hunt whitetails in Suffolk County parks, which include Sears Bellows and Hubbard County Parks (in Hampton Bays) and Montauk County Park (in Montauk).

Sears Bellows and Hubbard County Parks are situated across from one another in Hampton Bays. From Riverhead, take Route 24 East. Turn right on Blue Pond Road. The entrance for Sears Bellows Park is on the right. Access to Hubbard County Park is obtained by first checking in at Sears Bellows Park. For more information on hunting the two parks, call (631) 852-8290.

Montauk County Park also provides hunting opportunities for Suffolk County residents. From Riverhead, take Route 104 south to Route 27 (Montauk Highway). Head east on Route 27 through the village of Montauk. Turn north on East Lake Drive. The park entrance is past Montauk Airport, on the left. The phone number for the park is (631) 852-7878.

Call the administration building for varying regulations and permit information. Contact the Suffolk County Department of Parks at (631) 854-4949 and ask them to send you literature pertaining to hunting opportunities for white-tailed deer in Suffolk County parks. The address is P.O. Box 144, West Sayville, NY 11796-0144.

Weather, Lodging, Seasonal Hunting Dates

In Suffolk County, weather conditions during January can range from 50 degrees Fahrenheit down to the low teens. At times, the wind chill factor might make the temperatures feel like they're below zero, especially along the North Fork, where winds whip across Long Island Sound. The opening day of the 1996 shotgun season delivered 24 inches of snow, which washed away a week later in a torrential downpour, so be prepared for any kind of weather. Hooded rain gear, as well as snowshoes, can come in handy. Layering will be your key to comfort afield. Having at least one insulated outfit (parka and pants, jacket and bib, or coveralls) will save the day. You can peel off or put on articles of clothing accordingly, but the point is to have them with you on your trip. See Chapter 8: Selecting Hunting Clothing, Footwear & Accessories for All Seasons.

If you are planning an overnight trip or staying for a week or longer, the East End of Long Island offers lodging and dining accommodations ranging from rustic to elegant. Whether you hunt private land, lands managed by the NYSDEC, or Suffolk County parks, you can be assured of a good deer population and scenic beauty.

Archery season for hunting whitetails in Suffolk County, Long Island during 2016 begins on October 1st through December 31st. The Special Firearms 2017 Season hunt will be in January, sunrise to sunset. Shotguns (with a single ball or rifled slug) and muzzleloaders are allowed, as are scopes (telescopic, red dot, and holographic sights). The bag limit is one deer of either sex unless otherwise allotted via special permits.

CHAPTER 18

SHOTGUNS

Skeet, Trap, Sporting Clays
Going Light For Ladies

Shooting skeet, trap, and sporting clays are great ways to practice, practice, practice—leading up to precision wing shooting, right down to small game ground challenges.

Having moved from Queens, New York to Suffolk County, Long Island in 1991, I eventually became a member of a sportsmen's club that offered several activities, skeet shooting being among them. A longtime member and instructor took Donna under wing. He initially gave me a rather impatient "you should know better" look," politely taking my Remington 12 gauge 11-87 out of Donna's hands and offering up his 20 gauge semiautomatic along with an afternoon of tutelage. Previously, under my instruction, if you could call it that, Donna had been peppering the blue horizon, shattering one or two skeet out of a box of twenty-five. With the shooting pro at her side, Donna was now shooting at least twenty percent better. She desperately wanted to find a gun very much like the instructor's vintage Remington 1100 Lite 20 gauge, light as a feather because it might have been built on a 28 gauge receiver, he had explained.

After numerous inquiries, another knowledgeable member of the club pointed us in the right direction: a Franchi [Brescia Italian semiautomatic] Model S.P.A. 48 AL 20 gauge, weighing in at a mere 5.7 pounds; 26-inch barrel—probably one of the lightest guns in that gauge on the market. Actually, the gun weighed a shy lighter than the instructor's little gem. Donna's Franchi featherweight is chambered for 2¾-inch shells; chokes come in Full, Modified, and Improved Cylinder. Needless to say, its recoil was far less than my 12 gauge. She can literally shoot her Franchi 20 gauge all day without flinching or fatigue, whereas before, she shied away from my heavier piece of artillery as well as the sport. Besides being lightweight, a Franchi long-recoil design shotgun (working in conjunction with the bolt) has it all over inertia-driven and gas-operated types of actions.

Donna does not hunt; however, she has helped me track deer over hill and dale, shooting a camera in lieu of a firearm in the field. If you want to keep your woman around and happy, keep things simple and light. If, however, you wish to keep her at bay by design, try sticking a small cannon in her grip.

Shotgun Gauges & Gauging Shot for Bird Hunting

A great all-around smooth bore shotgun for smaller upland game birds is a 20 gauge. Donna uses her Franchi strictly for trap, skeet, and sporting clays, employing either Remington Gun Club or Estate target loads in number 8 shot.

I have my 20 gauge Remington Arms Premier Model 11-87 semiautomatic chambered for 2¾-inch and 3-inch shells. Chokes come in Full, Modified, and Improved Cylinder; 27-inch barrel; 7.5 pounds. I suggest selecting 2¾-inch shells, number 8 shot, and Improved Cylinder choke when mainly hunting smaller marsh and upland game birds that range in size between 8 inches to just under one foot.

Such birds include sora rails (8¾ inches); Virginia rails (9½ inches); Northern bobwhite [aka bobwhite quail and Virginia quail] (9¾ inches); snipe (10½ inches); American woodcock (11 inches).

For gray partridge (12½ inches), purple gallinule (13 inches), ruffed grouse (17 inches), I suggest 3-inch shells, number 6 shot, and Modified choke.

For hunting large upland birds such as pheasants (33 inches) and turkey (46 inches), I set aside the 20 gauge and grab my 12 gauge, chambered for 3-inch and 3½-inch shells, respectively. Modified choke tube for pheasant; number 6 shot. Full choke for turkey; number 4 shot.

As these are only suggestions, not edicts written in stone, the bird measurements presented serve as a general guide for *you* to judge shotgun gauge, shell size, shot size, and choke selection. Bird measurements were taken from *An Audubon Handbook ~ Eastern birds*, by ornithologist John Farrand, Jr., may he rest in peace. I'm not quite sure how he or, for that matter, any birder would react to my citing from their work as it applies to *hunting* versus *studying* birds. Mr. Farrand may be turning, rolling, or spinning in his grave. Anyhow, I've lifted said information from the source for you to have a clear picture.

Whether brandishing the 20 or 12 gauge scattergun for bird hunting, I invariably stay with number 4, 6, 7½, or 8 shot for two reasons: 1) They are good all-around loads. 2) I have quite an ample supply on hand.

As a final note on scatterguns referencing upland bird hunting, the gun of choice held by many, if not most, is a double-barreled shotgun. Whether it be a side-by-side or an over/under, it is considered the quintessential gun to carry into the field for hunting upland game. Well, maybe yes, and maybe no. Consider one important factor when weighing in on both types of twin barrels. Can you guess what that might be? I gave you a hint. The answer is their weight. If you are going to be toting a double-barreled shotgun around for a good part of the day, through fields and over hill and dale, especially if you're climbing up there in age, you might want to rethink this *quintessential* gun of choice whether in 12 or 20 gauge. Try to imagine snapping that tool from port arms to your shoulder for immediate target acquisition after having traipsed through several lengthy fields over the course of a few hours. Too often I have seen both guys and gals working open territory with their gun slung over a shoulder—rather than at the ready—because of sheer fatigue.

Of course, one could argue the benefit of immediately having two choke selections at one's fingertip when toting a double-barrel shotgun, referencing patterning densities as well as a long list of related minutiae to beat about until the cows came home. Again, I'll defer to my KISS mantra: Keep It Simple System. I go middle-of-the road when it comes to scatterguns. Single-barrel shotguns prove more than adequate for knocking down marsh birds and upland game—without the unnecessary added weight.

CHAPTER 19

MIGRATORY WATERFOWL

Professional Outfitters Make the Difference

Well before daybreak, five of us busied ourselves by placing better than a hundred duck and goose decoys in a spacious, leveled cornfield surrounding our below-ground bunker blind. It had been and was a mild winter here on Long Island. But after several brutal wintry seasons, starting with the new millennium, where frigid temperatures dipped and were determined to remain around the freezing mark, I did not mind the unusually warm weather. Still, our licensed guide, Joey "Ducks" Privitera, along with Rob Pollifrone, was well-prepared. Our blind was equipped with a propane heater. Just in case. Instant warmth in a pinch. Actually, I had my jacket open through most of the morning, and I began to wonder how this temperate weather would affect our hunt.

"Not to worry," Rob had said, as if reading my thoughts. "It's going to be a good shoot."

The other two customers with whom I shared the bunker absolutely agreed, for they had been part of the hot action earlier in the week.

And so had Max.

Max looked up at me with his big brown eyes, as if to say, "All *you* have to do is knock 'em down, fella, and I'll retrieve 'em."

I had been looking forward to meeting Max all week, for within the Island Outfitters brochure it had stated, "Watching Joe work the birds of Eastern Long Island is truly a special experience. The only thing better is watching his dog, Max, retrieve our success!"

If Max could speak—English, that is—he would undoubtedly tell you that, "Rob is being modest because both he and my master, Joey, 'work the birds' like there's no tomorrow."

I can attest to the fact that this is, indeed, true. Both Rob and Joey are master waterfowl callers. Also, they are expert wing shots, only to be witnessed if you can coax them to join in on the fun after everyone else has limited out. Too, Max is nothing short of remarkable to watch in his own right. Observing a well-trained dog work is truly a sight to behold.

Speaking candidly, I had not hunted ducks and geese in many years; too many to mention. As a yearly tradition, around Thanksgiving, when my son was very young, I would take him with me out to Sammy's Beach in Amagansett, ten miles from the tip of Montauk, New York. There, crouched down in the reeds, I would pass-shoot some blacks and brants from the shoreline. If a duck or two hit the water, recovery, at times, would become something of a feat. Standing in a pair of non-insulated waders in the frigid water, I remember waiting a good half an hour for the tide to carry the bird to me. Also, I recall an early conversation with my son, Jason.

"Duck hunting, huh, Dad?" Jason remarked through frozen breath.

Quite frankly, I believe the highlight of the trip for the boy had been the time we spent together immediately following those hunts. For Jason, it meant warmth and refueling his body engine: a hot breakfast of bacon and scrambled eggs washed down with hot chocolate. Also, the two-and-a-half hour ride back from the south shore of Eastern Long Island to Bayside, Queens, New York was filled with joyous chatter and laughter . . . unlike the loud silence we shared on the drive out while en route to a sportsman's utopia at the ungodly hour of four a.m. Too, I was painfully aware of my son's frustration of being too young to legally wing shoot, although he could powder skeet with a 12 gauge at age nine and was quite capable on knocking down birds.

For me, the seemingly end-of-the-earth trek out to the Amagansett/Montauk area, after leaving the three-season fishing scene behind in Nassau (where our family kept a small boat), symbolized the start of a new season. Montauk is truly a sportsman's mecca: a four-season paradise filled with boats, and fish, and birds, and down-to-earth folks. By late fall, it is a waterfowl hunter's wonderland.

I recall a challenging conversation that my young son and I had one cold, crisp winter morning in the midst of Montauk after finishing up a hunt.

"So, where are all the people, Dad?" the boy wanted to know. "Looks like a ghost town, if you ask me."

"Sleeping in or still out hunting," I assured him with a smile.

"Well, I haven't even seen one duck today."

I gestured skyward. "Look, right up there."

"Those are seagulls."

"Can't kid a kid, I guess."

"Nope. But we did see tons of mallards in that pond back there."

"That we did, son. But on private property, I'm afraid."

"And plenty of geese in that farm field we passed earlier. Hundreds, if not thousands."

"True. Private land, too, I'm afraid."

Jason sighed with a child's disappointment.

"What's wrong, J?" I asked.

"You only knocked down three birds. One duck. Two geese. And that was *two* years ago!" He held up two fingers to emphasize the point.

"Meaning?"

"Meaning that I think you could use the help of someone who knows the area.

You know. Like a guide."

"A guide costs good money, son."

"Yeah, but I think it might be cheaper in the long run."

"Why do you say that?"

"Well, I've been doing this with you since I was five. Right, Dad?"

"And?"

"And it's only the third time you've ever shot anything!" Three fingers shot up.

Several years after that conversation with my son, and before hooking up with Joey and Rob, a guide was in the offing. Donna—my significant other and outdoor partner of thirty-four years at the time—handled the camera. I wielded a 12 gauge Winchester pump. We came away with some nice shots: picture-wise and otherwise.

Author with a Brace of Brant

Returning to that first outing with Joey and Rob, still feeling somewhat concerned that it had been a long while since I had hunted waterfowl, I briefly related these stories to Joey (more in the form of a confession), who told me to just relax and that we were going to enjoy a successful morning in the field. Well, we certainly did, indeed—so much so that one month later, I booked another hunt and, this time, brought along a friend, Gene, who also had not hunted waterfowl in many a moon.

Unlike other types of hunting, a *lot* of preparation and expense goes into waterfowl shooting. Unless you are willing to lay out a significant amount of money for equipment—be it for pass-shooting from a shoreline, jump-shooting puddle ducks along the marshes, calling in birds from a ground blind situated in the center of a farm field, or perhaps gunning from a bobbing boat—you are not going to have the necessary edge to practically guarantee success if left to your own devices.

Of the methods mentioned above, I feel that a below-ground blind along with a plethora of decoys offer many advantages necessary to give one the added edge. Here on Long Island, setups like that require leasing land from a farmer, along with securing permission to unearth a space in which to place the bunker. The framework, of course, first has to be constructed. In most cases, you will need a forklift, especially at season's end to remove the bunker. This is to say nothing of the cost in purchasing one hundred plus decoys of varying sizes, a Mojo or two (electronic-spinning wing decoys), flappers, and other ancillary items.

Consider the know-how involved in identifying and calling in those birds. A half- or full-day hunt with professionals will make you appreciative of the fact that a guide is the key to success. Joey and Rob called and flagged to those flocks from the time they were only specks in the distant sky, till the time they turned, headed for, then homed in on our sentries and feeding *friends* upon the ground.

And then it was showtime!

We all knew our shooting positions beforehand. Back. Front. Left. To the right was a farmer's house; *verboten* to even think about pointing a gun in that direction, although it was a safe and legal distance away.

"Get ready, Bob—" whispered Rob, "—front and center; twelve o'clock." The roof of the bunker/blind slid back. "Now!" I had a bead dead-on. "Lead 'im," I was reminded. I immediately swung ahead of the bird, squeezed the trigger and followed through.

"Gene," said Joey. "Back wall. Three o'clock. He's cupping, putting on the brakes. Take 'im."

Two birds down. And a moment later, Max was off and running. First came my plump goose; front door delivery. But Gene had the prize. Joey beamed with joy for his new client.

Max doing what he does best

"A banded goose!" the outfitter announced. "Fifteen hundred ducks this season, my clients have taken," Joey stated with delight. "Over five hundred geese. And I've seen my share of bands. Your friend comes along, first time in thirty years, and downs a banded bird. Fantastic, Gene. Great going, guy. You be sure and call that in. Number's right here on the band," he instructed.

Gene and I are primarily deer hunters; both with gun and bow. Neither of us had been duck or goose hunting in three decades. The two of us came away with several prizes apiece that morning. Gene had his banded and even bigger bird than mine, which he surely let me know. It was only a few days later when Gene received a certificate in the mail, suitable for framing. It gave a brief history of his bird: Band Number. Species. Age of Bird. Location. The Canada goose was hatched in 2004, or earlier—hailing from Ayer, Massachusetts; not too far from the New Hampshire border. It was banded by the Massachusetts Division of Fish & Wildlife, in Westborough. Recovery data listed the location of Gene's kill: Baiting Hollow, New York. You would have thought that Gene received an honorary degree from Harvard or Yale. That band and document are proudly displayed among his collectibles. The two of us will always have those memories of that special day burned into our brains.

The initial lesson I learned from Joey and Rob that first morning was the importance of a good duck and goose decoy spread. High visibility is the key; hence, the more the merrier when it comes to the number of bogus birds needed to attract a sky-filled flock. Predawn, again, we had all pitched in and placed well over a hundred plastic impostors. Standing back from our array, you would think they were the real McCoy.

Overall patterning is as important as individual groupings. First, forming a large U-shape, we spread the decoys around our bunker. Rob and Joey then tweaked the bevy—positioning half a dozen birds to a group in a particular manner, depending upon the prevailing wind and other factors. Sentries were set just so. Feeders were placed strategically, too. It appeared that no bird was placed randomly, for the spread had to appear natural.

Just as important as covering an overall area with the spread is the body of the decoy itself. Poorly colored and/or dirty decoys will significantly knock down one's chances for success—not the birds you wish to bag. Between dawn and dusk, clean, crisp black and white colors are the order of the day, as those contrasting shades can be seen seemingly light-years away. The condition of those fake fowl is certainly as important as the ammunition you pick, the clothing you choose, and the place you hunt. I believe by now, you are beginning to get a picture of the work that goes into preparing for a successful waterfowl hunt.

What many prospective waterfowl hunters do not realize is the necessary scouting involved to ensure success. For you to attempt this time-consuming exploration willy-nilly in the eleventh hour is flirting with foolishness. You may find one field, for example, where a flock comes in to feed and rest. Once that forage is eaten, those birds are off to another area. A professional guide will have several places lined up and sewn up. By the time *you* come around, asking a farmer or other property owner for permission, that land has probably been leased. And guess to whom? That's right. Professional guides/outfitters. I once put a small add in a few of our local papers, looking for a place to hunt, figuring that I would save some steps. I even offered a gratuity. I was honestly surprised that I did not receive one response. Land to hunt on is getting more and more difficult to find here on Long Island. I imagine it is getting harder elsewhere, too.

However, if you are like many of us and sometimes have to learn the hard way by going it alone—or maybe pure stubbornness has little to do with it so much as weighing in the cost factor of a guide—there are several important things to keep in mind to help put the odds in your favor. The following is knowledge freely passed on from Joey and Rob to yours truly.

Ducks and geese have a penchant for landing into the wind. Therefore, have the tip of your field decoy spread facing a blow. A **U** or **V**-shaped pattern is the ticket. When the wind is inactive or eddying erratically, **X** marks the spot so that bases are covered from all directions.

Waterfowl decoys are another kettle of fish, so think fishhook; that is, the letter **J**. The bend of the hook, just like the letter **J** or **U**, faces into the wind.

Place duck decoys in pairs, or sets of three to four.

Specifically, set goose decoys in family groups ranging from four to twelve, each bird separated by two to three feet, with each family spaced two to three yards apart.

Limit your use of sentry goose decoys. Too many sentinels indicate a 'heads-up' that spells trouble.

Do, however, use many decoys to attract large flocks.

If the birds have dropped from the heavens but are questionably high on their first approach, keep your head and hold your fire. They will more than likely take another swing or two around the area before heading in to feed and rest. Of course, the likelihood is drastically increased if you know their language. How many of you out there are multilingual? That is, how many of you speak Duck and Goose? I didn't think so. No, Max; that's a rather poor imitation.

In truth, Joey employs scores of techniques and tricks to all but guarantee your success. Once again, the bases are covered by professional guides, be it Island Outfitters of Long Island, or other well-endorsed outfitters.

In conclusion, I will readdress the concern of many. Cost. If I factored into the equation the amount of time spent in travel, researching, and purchasing equipment—only to realize I would need a warehouse and a dog to guard it, the latter of which could hopefully double as a waterfowl pal—all to down maybe a couple dozen ducks and geese over the course of decades, I could have well afforded many *memorable* hunts. By hunting up an outfitter/guide, if you divide, say, a half-day hunt by four people, it amounts to . . . well, chicken feed by comparison.

Be smart.

Be safe.

Go with the pros and score big.

For additional information, contact Island Outfitters
Professional Duck & Goose Guided Hunts
Joey "Ducks" Privitera
www.islandoutfitterli.com
631-445-6817

My choice of shotgun for ducks and geese is a good quality 12 gauge chambered for a trio of 2¾-inch, 3-inch, and 3½-inch shells, expressly utilizing the latter two lengths so as to "Reach out there and touch someone," as in the AT&T advertisement.

Winchester 12 gauge Super X Drylok 3½-inch shells discharging one 9/16 ounce BB steel shot go the distance in connecting with ducks and geese at a velocity of 1300 feet per second. Winchester 12 gauge Super X Drylok 3-inch shells with 1¼-ounce BBB steel shot are long distance communicators with a velocity of 1400 feet per second.

I have not yet tried the larger sized T shot shells and probably won't. Without getting technical, larger shot sizes carry more energy to the target while smaller shot sizes offer greater pellet count. Consider these differences, get to a range, and pattern your shotgun.

Simply as a point of information, not necessarily promoting any particular product, the Winchester ammunition mentioned here is what was available in the store(s) at the time of purchase. It is not an endorsement of one particular manufacturer. Other recognized brands of shotgun ammo such as Remington, Federal, Kent, et cetera, all get the job done quite nicely.

The same holds true for shotguns themselves; buy quality—not what you *think* you can afford at the time. It's better to wait and save up those dollars. You will be far better off in the long run. My old, trusty 12 gauge Mossberg pump gun, Model 835 "ULTI-MAG" ~ "ACCU MAG" chambered for 2¾-, 3-, and 3½-inch shells is used mainly for waterfowl. Also, it is a good backup gun for the woods and fields. In truth, I prefer shooting my 12 gauge semiautomatic for ducks and geese; however, I generally use the old Mossberg pump in muck and mire and aboard watercraft—especially during inclement weather—while reserving the newer Premier model 11-87 Remington autoloader for a more civilized environment. That's just me; to each his own.

What I know to be a great waterfowl gun is the Benelli Super Vinci 12 gauge chambered for 2¾-, 3- and 3½-inch Magnum shells. Perhaps it's time for another toy. Shhh. Don't tell Donna because she'll want equal shares—probably a *new* Franchi for sporting clays . . . in pink.

A great soft-type shotgun case for waterfowl hunters, especially when shooting from a boat, is Cabela's Floating Sleeve Case, which is constructed from a weather-protective polyester outer shell and a thick sealed-in layer of buoyant foam. It features an adjustable padded shoulder strap, carry handles, an external gear pocket with sewn-in elastic loops for six shotgun shells, and a stalwart Velcro fold-over hook-and-loop butt entrance opening. This 52-inch floatable sleeve-type gun case offers the best protection should your weapon fall into the drink. Usually available in two camo patterns: Mossy Oak or Realtree.

Duck Decoys

There are a good many brands of duck decoys on the market from which to choose. They range from cheap to expensive. You are wasting your money if you decide to go the cheap route because you will be sacrificing realism and quality construction. Referencing the latter, inexpensive decoys will more than likely experience cracking and chipping as a result of very cold days. Conversely, you need not spend a fortune for realistic-looking birds made of quality materials, anatomically correct body postures, perfectly matched plumage for down-to-earth early-season imitation, and weighted keels for lifelike motion upon the water.

After extensive research concerning overall quality and price, I decided on Avian-X Early-Season Mallard Decoys. For $69.99 from Cabela's, a six-pack comprised of two swimmer drakes, one high-head drake, one feeder drake, one swimmer hen, and one feeder hen is an excellent choice to either start or add to your spread. Ultra-realistic paint schemes coupled to innovative paint adhesion eliminate faded decoy color issues. The decoys' realism rests in the Avian "eclipse pattern" referencing the male during the first months of fall when the birds start to migrate. Avian-X Early-Season Mallard Decoys pairs standard hens with "eclipse-pattern" drakes, perfectly mimicking plumage. Drakes surrender their bright breeding plumage for dull brown feathers known as "basic" or "eclipse pattern" plumage. Make no mistake in that these decoys are authentic looking. Start your waterfowl season off with this set of six Avian-X Early-Season Mallard Decoys, or visit them at www.avian-x.com for other models. When it comes to bird decoys, be they waterfowl or turkey, Avian is certainly a wise choice.

Rigging Duck Decoys

Here is where you can save several dollars if you construct your own rigs. Or you can simply order ready-made rigs. Components may consist of wire cable, treated cord, braid or monofilament line; egg slip sinkers or keel-hook type decoy anchors; double-barrel crimp sleeves. If you decide to fashion your own rigs, which is easy enough to do, I'll run you through a set of step-by-step instructions. The only tools you will need are a pair of snippers, a graduated crimping tool, a tape measure, and a black permanent marker.

Your materials will consist of a spool of .065 or .080 diameter commercial grade string-trimmer (weed eater) line used for trimming and edging lawns. As we will be fabricating six rigs for a half dozen duck decoys, set for an adjustable maximum line depth of approximately 10 feet, you will need 60-plus feet of string trimmer line, allowing a few inches for small loops at each end. I actually have my line depths set and locked in at 4 feet for small pond applications; the additional 6 feet is wrapped around the decoy's keel should I need it. I know folks who wind on 15 feet for good measure and have employed those depths. But for most backwater and small pond applications, a range of 2 to 10 feet should suffice. The convenience of making your own rigs offers greater versatility.

Next, we'll consider color. Clear 400-pound test monofilament is a popular material line choice among many duck hunters. However, for murky shallow water depths, I keep costs down and the rigging simple with lengths of green .080 string trimmer line, readily available at Home Depot. For deeper, clearer water conditions, where a green line may become an issue, you might want to consider clear string trimmer material. Lowe's carries *replacement* spools of Black & Decker .065 string trimmer line in 30-foot lengths, so you would need two spools for six decoys rigged to a maximum of 10-foot lengths. You would probably be better off selecting a spool of 400-pound test clear monofilament line. Personally, I prefer the tangle-free string trimmer material. Therefore, for those murky shallow water applications (as well as purposes of demonstration), I'll be illustrating a rigging system with 10-foot lengths of green .080 string trimmer line from Power Care, manufactured for Home Depot.

As an aside, I never had an issue using this material in clearer, deeper waters. The ducks were focused on those fine-looking Avian-X decoys and not necessarily any submerged lines. Your call at this point. I suggest buying a large enough spool to accommodate your spread. Home Depot sells a 1,152 foot spool of the commercial grade .080 green string trimmer line, enough for approximately 75 decoys holding a maximum of 15-foot lengths should you decide on a significant spread. Keep in mind that more decoys are always better. Expanding your duck decoy spread, or branching out by enlisting a legion of goose decoys for an over-water shoot, you'll be surprised how fast that line will disappear from the spool.

For ease of adjusting line depths, I recommend large (oversized) heavy-duty fishing line-sinker slides (catfish rig-type wire clips). They are to be clipped through either the front or rear of the decoy's keel (not to the sinker) and used to preset line depths in a fixed position. A package of 20 slides (approximately 2¾-inches long and wider than standard clips) from Amazon will run you $14; sold by Peter Tackle Place. Forget about those smaller #6 size sinker slides. They'll work in a pinch, but in *cold* weather, you will experience finger-numbing frustration when opening and closing those smaller clips. You'll need one sinker slide per decoy. Again, you will find that the larger-size clips will facilitate ease of handling when changing line depths. I prefer these clips to the carabiner-style hardware used in some duck decoy rigging. I'll also cover an alternative way to rig the line-sinker slide, which will allow you to quickly lock in a series of preset depths.

I use 4-ounce egg style slip sinkers from Sinker Supply, www.sinkersupply.com. A package of 10 ran $12.

Double-barrel aluminum cable ferrules for crimping lines are easily obtained and inexpensively purchased from your local hardware store. Two dozen cost me just under a dollar. Whatever line you decide, I suggest taking at least a 12-inch length to the store for perfect sizing, making sure that it passes through both sleeves of the ferrule, the line-sinker slide, as well as the sinker. For ease of assembly, it's better to select a slightly larger diameter ferrule for the line as you'll be forming a small loop at each end. The .080 string-trimmer line fit snugly into the sleeve's 3/8 inch length by 1/16 inch diameter holes.

Those are your materials. Let's see how easy it is to rig your own decoys. You have two choices. Read both procedures before deciding which rig you would prefer. The first procedure allows you more versatility in terms of desired depths.

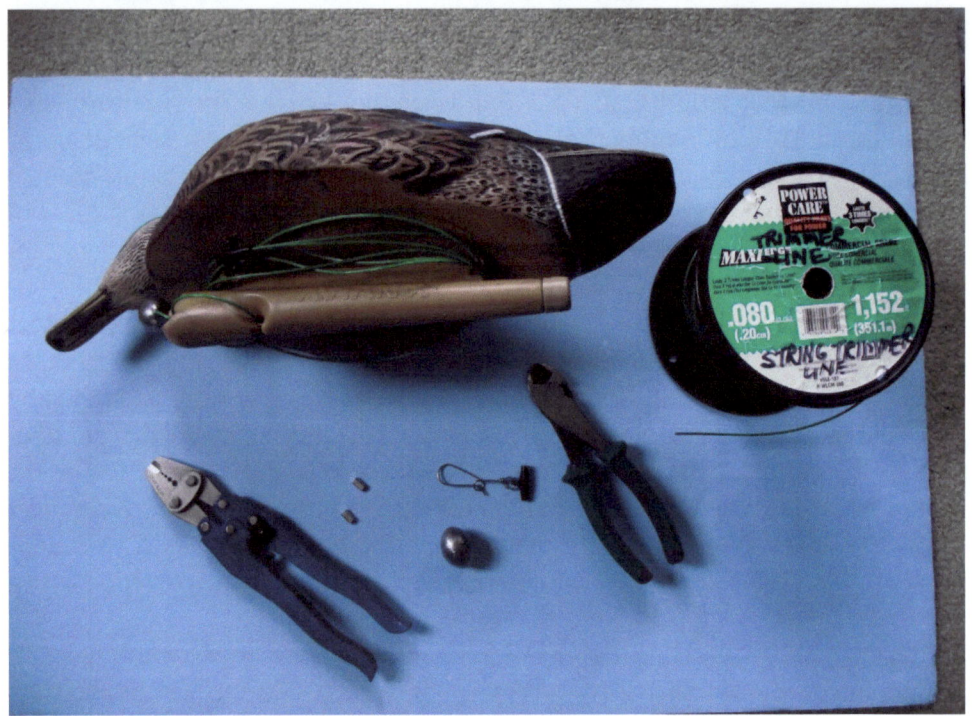

Duck Rigging Tools & Materials

Procedure I

Step 1. Pass an end of a 10-foot length of line through one of the doubled-barreled cable ferrule sleeves, forming a small ½-inch loop by passing it through the other end of the adjacent sleeve. Crimp the top and bottom of the ferrule firmly.

Step 2. At the other end of the line, slide on one line-sinker slide followed by the egg sinker. Repeat Step 1 by forming a second loop as before. These looped ferrules serve as stops, preventing the line-sinker slide and sinker from falling off. I do not bother fashioning larger traditional loops for tossing decoys as the loops tend to collect and hold onto slimy seaweed, grasses, weeds, and such.

Step 3. Clip the line-sinker slide to the hole in either the front or rear of the duck decoy's keel. Leave the clip open.

Step 4. From the sinker-slider clip, measure off approximately 6 feet of line and mark that spot with your permanent marker. Wrap that 6-foot section around the keel of your decoy and lock it into the clip. You now have a 4-foot section with the egg sinker suspended at the other end of the line—a suitable length for most applications. Continue wrapping the remaining 6-foot length of line around the keel, keeping it in place in either of two notches (swim clips) molded into the forward keel of Avian-X's Early-Season Mallard Decoy lineup for easy transport. Need more than a 4-foot depth? Unwrap the 6-foot length, open the clip, remove the remainder of line, and you now have a 10-foot length, which can be set to any desired depth between mere inches to 10 feet.

Keep in mind that there is plenty of room to *easily* accommodate an extra 21 feet of .080 commercial-grade string-trimmer line; that's 40-plus feet of depth for some deep-water rigging. I know of some guys who rig in 20 to 30 feet. This rigging system offers some real versatility.

The author with a rigged Avian-X Early-Season Mallard (drake) Decoy

Procedure II
Conventional Texas Rig
Suitable for a Single Preset Depth

Step 1. Rather than attach a sinker-slider clip to the line as explained in the first procedure, simply pass an end of a desired length of line (generally 4 feet) through one of the doubled-barrel cable ferrule sleeves, forming a larger 2-inch loop by passing it through the other end of the adjacent sleeve. This will facilitate in tossing the rig. Crimp the top and bottom of the ferrule firmly.

Step 2. Pass the other end of the line through either the front or rear hole in the duck decoy's keel, forming another two-inch loop by passing the same end through the adjacent sleeve, securing the ferrule by crimping both top and bottom firmly. This is obviously a more permanent method but does not allow you to readily change the line's position from the front of the keel to the back; nor does it allow you to change depths as in **Procedure I**.

CHAPTER 20

HUNTING DIMINUTIVE MARSH BIRDS
[Presented in Size Order]

Sora Rail

Sora rails are the smallest of the migratory birds discussed in this handbook. They are both freshwater and Atlantic Intracoastal Waterway marsh birds that provide fine wing shooting for hunters. The adult bird is identified by a gray-brown body with a black patch on its face and throat, a short stubby chicken-like yellow bill, and greenish legs. Hunting is often approached by poling a flats skiff through shallow wetlands, gunner seated up front, navigator perched high upon an elevated platform at the rear of the boat. As an aside, this shallow-draft poling method is great for fishing shoal areas in clear waters where fish would otherwise be easily spooked. Used for bird hunting purposes, the skiff will effectively help flush these birds from their cover.

  A good many hunters not only shy away from the golden age of pursuing rail birds, they also steer clear of eating these plump, miniature morsels simply because they can't be bothered with plucking or skinning procedures; others because they've failed to find a palatable recipe. Breasting the birds rather than cooking them whole is a quick and easy way to proceed. Pluck only the breast feathers then use small kitchen shears or a small knife to remove the breast. See my marinating magic and sautéing procedure in the recipe section of this handbook.

Virginia Rail

Virginia rails are the next up in size—slightly. They are easily identified by their long, angled-down, reddish bill. The bodies of adults are mainly brown, but darker on the back and crown, while their legs are an orange-brown. They are hunted and prepared for table fare in much the same manner as the sora rail. Again, please refer to the recipe section of this handbook for various cooking methods.

Northern Bobwhite [Quail]

Northern bobwhite [aka bobwhite quail and Virginia quail] are well-known for the male's familiar onomatopoetic call: *bob-white* or *bob-bob white*. You'll find them in grassy fields, along its edges, open pines, and through scrubby, bushy areas. They'll travel in coveys, running along the ground from one scruffy area to another—the flock taking to flight with rapid wingbeats when flushed. Donna will walk ahead of me, but off to one side, beating the brush and grasses with a long stick. I'll be following close behind, alert and ready, gun held at port arms. However, a bird dog such as a setter or a pointer would certainly facilitate matters.

The male bird is identified by its reddish-brown back, a lighter shade with white scaling and spotting along its breast, a broad white eyebrow with a throat patch below a blackish-brown crested poll, and a broad black-and-white collar ringing the bird's neck. Its rotund upper body sports round-tipped wings, striped flanks, and a stubby tail.

These birds make for excellent table fare.

Common Snipe

The common snipe may be found from marsh to wet, grassy swales and meadows. The bird flushes with amazing speed and a piercing call. Its erratic flight is surprisingly fast—undulating, zigzagging—offering shooters a true challenge. Hence, *snipe* is the origin of the word sniper, for one has to be an exceptional shot to knock down these birds.

Snipe can be identified by their extremely long, straight, dark bill, approximately twice the length of its head. The adult's body markings are black-brown, with stark off-white striped scapular feathered wings and brown rounded tail. Contrary to folks with certain mindsets, snipe make fine table fare.

American Woodcock

Woodcock are another of our long-billed shorebirds, similar to the common snipe. However, woodcock do not reside in marsh areas as their diet consists mainly of earthworms, their favorite food. Hence, they are found in wooded swamps, wet forested areas, and dense growths of bushes along shorelines. Adults are identified by four rust-colored lateral bars across their back, eyes set far back. Females (averaging 7.3 ounces) are larger than the males (averaging 5.8 ounces).

Woodcock are highly praised among game hunters as the bird's flesh is rich and flavorful—unlike any other of its kind.

Gray Partridge [aka Hungarian partridge]

Gray partridge have quail-like bodies and are a similar species to the Northern bobwhite, but without the heavy black-and-white collar markings that ring the smaller bird's neck. The gray partridge is an open-country upland game bird found in grassy, flourishing, cultivated fields. The adult male has a grayish-brown body with a short gray bill, an orange face and throat, a distinct brown patch below and to the rear of the eye, a gray breast finely barred with brown, and a white belly. Its flanks are crosshatched with reddish bars and buff-white streaks, along with chestnut-brown abdominal tail feathers.

These birds are best pursued with pointer dogs bred for endurance because a good deal of ground will need to be covered. In fact, these birds are generally garnered as a result of hunters taking aim at quail and pheasant. One such breed of dog with stamina to go the distance was our short haired German shepherd, Max, who is no longer with us. Donna and I miss Max terribly. He was the best—not only for hunting, but for his companionship. He was truly our canine friend.

Areas comprised of stubble (defined as the short, stiff stumps or stalks of grain and forage crops that remain after cutting and harvesting) are prime tracts of land to harvest these fantastic upland game birds. Hunt these fields and pastures in the fall, and you'll find partridge. As table fare, these birds are most favorable and flavorful.

Purple Ganninule

The purple ganninule (larger member of the rail family) is a heavier-bodied bird than the previous six covered. It is found in both saltwater marshes, freshwater swamps, as well as other wetland areas that provide abundant vegetation. The adult is readily identified by its blueish-purple head, throat, and breast, a red bill with yellow tip, pale-blue marking atop its crown, and a dusky-black back merging into glossy-green flanks and wings. Its yellow legs and feet are visible as it walks upon dense stands of floating vegetation. This fundamentally tropic marsh bird unmitigatedly ventures into the northern United States and southern Canada.

Often, the best way to hunt these migrant winged wonders is by poling a flats skiff as explained in the first entry referencing sora rails. Otherwise, you'll be traipsing through muck and mire and putting yourself at risk.

CHAPTER 21

TOP-FLIGHT UPLAND ACTION
[Presented in Size Order]

Ruffed Grouse

Ruffed Grouse are named for their long, black feathers that rise into a ruff; that is, tufts of broad black feathers which form a fringe around the bird's neck. The adult's body is a chestnut-colored pattern with predominately reddish-brown bars alternating between light-gray bands and spots. Another distinguishable feature is a peaked crest and a broad, dark, subterminal band at the tip of its tail, quite discernible as when fanned in flight. The male can be seen perched on fallen logs, beating its wings and sounding very much like a small, muffled engine starting up. When flushed, these forest dwellers explode in a startling thunder of pounding wings, making the unmistakable sound of a drum roll. They are often referred to as the king of all game birds and make excellent table fare.

Although a forest inhabitant, it prefers its edges and openings for cover. I would strongly suggest hunting ruffed grouse with a pair of well-trained Brittany spaniels for the best in flushing grouse. Actually, a Brittany is the *primo* gun dog, bred primarily for bird hunting.

Ruffed Grouse Wall Mount

Pheasant

The brightly colored ring-necked pheasant (male) is unmistakably one of our most recognized game birds. The hen (female) is drab in color and smaller than her mate. Males sport a long pointed tail, iridescent copper and gold plumage, a red face, and a bright white collar. Although they may be seen strutting their stuff along country roadsides, pheasants love cover and are therefore hunted in weedy fields, along overgrown ravines, through thickets, beside densely screened fence lines, on the periphery of marshes, meadows, and within cornfields—provided that they offer abundant *cover*. Concealment is the name of their game. Pursuing pheasant is right up there amid my favorite upland birds.

As professional outfitters offer opportunities for hunting hens and ring-necked pheasants on private preserves, a friend of mine and I made the most of one such outing. It was a snowy, cold wintery morning in 1996 when I first had the opportunity to hunt pheasant with a dog. I teamed up with my butcher buddy, Ken Birmingham (always good to know a butcher), and his companion Emily (and especially a butcher who owns a well-trained hunting dog) for the day. Emily was a young springer spaniel born to flush and retrieve game birds. I had hunted pheasants in many a field when I was a youngster, occasionally meeting with success. But to hunt with a trained pooch and at Greenfield Outfitters in Aquebogue, New York (now defunct), well, it was like the difference between night and day. Ken and I each limited out early in the game, which was fine with us because another winter storm would be soon be upon us.

Author with Emily & Pheasants Hanging in Background

Backing up a bit in narration, just like those ducks and geese I wrote about earlier in the waterfowl section of this handbook, I hadn't hunted upland game, especially pheasants, in many a moon and had to be reminded when I missed the first shot to, ". . . lead that bird considerably, Bob. Remember, they're half tail."

"Right, Ken."

Emily just looked from me then back to Ken as if to say, "This guy needs some serious remedial training."

I lead the next bird by a good margin as well as following through smoothly with the shot. I didn't want to have to be *reminded* of this latter point. Feathers blew, the bird went down, and Emily looked satisfied as Ken gave her the command to retrieve my prize.

Hunting pheasant without a well-trained dog is tough for the simple reason that the well-camouflaged bird will remain hidden and sulk (remain perfectly still) until earnestly flushed by a relentless hound.

Turkey

There is no question that wild turkeys are the largest of our North American game birds. Turkey hunting is both a spring and fall game, with spring being the prime time to hunt these gobblers because it is their mating season. Receptive hens [not unlike breeding does during the rut] make toms (adult male longbeards) and jakes (male juveniles) turn careless. Turkey hunting in the fall is not as productive as during their springtime mating season. They are on high alert and will spot you in a heartbeat. What to do? A trick I use is to locate a flock and *purposely* scatter them in all directions. I immediately move away from that spot and walk approximately sixty yards off in another direction that will provide adequate cover. I quickly settle in then sound a call that is used to reunite the flock—a call that says, "Hey, I am over here; let's get with the program and assemble, now!" It is the call of a mature hen sounding off with long, rhythmic series of yelps to pull the birds back together. It is *not* an "I am lost" distress call made by a poult (a young bird). More on turkey calls in a moment, but first an important note.

One fact I'd like to stress is that hunting turkey can be dangerous. The danger is presented from another hunter stalking turkeys. You should *not* stalk turkeys for safety's sake. The approach to turkey hunting is to hunker down in your blind or simply sit still and at the ready with your back against a tree. Full camo is the dress code of the day. You are not wearing a highly visible blaze-orange vest or jacket that would spook a gobbler in a nanosecond because their eyesight is extremely keen. Hence, you are not visible to other hunters in the area; consequently, accidents occur. If you spot another hunter, do not move or signal with your hand or nod your head. Instead, announce your presence in a loud, clear voice. A sudden movement on your part could result in injury or death. There are more accidents as the result of turkey hunting than any other type of hunting. Do not become a statistic. With that important message aside, let's see how we can outsmart turkey.

Chris Paparo's tom

Let's Talk Turkey
Turkey Calls

Mouth Calls

Talking their language is the first step in summoning forth these big birds. There are a plethora of turkey calls on the market. Professional callers often narrow the playing field by eliminating those calls that require two-handed operation (unless they have a partner who is going to do the calling). Professional callers generally employ the multi-reed, diaphragm-type mouth call so that both hands are free to handle the gun. Using the call effectively takes practice, practice, practice—practice to make five basic types of sound to imitate hen calls: a high-pitched to a low-pitched sound (yelps), a clucking sound, a cutting sound, a purring sound, and a regrouping sound. For the beginner, these basic calls are best learned from CDs and DVDs. Learn to make these five types of sound then enjoy the rush of toms and jakes heading toward your decoys.

One and/or Two-Handed Friction Calls

But what if you don't have the time, patience, or inclination to learn what may take months or maybe years to effectively call in turkeys with a hands-free turkey mouth call? Then what?

The Box Cutter by Primos is a great call. Easy to learn; easy to use. Just holding it in your hand for the very first time tells you that it is slightly different from the rest. How so? Well, it's the call's configuration in that it is angled with thumb-hole grooving, which allows your thumb to operate the Jatobá lid of the box like a spring, producing perfect cuts (pitches) that will get a gobbler's attention.

Jatobá, also known as Brazilian Cherry, is a hardwood tree found along the riverbanks in tropical Central America and is known for its durability: hard, heavy, and tough. The call's box (base) is constructed of solid mahogany. This single-sided call is to be ordered in either a right- or left-handed model, so be sure and specify. As the bird approaches, keep him coming with a series of yelps, cuts, clucks, and purrs that will draw that bearded boss in your direction like a magnet. These four basic sounds are easily learned by surfing the Internet and viewing a few videos. You will quickly learn, too, that each person has their own technique. When in the field, listening to the birds' language and imitating those sounds will make you a pro in no time. At some point, you may even be able to claim that you are bilingual and fluent.☺

Note: To give you some idea of these four basic calls, an alternating mix of high to low notes is the <u>yelp</u> of a wild turkey; a <u>cut</u> is a more excited, aggravated sound; an answering call from a hen asking where are *you* are is a <u>cluck</u>, which is a fractional sound with not as much sharpness or excitement to it. A <u>purr</u> is a low, soft series of sound. Again, view videos for an eyeful and earful. Cadence is the key and is mastered through practice.

There are other types of box calls by Primos that you may want to consider. They are those referred to as two-sided calls, meaning that the lid (striker) can pass in either direction above the box. One of these calls is designed for wet weather and is appropriately named the Wet Call. If you hunt turkeys in an area where you will encounter wet weather on a regular basis, not only from rain, snow, and mist, but from a morning frost melting and dripping those elements upon you, you may want to consider the Wet Call. Unlike other box calls, the Wet Call does not need chalk (which creates needed friction) to keep it in tune. In wet weather, box calls utilizing chalk will create an issue. The underside of the Wet Call's lid is treated so that it is not affected by inclement weather.

If you hunt in a constantly windy region, you may want to think about the Battleship Heartbreaker box call. As its name suggests, it is big, and its high pitch will reach out there and be heard. If wind is not an issue, you would want to select from the more compact calls covered here.

The Chick Magnet box call is actually two calls in one. Unlike the other three, this call works by magnets. It comes with two magnetic lids (strikers) that operate independently of one another, not like the other calls that have a single lid fastened to the box with what is called a chasing spring. The box itself incorporates a magnet, too. One striker produces a coarse sound while the other creates a softer, sweeter, high-pitched sound. You simply select and place one of the two strikers atop the box and operate the call as you would the others, passing the paddle back and forth. Those powerful magnets hinge the handle in place, holding both paddles when transporting.

To keep things simple, I suggest that beginners choose the Primos single-sided Box Cutter because it is an easy call to learn how to use. Once you are familiar with this call, lodging it between your knees for one-handed operation becomes second nature. Its thumb-slot design and sideboard prevents overriding the striker and breaking cadence. Sounds ranging from a raspy yelp to a smooth purr are produced effortlessly. You'll quickly learn how to handle a box call. For example: when to pass the hinged paddle (the lid's striker) lightly or more aggressively for the desired sound; and with practice, knowing the proper pressure to be applied; finally, picking up a rhythm. Given the *types* of turkey calls on the market today, a box call (which has been around since 1897) sounds most like a turkey. Given the *styles* of turkey calls, the Primos Box Cutter is a cut (no pun intended) above the rest.

The level of proficiency you'll obtain through imitating, articulating, and understanding yelps, cuts, clucks, and purrs—instead of just talking gobbledygook—will be the true measure of your success. The satisfaction you will receive in calling in your first tom to a decoy spread will be unforgettable. I equate it to my first experience rattling in an eight-point buck that stopped dead in its tracks after eyeballing my six-point buck decoy . . . maybe even tying my first fly that caught a trophy trout.

Turkey Tactics

Unlike waterfowl hunting where you may need dozens of decoys to form an inviting spread, two or three female imposters (hens), along with a jake and/or tom (males), are all that's needed to draw turkeys to within shooting distance. I like to set out decoys approximately 20 to 30 yards from me. This distance provides for good coverage (density pattern) of shot via a Full choke, ensuring a clean kill. I aim for the base of the bird's neck (wattles) rather than taking a full head shot, blanketing both body and brain. Such shot placement allows for a moderate margin of error should the bird suddenly turn cautious and hold steadfast but is in sufficient shooting range of the decoys. My Remington 12 gauge semiautomatic is loaded and chambered with 3½-inch shells, number 4 stainless steel shot. To date, no gobbler has escaped that pattern because I don't shoot beyond 40 yards, although I certainly could kill gobblers out to 50 yards with the right turkey loads. Again, I keep it simple and humane by employing the KISS concept (Keep It Simple System). Although tom turkeys are tough ol' birds, you do not need a 10 gauge shotgun combined with special handloads to effectively terminate turkeys.

Patterning your gun is the key to success. Referencing the above, if I can count approximately 210 pellet holes out of 256 in a turkey-sized paper target at 30 yards, I'm good to go.

Turkey Decoys

Turkey decoys are a must and should be lifelike and durable for continued success. There are basically three types: hard shells, soft shells, and soft-shell inflatables. Whether you are a first-time purchaser or adding to your spread, please read through this **Turkey Decoys** section before making a decision. I saved my best for last in terms of what is best for *me*, along with the reasons why.

Inflatable-type turkey decoys make for easy transport because they deflate. If you do not have to travel far afield, hard shell types will save you approximately a dozen breaths per decoy, for you won't have to keep inflating them when afield.

Referencing the inflatable types, allow me to suggest Avian-X LCD turkey decoys, made of rubber. For the hard-shell plastic-blend types, I'd recommend DSD Decoys and Dakota Decoys. Forget about those other flimsy foam, cardboard, paper, and cloth material sorts, including pull-string type silhouette forms (you want the whole bird)—unless, of course, you're on a strict budget. On the flip side, no need to go crazy with expensive remote controlled Mojo-type decoys, but with one exception: Mojo Outdoors' Shake-n-Jake. More on that particular bad boy in a moment. Realism combined with durability is your main consideration.

There are five basic body styles and positions that offer lifelike appearances to your setup: alert <u>sentry</u> (head held high); relaxed <u>feeder</u> (head held low); <u>breeder</u> (posed with lowered head forward, extended body, raised rump—ready for action); <u>strutting</u> hen, jake, or gobbler; <u>dominant</u> strutting gobbler with long beard and fanned tail.

Author Placing Avian-X Turkey Decoys (right to left): Strutting hen, Jake, Dominant Strutting Gobble with long beard and fanned tail

The New Hatch of Avian-X, LCD inflatable turkey decoys are unquestionably realistic. A valve on the bottom is used to inflate and deflate the body. When you first unpack your deflated folded decoy, it is suggested that you initially allow it to get to room temperature before running hot water from a shower upon the body for about fifteen minutes so that the rubber becomes more pliable. This will remove the folds and creases formed when they were packed for shipping. Also, it will facilitate inflation. If you do not have the need to carry the decoys far, I'd leave them inflated. Had you the need to travel good distances, you would, of course, deflate them. Because of their versatility, you may prefer these rubber inflatables over the plastic hard shell types. Motion stakes and carry bag(s) are included. Check them out at www.avian-x.com.

DSD (**D**ave **S**mith **D**ecoys) are very pricey; however, the cost is justified not only in terms of realism, but with impressive durability. I have seen a DSD hen decoy purposely shot at from 12 to 15 yards with a Magnum 3-inch, 2-ounce, number 5 shot shell. Although the decoy flew back on impact and was riddled with shot, pellets rattling inside its cavity when picked up and shaken, the outer surface self-healed and the pellet marks were hardly discernible. This is made possible via A.C.E. (**A**dvanced **C**rosslink **E**lastomer) technology. A.C.E. is a thermoplastic/elastomer process and is not to be compared to typical polyethylene pure plastic processes, which comprise virtually all hard shell production decoys manufactured abroad. The decoy's painted finish is superb. Once again, you get what you pay for. Hence, DSD decoys are paradoxically a soft/hard shell body; they are <u>not</u> foldable. Motion stakes and carry bag(s) are included, too. Check them out at www.davesmithdecoys.com.

Dakota Decoys' X-Treme Jake and Dual Purpose Hen Decoy are made from an EVA-blend (**e**thelyne-**v**inyl **a**cetate) plastic process. Capturing the body language of an arrogant jake (a young male wild turkey), world-famous decoy carver Dave Constantine has replicated the bird's features by fashioning its slightly rearward head-tilt, freezing its open gob in an about-to-gobble manner, while producing a partial strutting pose that drives mature toms crazy. Likewise, the realism of Dakota's Dual Purpose Hen Decoy gives you the option of either positioning the bird in a standing position or placing it upon the ground in a receptive breeding profile. They are <u>not</u> foldable. Metal stake(s) included. Check them out at www.dakotadecoy.com.

Now, back to that one mojo mentioned a moment ago. World champion turkey caller and consummate hunter, Preston Pittman, teamed up with Mojo Outdoors to create Pittman's signature series Shake-n-Jake lifelike turkey decoy. From up to 150 feet away, the motorized unit allows you to raise and lower the decoy's tail as well as simultaneously turn its head. It operates on four AA batteries. This motion dude is a winner. It is costly, but to be seriously considered for your setup. It is <u>not</u> foldable. Steel stake and blaze orange carry bag included. Check them out at www.mojooutdoors.com.

Saving the best for last, my choice of a turkey decoy selection was a no-brainer.

It may or may not be for you. That is why I first had you take a close look at the other types of turkey decoys and manufacturers. Not until Donna and I visited Cabela's in Hamburg, Pennsylvania and laid eyes and hands upon several of those decoys mentioned did I decide what was best for *moi*. I took into consideration their construction, exactly where I would be using these turkey decoys, and their cost.

In a nutshell, Primos Hunting products are hard to beat. Their slogan is, "You can pay more for a premium decoy, but why would you?" That phrase says it all, but you wouldn't know that unless you had the benefit of an eyes-on, hands-on experience. Those decoys are, most importantly, realistic. They are lightweight, durable, and far less expensive when compared to the other decoys mentioned. More on that point later when we'll weigh in on dollar-for-dollar.

As I do not have to travel or walk any significant distance with my decoys, I need not pack or roll them up to carry in a vest or bag, although I could, since the decoys are made from a proprietary material that allows you to do so, making them quite versatile. Since the decoys are not the inflatable type, you need not waste your breath and time. Simply remove them from your vest or bag if needed, unfold, and pop the birds back into shape. I carry three decoys fully-formed. Admittedly, I am spoiled in that I only have to carry the trio (hen, jake, and a strutting mobile gobbler) from cabin to a nearby blind. Then it's simply a matter of placing or staking them to the ground.

Let's begin with the Gobbstopper Hen decoy; realistic as they come. She is custom-designed by world-class sculptors. William Primos boasts that the decoy "features the detail and paint scheme quality you would expect from a taxidermist. Its ultra-realistic look will fool the leeriest toms and rival the competition's best looking decoys, at a price virtually any turkey hunter can afford." Well, William, I concur wholeheartedly. With a motion stake that comes with the bird, you can place her in an upright position, a contented stance, or simply remove the stake and set her in a submissive spot upon the ground.

The Gobbstopper Jake is so realistic that a WARNING on the box in which it comes states that the hunter needs to use a blaze orange flag when carrying the decoy through the woods. Better believe it. Placed and paired with the hen, this dynamic duo soon becomes a turkey magnet. Motion stake is included.

The Killer B Strutting Decoy Gobbler completes my setup. With a 90-foot pull line, this mobile bird raises and lowers its realistic fanned-out silk tail to *any* appropriate position: tail fan down, tail fan at ¾ strut, tail fan at full strut, and back down again if you want—without leaving your position. After harvesting a tom, you can substitute the silk fan with plucked feathers from the real McCoy via a plastic fan holder in which to form an even more earthy appearance. If you wish to go all-out, you can remove the secondary feathers from the harvested bird then use a glue gun to stick them in place at the base of the fanned tail. Too, you could replace the decoy's beard with a genuine one from a dispatched tom. You're not going to get much more of a bona fide bird unless you fettered a live one to a stake.

The Killer B Strutting Decoy Gobbler comes complete with fold-up, stow-away silk fan, ancillary fan holder for real feathers, fan hardware, 90-foot pull line, printed and illustrated instructions for setup and operation, additional instructional DVD, motion stake, and carrying bag with blaze orange flag.

As with the rubber-bodied type decoys covered earlier, Primos turkey decoys are initially to be run under hot water in order remove the folds and creases from packing and shipping. I placed my trio under a hot shower for about fifteen minutes then lightly towel dried their bodies before using a hair dryer to warm the surfaces, which facilitated in popping the bodies back to their original shape.

Let's now do a dollar-for-dollar comparison among all the decoys listed.

Avian X, LCD: Hen $80 ~ Jake $100 ~ Gobbler $120
DSD Decoys: Hen $120 ~ Jake $160 ~ Gobbler $200
Dakota: Hen $100 ~ Jake $110 ~ Flocked Back Jake $130, [no gobbler available]
Mojo Shake-n-Jake: $150, [no gobbler available]
Primos Hunting: Gobbstopper Hen $64 ~ Gobbstopper Jake $42 ~ Killer B Gobbler $90

The way I see it is that unless you are going to shoot-up DSD's turkey decoys, either purposely or inadvertently, there is no need to pay those higher prices, or for other name brands, either. Primos turkey decoys are not cheap substitutes. Just like their competitors, Primos turkey decoys are made from a proprietary formula, along with a paint process that rivals the competition's attention to fine detail. Too, the company is always striving to improve their product line. For example, the new Killer B Strutting Gobbler mobile model has been created from the prior spring season's B-Mobile model. The new bird has been given a complete body makeover, intensifying its iridescent colors throughout the body and head, bringing out more of the red tones. Additionally, it was gifted quality eyes from the taxidermist to give it realism personified. You'd swear the tom was looking directly at you. Very cool. Even the bird's posture has been updated to have him seemingly, pompously strut. So, too, is the mobile tail fan new. In short, Primos Hunting products are terrific, and that's no gobbledygook.

Check them out online at www.primos.com.

Turkey Decoy Spread

Your decoys should be set up in an area where they may be seen from a good distance, such as a wide logging trail or a clearing. If the approaching turkeys suddenly shy away from your setup, evaluate the situation and try a different approach. If you have a dominant jake or a boss-sized tom in your spread, it may prove intimidating to a less aggressive bird. Remove that bird from the equation. Too, if you have a breeder staked high and sitting pretty, lower her to ground level so that she appears even more submissive. Then when a jake or longbeard comes calling and mounts your receptive hen, she'll roll with the gobbler and drive him crazy. These are tactics that rarely fail.

Vested Interests

A good turkey vest is a must-have item, which can also double when stalking game and needing an occasional rest. For example, while still-hunting deer, there will be times you'll just want to sit for a spell instead of standing endlessly on your feet. Perhaps you can't find a suitable dry spot after a recent rain or snowfall. Or in addition to a soaking-wet ground, the base of that perfect tree—against which you'd like to sit in wait to ambush a buck or tom—has gnarly knots that dig into your butt and spine. A good turkey vest would make life considerably more comfortable for a long day in the woods.

When I go hunting, it's usually for a good half or full day, so I make no excuse or apology for wanting to be comfortable. Cabela's Men's Minimalist Turkey Vest, with its cushioned seat, affords me a dry seat or good back support.

Although the vest's model name (Minimalist) connotes something that is barely adequate, referring to its number of pockets, they are more than sufficient, both in terms of number as well as size. For an MSRP of $80, it is a moderate price to pay for such a fine product. There are turkey vests that cost close to double that amount, and what you're really paying for are more pockets. As it is, Cabela's Men's Minimalist Turkey Vest has ten pockets: a huge, nylon-taffeta, blood proof, expandable decoy/game bag pocket in back (two drain holes); two big foam-protected (8 x 8 inches) zippered utility pockets in front (which also have three sewn-in elastic loops on each side for shotgun shells); horizontal friction-fit box-call pocket with silent-close flap, adjustable cord and elastic accessory loop; small elastic pocket for chalk; a slate call and striker pocket; one-quart water bottle pocket; easy access pocket for a cell phone/GPS; plus two other small utility pockets. Tell me you need more and bigger pockets. If you do, consider Cabela's Men's Tactical Tat'r II M.O.R.E. Vest for a lot more money.

In terms of comfort and convenience, Cabela's Men's Minimalist Turkey Vest has a detachable Speed (buckle strap) Seat, 2½-inch thick [not 3-inches as advertised but perfectly suitable] tri-layer, open/closed-cell Memory Tech foam seat with Ultra-Grip, rubber-coated bottom. Well-appreciated on cold, wet, hard ground. Cabela's boasts its Couch Cushion Comfort System with raised closed-cell, foam-padded mesh back panel and 3-inch wide, cushioned shoulder straps. Two handy D-rings are located at the bases of each shoulder strap along with large front zippered pockets. Adjustable sternum and waist buckle straps provide for a comfort fit. Last but not least, the back of the vest has a tuck-away flap to either display or conceal a sewn-in, 12-inch long, blaze orange safety flag. How cool is that? This is truly a lightweight, practical, comfortable vest. Its outer shell is constructed of 60/40 cotton/polyester twill; the lining is made of a durable polyester Oxford weave with a water-resistant finish. It comes in a Mossy Oak-Obsession camouflage pattern.

Cabela's Men's Minimalist Turkey Vest

Gloves, Hats, Masks & Other Clothing

Gloves, hats, masks, and other clothing are a must for turkey hunting because these wild birds have terrific eyesight, better than 20/20 vision. They also see ultraviolet light in the UVA range—especially during low-light conditions— so be sure to wash all hunting clothing in laundry detergents that are free of brighteners (dyes), chlorine bleach, fabric softeners and, of course, perfumes. Turning garments inside out then zipping or buttoning closed before washing accomplishes two things: prevents any loop fasteners, drawstrings, straps, et cetera from tangling or snagging, and adds longevity to the patterned fabric. Washing in cold water and allowing the garment to drip-dry will also add longevity to the article of clothing. Although not a laundry detergent per se, I suggest Arm & Hammer Baking Soda, or 20-Mule Team Borax.

For springtime turkey hunting, I selected Cabela's Ultimate Mesh Half Facemask, featuring a light, soft, breathable, bug-resistant polyester material with Lycra added (92% poly/8% Lycra), which conforms to fit your face whether or not you're wearing glasses. The half-facemask style is available in a Realtree pattern, draping 20½-inches. MSRP: $15. For the fall, I'd suggest hunting around for a neoprene full facemask.

Gloves: camo mesh for the springtime; neoprene camo for the fall.

You're good to go, for everything will be neatly arranged in the Cabela's Men's Minimalist Turkey Vest.

CHAPTER 22

WILD BOAR [incl. Feral Hogs & Hybrids] & OTHER GAME

Hunting wild boar can certainly present a challenge. For openers, it can prove dangerous, especially if a female swine (sow) feels that her piglets (young swine) are in peril. I have read accounts and seen videos where hunters have encountered wild boar and feral hogs and were suddenly attacked. In one incident, the charging animal ripped open a man's leg. In another occurrence, a hunter received over three hundred stitches. In still another, a boar killed a hunter's dog. Here in the United States, an average female wild boar can weigh anywhere between 77 to 330 pounds; around 165 to 440 pounds for a male. That's a pretty big boar for here in the States. In parts of Eurasia, wild boar can tip the Toledo at 600 pounds. In any event, you're talking about a worthy opponent if push ever came to shove.

We have three basic types of wild swine referencing the cloven-hooved pig family: Eurasian wild boar (often called Russian boar), which were first introduced to North America in 1893; feral hogs of domestic ancestry that escaped from farms and preserves; and hybrids that are a cross between the two.

Generally, a wild boar is black in color but can also be brown or gray. It has a long head with a flexible, cartilaginous, disc-like snout. Its upper tusks (a form of canine) run approximately 3 to 5 inches on average. Big tuskers can grow to 9 inches. The tusks curl outward and upward along the side of its mouth. The lower tusks are smaller and turned slightly outward, pointing rearward toward the animal's eyes. Boars attack by charging while pointing their tusks towards the intended target.

In April of 2014, the New York State Department of Environmental Conservation set a new regulation that prohibited the *hunting* or trapping of Eurasian *boars*, feral hogs, et cetera. This caused quite a controversy among many landowners, not only farmers but residential property owners as well. Wild boars are fast becoming prolific creatures that are considerably destructive, uprooting anything from home gardens to entire pastures, mowing down corn stalks and breaking through levees and other structural, protective barriers. The list is endless. When a large family group (called a sounder) joins together, they create utter havoc.

Yet you can't hunt them in New York, except with a special permit issued by the New York State Department of Environmental Conservation. They have their own *game* plan. You were allowed to hunt them on certain preserves in New York State until 2015. But then *that* was put to a stop. Rather than get into the politics on this particular issue, I'll simply say that wild boar are delicious. I'll only add that outsourcing the animal to specialty restaurants and related kitchens is big business.

So where does one go in our geographical area to hunt these sought-after big beasts for a wild challenge as well as fine fare? The closest and best preserve in our tri-state area (New York, New Jersey, Connecticut) lies in another state just to the west of New York, which just might be the ticket for you. For big game trophies (including exotics), check out the fully-guided Tioga Boar Hunting Preserve in Tioga, which is located in the Allegheny Mountain Range of North Central Pennsylvania. Weapons of choice are varied: rifle, bow, crossbow, muzzleloader, handgun, or shotgun—employing rifled slugs that you would normally use for hunting deer. If using a handgun, a .357 or heavier caliber such as a .308 is a good choice. Actually, these handgun calibers are recommended for boar by the ranch. Guides will cape out your animal for mounting if you so desire; the meat will be cut into standard cuts: steaks, chops, roasts, and spare ribs. It will then be bulk packaged in ice (within a 64-quart cooler that you'll provide). Once home, all you'll need to do is vacuum seal for best long-term results or simply freezer wrap for a shorter duration. See Chapter 16 referencing packaging.

In addition to wild boar and whitetails, get a load of the following big game animals that head the list: fallow buck, sika buck, elk bull, elk cow, red stag, buffalo, Rocky Mountain ram, mouflon ram (a subspecies group of wild sheep), Corsican ram, Texas Dall ram, Spanish goat, and black Hawaiian. If overwhelmed with that prodigious big game lineup, wild turkey might be in order. Of course, you could travel thousands of miles to Eurasian countries for exotics and spend many thousands of dollars for what is virtually in your own backyard. How do three squares a day at the lodge and overnight accommodations for a $100 a person grab you? Incredible! We're talking delicious, all-you-can-eat home cooked meals prepared by their chef. These guided hunts, conducted by some of the best professionals in the business, range from $400 to $2,000 and up. A Russian/European trophy boar hunt will cost between $750 and $900 (super trophy hunt), depending on the size of the animal.

Let's take a moment and stand back from what some may pejoratively refer to as "canned hunts." Seeing as how New York State is limiting a hunter's ability to hunt wild boar, feral hogs or hybrids, preserves like the fully-guided Tioga Boar Hunting Ranch in Pennsylvania are filling a sorely needed niche for those who wish to pursue this challenging animal—challenging in the sense that it can be considered dangerous game. For an inexperienced hunter, this would prove a foolhardy pursuit without the presence of a professional to *guide* and educate you along the way.

For a first-time hunter, perhaps a youngster looking to harvest his first deer, this ranch may be a good beginning to make one's bones, so to speak. From $400 to $500 (based on the size of a whitetail doe) for a fully-guided hunt, this is a great deal. Hunting is offered seven (7) days a week, and no license is required. Without question, Tioga Boar Hunting Ranch is one of the premier preserves in the northeastern United States.

Hunting whitetail bucks includes one to two nights lodging, all meals, and skinning; butchering of meat is $50 additional; caping for shoulder mount, $60. Cost for the hunt is priced according to the size of the buck's rack, ranging from 110 inches to over 210 inches. The Tioga Ranch website is www.tiogaboarhunting.com. Click on their Rates link, then look down the list for Whitetail Buck and click on the adjacent link for specific information regarding whitetail rates.

CHAPTER 23

ELK HUNTING

For an adrenaline rush, drawing a bow and dropping a 700-pound rut-crazed bull heading toward your caller will definitely do it for you. Teamwork between bugler and shooter is the name of the game for greater success; archer up front, caller positioned several yards back. Once pretty much a west of the Rocky Mountains adventure, the eastern states offer many good elk hunting opportunities, too. But don't think it's anything like deer hunting. That would be your first mistake. Knowing when to pick the right moment to draw and release is of paramount importance. If you're made, a spooked bull does not necessarily mean "game over," for during the rut, that single-minded male has one thing in his brain, and your caller can likely bugle him back in for a kill shot. Hunting solo with a bow and arrow greatly diminishes your chances of success.

Classifying the elk population, there are four of several subspecies that are hunted in North America: The Rocky Mountain elk, The Roosevelt elk, the Tule elk, and the Manitoban elk. The Rocky Mountain elk (aka American elk) is found west of the Mississippi and are the most widespread, boasting the biggest antlers of the four subspecies. The largest herds are found in California. The Roosevelt elk (aka Olympic elk) is the largest in body size but not antler size. They inhabit areas of Oregon and the state of Washington. Smaller herds inhabit parts of California and British Columbia. Tule elk, named after tules (large bulrushes that grow in marshes) are the smallest in size and found only in central California. Manitoban elk predominately inhabit the western Canadian prairie provinces of Manitoba, Saskatchewan, and Alberta, as well as the Midwestern United States.

Unless you're on a canned hunt, or covering steep terrain on horseback, be prepared to do some serious walking, especially out west. You'd better be in good physical condition. If hunting public land, apply early for those special draw permits. You may get lucky. Each state has different regulations and deadlines, so get started researching sooner than later in planning your hunt.

If you plan on hunting a reserve with a guide through an outfitter, do your homework. Thoroughly research an outfitter's reputation before laying down a deposit. Understand the complete package, meaning exactly what the outfitter will provide; what the guide is responsible for; ambient temperatures and type(s) of terrain to be covered: low-rolling mountains, steep limestone peaks, open plains [grasslands], Arctic tundra [10–20 degrees Fahrenheit]; duration of the hunt; and, of course, price, including the cost for extras such as caping, skinning, butchering, et cetera. Be completely up-front regarding your physical health, abilities, limitations, as well as what you expect from the hunt. This open approach will better serve both parties. Be sure there are no lingering questions left in your mind. Lastly, get everything in writing—before booking.

Unless you are dead set on shooting a trophy bull, consider taking a respectable size cow (female antlerless), especially if you're hunting on a draw permit and have a limited amount of time. Those steaks are going to taste delicious. If you are set on seeking that trophy bull in those wide open western spaces or northern territories, many professional elk hunters feel that a week is needed to give yourself a fair shot. Pun intended. That opportunity comes with the territory. Again, pun intended. But both are very valid points. Remember that this is most likely a one-time opportunity.

Understanding the Wind

One of the best advantages you can give yourself when hunting elk, particularly in those mountainous areas where the wind is continuously shifting, is to have the wind in your face wherever possible. Your scent is carried downwind; therefore, you want to be upwind of your target. If your olfactory sense was as acute as an elk's, you would smell him or her coming as they will certainly smell you. It is arguable as to which animal has the keenest nose; deer or elk. Folks who understand and pay attention to the wind then act accordingly will be more successful than those who walk around hunting aimlessly.

A puffer bottle or simply a plastic .35 millimeter film container (remember those?) filled with milkweed seeds are far better to use than any powders because you can see and study the seeds drift through the air over longer distances. Instead of using chemical agents such as baking soda, wood ash, ground up chalk, et cetera, which only indicate the direction of the wind in relationship to your immediate body, try using milkweed seeds. Wind can be tricky, especially in those elevated areas.

Gather seed pods in the early fall as you'll have no mess from the fluff on your clothing. Merely pop open the shell along its lateral seam and carefully separate the brown seeds from the white fluff by using your fingernail to scrape downward. Deposit the seeds into a container; discard the fluff. A ripe seed pod will have a discernible open crack running along its shell.

If you are hunting from a treestand, hang it facing downwind toward where you expect the elk to appear. Again, you want to be upwind (meaning, wind in your face) from your target. Upwind, crosswind, and downwind currents will determine stand placement.

Generally speaking, during the early morning, and as the day progresses, a body of warm air rises. Conversely, as the day heads toward late afternoon, a body of cooler air descends. We know that hot air rises and cold air descends. Apply this to hunting situations during the course of the day, and you now have a basic understanding of thermals: the rising and falling of a mass of warmer or cooler air. It can swirl, eddy, or switch direction in a heartbeat.

These thermals can sometimes be stronger than the prevailing wind: a wind that blows predominantly (mainly) from a single direction—depending on geographical location and time of year. For example, on Long Island in winter, the wind chiefly comes out of the northeast. Hence, we can get hit with a nor'easter when the prevailing winds are truly cranking, resulting in severe storms along the east coast of the United States and Eastern (Atlantic) Canada. During the summer months, the prevailing wind generally comes out of the southwest. But these dominant wind directions, too, can change in a heartbeat.

Sweeping from west to east and top to bottom are five contiguous states to consider when looking to book and take a prize elk. The Salmon River area in the town of Salmon, Idaho is a fine choice, followed by the Lee Metcalf Wilderness area near Yellowstone National Park, Montana. Saratoga and Cody, Wyoming are promising areas, too. Grand Junction in Colorado is a great area. And don't let the word *city* as in Rapid City, South Dakota fool you. Elk abound in these areas and avail themselves to excellent opportunities.

Some states require your entering the lottery process, building up necessary points over a period of time. A good many folks do not realize that there are states that offer Over-the-Counter tags to non-residents as well as residents. Contact the Department of Fish and Game in one of these eight states if you are considering hunting elk: Washington, Oregon, Idaho, Utah, Arizona, Montana, Wyoming, and Colorado. You may be surprised to learn that you can circumvent the lottery process. Rules and regulations can change from year to year, but you have a good chance or receiving a tag for a cow (female) and possibly a bull (male). Specifically inquire about Over-the-Counter tags for elk and combination hunts. Again, you might be surprised.

CHAPTER 24

MOOSE HUNTING THE CANADIAN NORTHWEST TERRITORY

Planning a Fly-In

Of the deer family (Cervidae), including, for example, Florida's Key deer [smallest], fallow deer, mule deer, Virginia white-tailed deer, caribou, elk and such, moose reign supreme. They are the largest of the deer families on the face of the planet, weighing as much as 1400 pounds.

Imagine hunting for a truly trophy bull moose in the heart of Canada's Northwest Territory—with a bow and arrow! Once you harvest a monster bull, it's time to return back to base camp. But envision a rack so big that it won't fit into the outfitter's helicopter that just choppered in to lift you out, post hunt. What to do? Plan B. Here is an example:

Shawn McLean (hunter) and Brad Tylor (cameraman and hunting partner) break camp and hike toward a nearby lake to be picked up by the outfitter's float plane— Shawn carrying a huge set of paddle horns across his back.

Note that I haven't quite turned this handbook into an outfitter's advertising directory. However, when an outfitter comes along with such endorsements as Stan and Helen Stevens of MacKenzie Mountain Outfitters, I'd be remiss not to include them in this text. Visit the team on the Internet at www.mmo-stanstevens.com or write to Box 175, Dawson Creek, British Columbia, V1G 4G3, Canada. This is not a canned, high-fence hunt by any definition or stretch of the imagination as the Stevens' have 9000 square miles of untouched wilderness available to them (150 miles by 60 miles). These bulls and cows range freely. This is a world-class hunt in the heart of the Canada's Northwest Territory, running from Norman Wells to the Yukon border.

Shawn shot the bull clean through at 40 yards with a Mathews bow and Muzzy arrows. Sixty inches (5 feet) at its shoulder is a good size moose. Shawn's was much larger.

Dall sheep, caribou, wolf, and wolverine are also among the game animals that MacKenzie Mountain Outfitters Ltd. offers. Quoted from one of their information pages, "All non-resident hunters are required to hunt with an outfitter licensed by the Government of the Northwest Territories. Mackenzie Mountain Outfitters holds the sole right to take out non-resident hunters within an assigned area. There is no chance of encountering another hunter while hunting in this vast space." The operation boasts a 95–100 percent success rate for their customers.

2016 will be Stan and Helen Stevens' 40th year as outfitters, operating Helio Courier STOL (Short Take Off and Land) aircraft on both wheels and floats in addition to a R44 helicopter. Stan is an experienced bush pilot who has been flying and guiding hunters in Canada's Northwest Territory since 1972.

Average September temperatures for moose hunting in the area range between a daytime high of 60 degrees Fahrenheit to a nighttime low of 15 degrees Fahrenheit. Selecting your hunting clothing to be worn in layers as opposed to packing bulky apparel is the smart way to travel to your initial destination. Keep in mind that once you arrive, you'll be separating items to accommodate transportation via a small bush aircraft. Suggested below is a *general* clothing and gear list to help plan your hunt.

General Clothing & Gear List

- airline tickets
- passport
- backpack; internal or external frame ~ 3500–5000 cubic inches
- sleeping bag rated to 0 degrees Fahrenheit thermal pad
- 1 pair leather (snow sealed) hiking boots
- 1 pair rubber hiking boots
- rain gear
- long underwear (synthetic)
- wool/synthetic socks (several pairs)
- wool/fleece shirt
- wool/fleece pants
- insulated vest
- wool or down jacket
- insulated hat & gloves
- water shoes or Crocs (to wear while boots are drying)
- camera
- extra memory card and batteries
- firearm
- 2 boxes ammunition and/or bow & arrows
- binoculars
- flashlight (extra batteries)
- headlamp (extra batteries)
- personal articles

- compact first aid kit
- ChapStick
- medication if applicable
- extra duffle bag and duct tape for cape and horns
- hunting knife

Optional Gear
- shooting sticks
- spotting scope
- range finder
- lightweight travel rod/reel
- fishing tackle (flies, plugs, et cetera)

CHAPTER 25

EXPLAINING RIFLE CALIBERS, CARTRIDGES & CONFUSION

Before going after truly more dangerous game—a quick word about firearms whether we're looking at rifles, muzzleloaders, or handguns. A good deal of confusion surrounds calibers and cartridges, mainly because the two terms are often mixed in the mind and sometimes thought of collectively, especially among novices. So let's clear away the cobwebs. A firearm's caliber refers to the inside diameter of its barrel; that is, its bore. The interior of the bore throughout its barrel length is rifled, meaning spiraled with lands and grooves in order to give a bullet spin, thereby creating far greater accuracy than a smoothbore weapon. The corresponding diameter of the bullet is its caliber.

Cartridges on the other hand refer to the entire brass casing, comprised of the primer at its base (whether centerfire or rimfire), the powder within the case, and the bullet to be projected. Cartridges are also referred to as rounds. Confusion often arises between the two terms via abbreviations applied to caliber/cartridge.

A person new to the sport may hear that a friend's rifle is a Marlin .30-30 Winchester, shooting nice groups with Remington 170-grain Core-Lokt soft points. Marlin? Winchester? Remington? Core-Lokt soft points? Huh?

Marlin Arms is the name of the firearm manufacturer; .30-30 is the abbreviated combined form of caliber chambered for the Winchester barrel; Remington is the brand of ammunition; 170 grain is the weight of the bullet (not the amount of powder); and a Core-Lokt soft point is the bullet design.

Referencing calibers/cartridges, each company delights in applying their own numbers and names. Example: The well-known .30-30 rifle. The first set of numbers designates that it is a .30 caliber, shared with the second set of numbers signifying the weight [30 grains] of the Winchester cartridge bullet. To further illustrate the point that there is no industry system or standard but rather a code, let's look at the ever-popular .30-06 Springfield rifle cartridge. Instead of referring to the entire name of the .30-06 Springfield, we oft abridge it to .30-06. The first set of numbers [.30] designates that it is a .30 caliber. The second set of numbers [-06] signifies the model year of the cartridge; that is, 1906, when the U.S. Army employed it. Welcome to the confusing world of firearm caliber/cartridge nomenclature.

Only through reading, research, and experience will the beginner grasp caliber/cartridge nomenclature. So don't make yourself crazy if you find contradictions referencing what you thought a set of numbers and names meant. This is learned pretty much on an individual caliber/cartridge basis.

To keep these otherwise confusing descriptions referencing calibers and cartridges separate but clear in your mind, you may have noted (at the expense of repetitiveness—decimal point designating caliber) that I've simply signified calibers with a decimal point preceding it. When I am referring to cartridges, no decimal is shown nor should be, for they are not calibers but the rounds of ammunition. Examples: .308 caliber; 308 Winchester cartridge. European designations are given in millimeters.

Inquiries referencing the best arm's companies, types of guns, calibers, and cartridges for hunting anything from varmint to big game are loaded (pun intended) questions. They become highly subjective matters that boil down to a number of considerations; namely, a quality gun manufacturer, size of quarry sought, distance from which you'll be shooting, and intended use of the animal. That's about as basic as it's going to get. As this handbook is not a *Consumer Report* type of product review publication, per se, you and I can narrow a number of choices by placing them into a general category based on the KISS principle, which is the foundation of this compendium.

Let's begin by looking at a great single-shot handgun for hunting a wide range of not-so-dangerous game, whereas repeated shots from a semiautomatic weapon might be the order of the day if confronting, say for example, an African lion. Yes, some folks, who you will meet shortly, do hunt them with a handgun. However, we'll stick with this continent for the moment and examine a single-shot handgun that would be a fine choice. Few folks can or will argue that Thompson/Center Encore and Encore Pro Hunter pistols, in addition to the Thompson/Center G2 (2nd generation) Contender pistols, are par excellence. These two break-open (action-design) models will handle a multitude of cartridges via their interchangeable frame/barrel systems: ten choices of caliber selection for the Encore; eleven for the G2 Contender. The G2 Contender model has a manual firing pin selector for both rimfire and centerfire cartridges. Adding to unparalleled versatility are preferred barrel lengths, offered in blued or stainless finish, along with choice of grip and forend (rubber composite or walnut wood).

And for the *pièce de résistance*, the quintessential embodiment of all-around adaptability [just like its handguns], Thompson/Center rifles, shotguns, and muzzleloader barrels are interchangeable on their Encore and Encore Pro Hunter frames, incorporating, of course, a rifle-style stock and forend. The same applies to the G2 Contender; its frame will accept rifle, shotgun, and muzzleloader barrels.

In other words, my Encore .50 caliber Thompson/Center muzzleloader will accept *all* Encore rifle, shotgun, and muzzleloader barrels in a number of calibers. Had I a G2 Contender rifle-style stock, frame, and forend, I could interchange any number of rifle, shotgun, and muzzleloader barrels. There is no other all-encompassing firearm system like it on the face of the planet. It will meet, if not exceed, all of your small and big game hunting needs. For a complete listing of these fine firearms, check them out at www.tcarms.com.

Rather than specify what handgun caliber(s) would best be suited to cleanly dispatch a particular animal, as too many variables and, therefore, arguments would quickly come into play, we'll simply start at the lower end of the spectrum with calibers used to handle rimfire ammunition (easier on shooters' pocketbooks), work our way toward the middle-of-the-road with calibers designed to handle centerfire ammo (readily ready for reloading and for shooting a flatter trajectory), then head upward and onward with respect to larger, more powerful calibers/cartridges—loaded for bear, literally.

Once you have a sense of caliber size, common sense should dictate what round (cartridge) is suitable for the size of the animal sought. For example, squirrels, rabbits, woodchucks, et cetera; red and gray fox and raccoon; coyotes and bobcats; deer; elk and moose; big bear.

Both the **.17 HMR** (Hornady Magnum Rimfire) and the **.22 LR** (Long Rifle) **Match** rimfire calibers are great for inexpensive target practice and for dispatching small-sized game and varmint.

The **.204 Ruger**, **.223 Remington**, and the **.22-250 Remington** calibers are fine for mid-sized game and varmint.

Calibers such as the **6.8 Remington**, **7-30 Waters**, **.243 Winchester**, and the **7mm-08 Remington** are more than adequate for larger-sized game and predators.

Moving into big game calibers, the **.30-30 Winchester**, **.357 Remington Magnum**, and the **.308 Winchester** calibers will get the job done nicely.

Calibers such as the **.30-06 Springfield**, and the **.44 Remington Magnum** will handle even bigger-bodied game.

Heavier calibers like the **.45/70 Government**, the **.460 Smith & Wesson**, and the awesome **.500 Smith & Wesson** (the world's most powerful handgun) have their place, especially the latter two being the weapon of choice for knocking down and killing a potentially dangerous bear that does not want you in its neighborhood. I'll make but one proviso here. Better to have a double-action revolver in hand during this scenario rather than a single-shot pistol because it just might take more than one bullet to convince a charging Alaskan brown bear (grizzly) that it has been lethally shot with that first round but just doesn't realize it's dead yet.

Now, based on your shooting ability (accuracy at distances from which you'll be shooting ~ near and/or from afar), how much gun you can handle (recoil-wise), where you are going to hunt (heavily wooded areas, brush, or open fields), size of the quarry you're hunting (squirrel, rabbit, woodchuck, red and gray fox, raccoon, coyote, bobcats, deer, elk, moose, bear or *big* bear), what you plan to do with the animal (harvest it for its pelt or for the pot), et cetera, will determine your handgun caliber.

Fourteen of the fifteen calibers listed are available in one or the other Thompson/Center handgun models: Encore/Encore Pro Hunter, and G2 Contender. The exception is the 500 Smith & Wesson. Saving an interesting combination for last, both the Encore and G2 Contender models offer a .45 Colt/410 bore for double-duty action, shooting either a .45 caliber round or a 410 shotgun shell.

Thompson/Center handguns are chambered for some of the more common, high-performance *rifle* cartridges in the United States, guaranteeing long-range, MOA (**M**inute **O**f **A**ngle) accuracy [covered earlier in Chapter 5] in the hands of a capable shooter. What more could you ask for in a single-shot pistol? Keep in mind that a Thompson/Center single-shot, break-open style handgun, in your preferred caliber, is "dead-on-balls accurate"—an industry term as explained by Marisa Tomei in the movie *My Cousin Vinny*. ☺

More On Rifles

For extremely long shots over 200 yards, if I had the inclination, which I do not, I'd set aside the handgun and pick up my trusty Remington Arms .30-06 Springfield 742 Woodmaster semiautomatic with its Redfield 3x-9x telescopic sight. Good to go. For in-close brush work, I'd grab my Marlin Arms .30-30 Winchester 336CS lever action. Unfortunately, rifle hunting is illegal in the areas where I hunt. However, to get around that matter, I reach for my black powder Thompson/Center Arms .50 caliber Encore 209 x 50 Magnum muzzleloader (employing Pre-formed Pyrodex Charges and ShockWave Sabot projectiles) during the special firearms seasons in Suffolk County, Long Island and Tomkins, County, New York.

For the occasional varmint in the backyard on Long Island, eating virtually every flower, fruit, and vegetable, I reserve a .22 pellet fired from a most accurate RWS air rifle; Model 34 break-barrel Abzugsvorrichtung T06 Diana. Finally, serving as a learning tool for newcomers for many, many years, I lead folks to the range and introduce them to my bargain Marlin Firearms .22 Glenfield, Model 25 bolt action with a Glenfield 4x-15x telescopic sight, bought new at Leslie Edelman's Gun Shop at around the time man first discovered dirt; $29.95, would you believe? It was the first gun with which my son learned to shoot.

It's certainly worth mentioning that Thompson/Center Encore and Contender models offer a vast selection of interchangeable barrels, covering the entire gamut of gunning situations—from vaporizing varmints to hunting small and big game. Instead of buying several or many guns to suit each occasion, you can simply select the necessary barrels needed. Two frames [Encore and Contender], and you are home free. It's a win-win situation. Let's see how all this comes into play.

Firearm Conversion

Instead of owning several different guns, imagine being able to convert a rifle into a muzzleloader, a shotgun, or a handgun—or any other way around—in less time than it takes to brew a pot of coffee. Envision changing barrels for that respective firearm —rifle, muzzleloader, shotgun, handgun—in less time than it takes to pour coffee, stir in milk and sugar, pull up a chair, and take your first sip. Exaggeration? Well, maybe yes if you take your coffee black. All you do is pop one pin from the firearm's frame, remove two screws from the forend, pull off the barrel, and replace it with another. Done. Later, we'll do a conversion. But first let's open up a can of worms.

Let's suppose I want to convert my Thompson/Center Encore .50 caliber Magnum muzzleloader into a Thompson/Center Encore or Encore Pro Hunter .308 caliber Winchester pistol, or any Encore or Encore Pro Hunter handgun model for that matter. I could do so physically, but not legally in the United States. Therefore, it is important that you check your laws and regulations when converting elsewhere.

However, shooters and hunters can legally convert that muzzleloader into a rifle or shotgun configuration. Too, Thompson/Center pistol shooters and hunters can legally (licensed, of course) convert those handguns into long guns by installing a buttstock and a barrel of 16 inches or longer. But here's the rub. Once the firearm is configured as a rifle from a handgun, converting it back to a handgun is considered affecting a handgun from a rifle! That's the law promulgated by the Bureau of Alcohol, Tobacco, Firearms and Explosives (BATFE). It would certainly be apropos to quote through one of Charles Dickens' characters from *Oliver Twist*. "If the law supposes that, the law is a ass—a idiot." Poor grammar notwithstanding, this asinine law enters into gray areas that are convoluted in reasoning, confounding, and contradictory in its explanation.

To stay within the parameters of the law, I simply have my Thompson/Center Encore muzzleloader frame dedicated—as about to be carefully explained—whereby I can legally interchange rifle, carbine, shotgun, and slug gun barrels. Had I the need for a G2 Contender frame for a rifle and associated long guns, I'd have one such firearm dedicated as well.

Regarding my Thompson/Center Encore Pro Hunter handgun, I have its frame registered and dedicated to an Encore .308 caliber barrel. Similarly, I'd have the G2 Contender frame registered and dedicated to say a .357 Magnum barrel. I could then legally interchange a series of pistol barrels for each model without worry of winding up in the Graybar Motel.

But let's belabor this scenario and just suppose that you were outside the United States where such conversions were legal and you wanted to convert your Thompson/Center handgun to a T/C long gun or vice versa; that is, a muzzleloader, rifle, shotgun, slug gun, or carbine. As expressly explained and illustrated in T/C's catalog, you would simply swap out the pistol grip and pistol forend and replace them with the appropriate stock and long-gun forend. Four tools, approximately ten minutes, and you're done. Recall? In the time it takes to brew a pot of coffee. Whether for pistol or long-gun configurations, butt stocks and forends are offered by T/C in either walnut or black composite (rubber).

Let's take a quick look at converting a muzzleloader rifle to pistol. Working over a terry cloth towel, I remove one of the two Phillips head screws that hold the grip cap located at the base of the muzzleloader's pistol grip; loosen the other and simply swivel it out of the way. This will give you access to the stock draw bolt that is removed with an Allen wrench, allowing you to separate the stock from the frame.

With a slotted screwdriver, remove the two panhead screws that hold the muzzleloader's forend to the barrel. Break open the breech, tap out the frame's hinge pin with a wooden dowel, and remove the barrel. [It upsets me when I see someone tap out the hinge pin with a metal rod or brass cartridge case. You can practically push the pin out with a finger, so you don't even need a rubber mallet.] You're done with step one. However, I prudently take the time to reassemble the muzzleloader forend to its barrel, set the stock draw bolt back within the grip cap and screw it in place so that I don't misplace or lose any parts.

Next, select an interchangeable Encore or Encore Pro Hunter pistol barrel (ten in all to choose from) and align it with the muzzleloader frame. Replace the hinge pin, close the breech, attach an Encore pistol forend and ambidextrous pistol grip (wood or synthetic), pistol draw bolt and grip cap (three screws). You have just converted a muzzleloader into a handgun in no time flat. This conversion assembly is basically the same for the older model Thompson/Center Contender as well as the newer G2 Contender model. But again, the issue of legality rears its ugly head. By following what I have outlined in paragraph four of this section, you'll keep yourself out of the slammer, for you'll only be interchanging barrels, not switching back and forth between or among frames.

After perusing the Bureau's legal language through its Gun Control Act (GCA) referencing rifle/pistol ~ pistol/rifle firearms conversion nomenclature, I suggest that the agency abandon the confusing term "short stock" as applied to handguns, adopting in its stead a clearer term: pistol-grip butt in lieu of "short stock." This would clarify matters. In other words, "Get a *grip*, guys!" Pun and fun aside, on a more serious note, what you do *not* want to do is assemble a pistol barrel that is less than 16 inches to a rifle-style stock, thereby creating a short-barreled firearm that is absolutely in violation of the Federal Firearms Law.

Thompson/Center Rifle, Muzzleloader & Shotgun Overview

Thompson/Center rifles are also offered in several types of actions. The Venture bolt action rifle (3-shot magazine +1 chambered round) gives you the option of selecting among sixteen calibers, running the gamut from a .204 Ruger to a .338 Winchester Magnum. However, the barrels are not interchangeable. Each rifle features 5R Rifling, which allows for greater bullet stability; that translates to MOA accuracy: 1 inch 3-shot groups at 100 yards using premium ammunition. Its cousin, the Venture Predator, comes in either Realtree camo or Snow camo patterns, offering four and six different calibers, respectively. Consult their online catalog for specific information.

The Thompson/Center Dimension bolt action rifle offers interchangeable barrels in ten calibers ranging from a .204 Ruger to a .300 Winchester Magnum. It is important to note that although the barrels are interchangeable, four (4) *different* bolts fit within a "family" division of four, grouped and stamped "A", "B", "C", and "D". In other words, you need one of four bolts to fit a particular barrel series, correspondingly stamped "A", "B", "C", and "D". So, too, are the magazine and magazine housing components. See their catalog for caliber classification. But to give you a quick reference, the "B" family would cover the .22-250, .243 Winchester, 7mm-08 Remington, and the .308 Winchester calibers, for which you would only require the one "B" bolt and corresponding "B" magazine components. The firearm's stock and receiver are universal and available in either right- or left-handed models. Accessory camo stocks in either Realtree or Mossy Oak Break-Up patterns are also available. The Dimension component series certainly makes sense if you want a range of rifle calibers to cover anything from small to big game hunting.

There are several Thompson/Center .50 caliber muzzleloaders from which to choose: the Encore Pro Hunter XT, the Pro Hunter FX, the Triumph Bone Collector, and the Impact. The company offers either fixed or interchangeable .50 caliber muzzleloader barrels. The Encore Pro Hunter XT .50 Caliber Magnum Muzzleloader will accept any Encore or Encore Pro Hunter single-shot barrel, such as the Encore Pro Hunter Turkey shotgun, chambered for 12 or 20 gauge 3-inch shells, Extra Full Turkey Choke, complete stock, forend, and barrel camo design. For the Encore Predator single-shot rifle, full-camo design is available in .204 Ruger, .223 Remington, .22-250 Remington, and .308 Winchester calibers. The Encore Pro Hunter Katahdin big-bore compact carbine boasts a trio of serious calibers: .45-70 Govt., .460 S&W Mag., and the .500 S&W Mag. The options are endless.

Thompson/Center firearms are guns for all reasons and seasons. With an Encore or Encore Pro Hunter system, one can easily convert a muzzleloader to a rifle, to a shotgun, to a slug gun, to a carbine and back again. Dedicate an Encore or Encore Pro Hunter pistol to a single frame, grip, and forend, and enjoy the benefits of interchanging many barrels to suit the situation. Dedicate a G2 Contender pistol to a single frame, grip, and forend, and enjoy the benefits of interchanging several barrels to suit the situation.

Among the many features Thompson/Center offers throughout their wide range of firearms (too many to list and delve into at length in this handbook), I'll home in on several specific and important elements that are either built in or advanced as options: Hogue Overmolded traction panels for a sure grip; Weather Shield protection, virtually impervious to rust; FLEX Tech recoil pads; adjustable recoil-taming stock spacers; several camo patterns from which to choose; M.O.A. guaranteed accuracy; wood or synthetic stocks, pistol butts, and forends; blued, stainless steel, or stainless steel fluted barrels; adjustable steel peep sights and fiber optic front sights; centerfire/rimfire selector; ease of cocking Swing Hammer for scope clearance; and, of course, Thompson/Center's unparalleled interchangeable/conversion barrel system. Mentioned here are just a few of their many features. Next, I could go on with the Thompson/Center accessory list, consisting of a plethora of items. I'm reminded of a sign in the window of an upstate hardware store. "If we don't have it, you don't need it." That's just about sums up T/C's list of particulars. Request a catalog or download their PDF catalog at www.tcarms.com.

CHAPTER 26

BLACK & BROWN BEAR (GRIZZLY)

An adult black bear weighs between 200 and 600 pounds; it is the smallest of three North American species: black, polar, and brown (grizzly). An adult female black bear weighs considerably less than her male counterpart, usually by about a third. Although *generally* considered nonaggressive toward humans—if not provoked—words like generally, rarely, and infrequently are adverbs that you should weigh in on very *carefully*. When hunting bear, and the bear is alerted to your presence, it may not behave passively; therefore, think of that animal as becoming defensive or predatory. I have seen instances of the hunter becoming the prey as the predator bear stalked him. You are on their turf. A bear is an unpredictable animal and is to be considered dangerous.

An adult Alaskan brown bear (coastal grizzly/Kodiac Island) weighs between 800 and 1200 pounds but can top the Toledo at around 1700 pounds. It is the world's largest terrestrial carnivore and can become an *extremely* dangerous adversary as the hunter can quickly become the hunted. A predatory brown will stalk and want to eat you.

Three caliber considerations for an interior Alaskan brown (generally smaller than their coastal Kodiac cousin) would be a .30-06, .338, or a .375. One would want to go up in caliber for a truly trophy bruin. A continuum of confusion exists among labeling these brutes: brown bear, grizzly, Kodiac. Rather than get into esoteric taxonomy (species and subspecies), think of Alaska's brown bears as the general classification; grizzly (interior bear) versus Kodiac (coastal bear) in terms of size. Captain Quint in the movie *Jaws* needed a bigger boat. You're going to be better off with a bigger caliber such as a .375 for the big boys. Once you peruse the tales of the professionals covered in the bonus section of this handy handbook, having traveled off the North American continent to hunt Africa's and Australia's most dangerous big game animals (elephant, rhinoceros, hippopotamus, Cape buffalo, lion, leopard ~ banteng and water buffalo), choosing calibers, cartridges, bullet designs, firearms, and actions is going to become far more clearer to you. In the meantime, sections covering deer, elk, and moose, leading up to pursuing small, medium- to prodigious-sized bear, hopefully have begun to illuminate what is only seemingly arcane. Size of the animal coupled to thickness of its hide is your starting point.

In hunting smaller black bear in the interior of Alaska, Canada, and the Eastern United States, a .30-06 would certainly be *adequate* as that gun has absolutely taken down bigger bear for nearly a century. But adequate doesn't quite cut it for me, and I'd be back to looking at a larger caliber. That's because even smaller black bear vary greatly in size throughout North America. Smaller black bears are considered 150 to 200-plus pounds. Larger coastal black bears can range between 300 and 600-plus pounds. And somewhere in the middle the twain could meet. A 201- to 299-pound black bear is a good mid-sized bruin.

Besides considering caliber and cartridge, et cetera, location should certainly factor into your planning. Know where you'll be hunting: Eastern United States, the Pacific Northwest (too general), British Columbia (more specific), coastal or interior Canada, coastal or interior Alaska. We're now considering terrain: mountains, plains, woodland. Coupled to cartridge choice is bullet design, to be determined by CXP classification: **C**ontrolled e**X**pansion **P**erformance. When hunting bear, select a cartridge/bullet classified for CXP2 or CXP3 game: CXP2 for smaller bear; CPX3 for larger bruin.

The .30-06 is a most versatile caliber. No question. With proper shot placement, it can take down anything in North America. A 180-grain bullet will get the job done quite nicely. That's certainly fine for the small- and medium-sized black and brown bears, but who knows what you may come across on the hunt. I read about a fellow who went deer hunting and inadvertently came across and killed a 600-plus pound *black* bear (not a brown). Therefore, I would want more of an insurance policy caliber-wise.

For your larger size black and brown bears, a .308, .338, and .375 caliber, are good choices—but with one proviso. You must be able to handle the gun comfortably. Can you manage more gun becomes the question. A larger caliber comes with more recoil. Flinching, jerking the trigger, or—God forbid—closing your eyes could likely lead to disaster. If you're afraid of the weapon's recoil, that firearm is not for you. Far better that you have the confidence to shoot a smaller caliber gun with exacting accuracy than to falter in the field. Your target is the animal's heart and/or lungs. Your objective is to do that with a single bullet at approximately 35 to 50 yards, with a follow-up shot if necessary. Long distance shots may result in a wounded bear that you really don't want to be tracking.

CHAPTER 27

HANDGUNS

Target Shooting

A .22 caliber rimfire handgun is the most sensible and inexpensive way to learn how to shoot paper targets—period. Next, one needs to decide what kind of handgun to purchase: single-action revolver, double-action revolver, single-shot pistol, or semiautomatic pistol.

The year was 2003. For openers, I chose a revolver for Donna over the other types of handguns for a few sound reasons. The number one reason being safety. Safety is paramount. A revolver is a far safer handgun to handle than a semiautomatic pistol, especially for a beginner. I chose a double-action revolver for Donna over that of a single-action revolver or a single-shot pistol for its versatility. A single-action revolver or pistol can only be fired by *manually* cocking the hammer (rearward) then squeezing the trigger, whereas a double-action revolver can repeatedly cycle rounds by each pull of the trigger—but with greater pressure and travel distance than through a single-action firing mode. I wanted Donna proficient in both methods of operation.

Small caliber handguns such as Donna's .22 Smith & Wesson Model 617 stainless steel revolver was a nice way of introducing a newcomer to target shooting. It wasn't long before she graduated to a Sig Sauer P232 SL 9mm semiautomatic for concealed carry and home protection. I created a friendly monster. It's certainly nice to have a partner (especially one of female persuasion) to share similar interests.

Laser Sights as Learning Tools

Purchasing a pair of laser sights for the added edge proved a most rewarding experience, positively augmenting Donna's handgun proficiency at the shooting range by a considerable margin. A pair of Crimson Trace Lasergrips was eventually ordered to fit her S&W Model 617 .22 LR (Long Rifle cartridge) revolver. Talk about tack-driving accuracy and upping one's score. Actually, I was a bit envious. Jealous would be more to the point. When Crimson Trace Lasergrips became available to fit *my* handgun, I ordered the coveted item expeditiously. But I'll start at the beginning of the story.

As my soul mate, Donna and I have been doing what we truly enjoy; that is, spending a great deal of time together in the great outdoors. On the gunning front, we shoot skeet, trap, and sporting clays; rifles, and bow and arrow; following up with handguns. Referencing that latter arena, I had some military training . . . many a year ago. Pistol shooting was a sport that the two of us had talked about getting into for quite some time.

Donna's first handgun was the Smith & Wesson Model 617 .22 caliber, 10-shot stainless steel double-action revolver with a six-inch barrel. It proved to be a good choice for a beginner, especially in terms of safety, as there is less chance of mishaps. The six-inch barrel, of course, gave her an advantage with regard to accuracy over shorter barrel lengths. She was not initially concerned with carry and concealment so much as she was with learning the basics of shooting, and rightfully so. In addition, with the smaller caliber, she could shoot all day without breaking the bank. Her choice of stainless steel over that of a blued finish was not so much a matter of aesthetics as it was its practicality in terms of protection from the elements, for we live in a marine environment.

"Cool, real cool," she said, nodding her head in appreciation when first examining the model on display at our local gun shop in Riverhead, New York.

The proprietors—Diane and Ron McGee of Edward's Sporting Goods—and I discussed other makes and models as well, but Donna was sold on that S&W from the get-go.

"So cool and shiny and less corrosive than carbon steel," she elaborated excitedly. "Easier to maintain."

"Sensible girl." I turned to Ron and Diane. "Sold American," I concluded. "Done deal. Please order the piece."

Donna's visit to the Peconic River Sportsman's Club pistol range in Manorville, Long Island proved a bit frustrating. I had given her a preliminary lesson on sight alignment the day her handgun arrived. Again, I offered remedial instruction before we left the house. Nevertheless, Donna felt she knew all about sight alignment, having first shot iron sights with a rifle some forty-plus years ago, and up through the years. A damn good shot she was and still is, too—with a rifle, that is.

"But this is a horse of a different color," I had tried to explain quite patiently. "This is not like shooting a rifle. I mean, well, it is and it isn't. What I mean is you still have to line up the front sight between the rear notch evenly, holding that sight picture perfectly level and pointed at—"

"Pointed at the **x** or six o'clock on the bull's-eye. I know. I know. Been there, done that. About a million times before."

"Still and all, you have to *hold* that sight picture, eye along the sight plane, aligned to the target and—"

"I'll be fine, dear."

Well, she was *not* fine. She wasn't even on paper after five shots at twenty-five yards. Frustration personified clearly defined her features.

"You put blanks in the gun!" she whined. "I just know you did. You're trying to drive me crazy."

"I told you it's not that easy, initially. I told you to practice sight alignment at home."

"Here, you take this and let me see *you* hit the target."

"I cannot shoot your gun. Technically, it's the law," I teased. "You know that."

"Just as I thought. Blanks," she complained.

From the same box of ammunition, I filled the clip of my new Smith & Wesson Model 41 .22 caliber semiautomatic, loaded the gun, and proceeded to place five shots at *my* twenty-five yard target. One was off the paper but still in the target board. Two were on paper but outside the last ring. One passed through the eight-ring. Another found its way most magically to a black nine. My grouping was about as tight as the mouth of a traffic tunnel.

"I think we both need lots and lots of practice," I admitted. "What do you think?"

Donna took her time and fired another five rounds, remembering everything I taught her about stance, breathing, sight picture, and trigger squeeze. She concentrated very, very hard. I patiently explained 'shooting through the wobble' at that point. This time she had three holes in the target board, two more on paper beyond the outer ring, another in the nine ring at nine o'clock.

"There may be hope for you yet," I said encouragingly.

"Well, you're a lot more optimistic than I am."

"Show you something?"

"Sure."

"Reload first, then sight in."

After Donna reloaded the revolver and it was pointing safely down range, I cocked the hammer on her piece, explaining single and double action, instructing that I wanted her to *squeeze* the trigger slowly without even thinking about when the hammer would fall. Without flinching, she placed that bullet and the next four (after cocking the hammer back herself each time) on paper. Three were outside the outer ring, two within; spread out over four inches.

"You don't tell me about this single/double action business until I make a complete fool of myself first time out?"

"If you want to master rapid fire someday, you're going to have to learn trigger control," I stated.

Only then did it fully dawn on Donna, that, unlike my semiautomatic, in order for her to cycle the action repeatedly, she had to pull the trigger *manually* and with greater pressure and travel distance than through its single-action firing mode.

"I want a semiautomatic like yours!" she suddenly demanded.

"And you'll have one, one day—after you first learn the basics and shoot double and single action with your revolver. There's a tool on the market that I'm considering to help us along."

"What?"

"Laser sights."

"Like I see in the movies?"

"Like you see in the movies," I confirmed.

"Do they make them for this gun in particular?"

"That's what we're going to find out."

Before we left the range that morning, I was placing most of my rounds in the black. My grouping, however, was far from satisfactory. Donna was on paper but barely, with most of her shots scattered around the outer ring. *Around* being the operative word.

Discounting the Buck Rogers era, laser technology has been around for about fifteen years at the time. There are the good, the bad, and the ugly from which to select. Actually, there is one laser sight that is great. After researching different types with respect to handguns, I homed in on Crimson Trace Lasergrips for Donna's new revolver. Out of the box from the factory, the Lasergrip is preset for approximately 50 feet; that is, just shy of 17 yards. As we shot from benches at 25 yards at a local range, I respectively made minor adjustments for elevation and windage for that particular distance and breezy day. It was late afternoon. I had Donna align her sights to the bull's-eye, having placed my forefinger to block the laser's light beforehand, releasing it the second she zeroed in on the **x**. There was nothing wrong with her sight pattern, for it was picture perfect. However, when she squeezed the trigger with the hammer cocked, you could see the red dot jump as she pulled the shot. In fact, she could see it, too. That is when we both first truly appreciated laser technology as a tool. Seeing is believing.

"Did you see that?" I asked.

"I saw it."

"You pulled the shot high and a little to the right."

"I know."

"Well, don't do that."

"All right, I won't."

Donna put the red laser dot back on the bull's-eye once again. I stood behind the spotting scope, watching her place the next four shots in the black, cocking the hammer back each time in single-action fire.

"That's better," I said reassuringly.

She stepped over to the spotting scope and examined her handiwork. "What do you mean, better? That's terrific!"

"It'll be terrific when I see a group the size of a silver dollar."

"How about I just shoot you now and place quarters on both your eyes."

"You better not talk like that."

"Why?"

"It could be misconstrued as a threat."

"Oh, I promise I won't miss at all," she quipped.

"Big shot now, I see. Let's see how you do with double-action firing. Do not cock the hammer back," I insisted. "Practice your trigger control."

"Fine."

Donna concentrated on pulling smoothly through the next five shots, watching the red dot flash further upward and over to the right. Yet all five rounds passed through paper: three of them within the seven, eight and nine ring.

Trigger control was clearly Donna's initial problem as it is for most folks starting out. With practice, by the end of the afternoon, she had improved dramatically. The following week we returned to the range. Donna was placing seven out of ten shots in the black utilizing single-action fire; five out of ten were in the black, employing double action. The last five rounds were well within the eight and nine rings. More importantly, her groups were getting tighter. As the afternoon waned, that red dot became brighter and brighter. We realized the advantages of lasers as a low-light or no-light tool for law enforcement personnel, especially after considering when most crimes are committed, that being after-hours or very early in the morning when most law-abiding folks are home asleep in bed.

Laser Sights for Home Protection

For home protection against an intruder, a handgun fitted with a laser sight would more than likely prove a serious deterrent. A radiant red dot holding to the center of a burglar's chest in the dark could possibly de-escalate what might otherwise be a highly volatile situation. However, keeping a loaded handgun in or on a nightstand without the benefit of laser technology is not wise. An FBI friend of mine as well as other law enforcement personnel will state that you are better off having a shotgun handy in such a situation. With the adrenaline going, having to handle a handgun in total darkness, or having to turn on a room light or even activate a switch on a laser could prove futile and even fatal. But having a handgun where all you have to do is grip the weapon's handle to direct and deliver a deadly dot and then a bullet if necessary—a missile that will unquestionably find its mark without traditional sight alignment because that part of the equation is altogether eliminated—well, quite frankly, that's a tool you would want to have at the ready. All you have to do is point (not aim) that red dot of light no differently than if you were presenting with a laser pointer during a talk or lecture.

Actually, the above is a perfect example to illustrate the versatility of lasers. For when standing before an audience, it would not be an unusual move to direct the dot —without turning completely around to face the screen—obliquely to the *target* of attention, be it a bar graph or other statistical table. If it were a handgun equipped with a laser you were holding askew, followed by a bullet, the projectile would hit precisely where you pointed, provided you exercised proper trigger control. That is the beauty of lasers.

In my opinion, after doing the initial necessary homework and extensive research, Crimson Trace Lasergrips exceed in all areas such as fit, finish, and function. The company has wisely aligned itself with the National Rifle Association, offering its instructors training in this technology. Believe me when I tell you the two teams are right on target. A match made in heaven. Crimson Trace also offers instructional tapes: *Shots in the Dark: A Complete Guide to the Tactical Use of Laser Sights* (Paladin Press), as well as *Laser Training and Defense Techniques* (Crimson

Trace Corporation), both with Clyde Caceres, veteran law enforcement trainer. When employing the use of cover, applying laser technology greatly reduces the risk of exposure for the simple reason that less of your body is visible, the head and arm in particular, giving you the deadly added edge.

In just three visits to our local pistol range, Donna had improved her marksmanship unbelievably. Why do I even bother to continue to train her in the use of traditional sight-picture patterning, stance, et cetera, when all she has to do is point and shoot? The answer is because one must always learn and hold in mind the basics.

The arguments against laser sights are truly inane when put in their proper context. There are those who feel that laser sights will create an unhealthy dependence. Keeping in mind that laser technology is a tool to augment the capability of professionals and novices alike, who would not want the added edge, particularly when the advantages are significant? In an imperfect world, equipment is subject to failure, your handgun and laser sight included. If the latter tool failed, you would, of course, rely on your traditional sight-picture patterning. Training traditionally, while employing new methodology as viewed in those videos just mentioned, absolutely increases your chances for success. Training conventionally in tactical situations while applying laser technology could help you survive a gunfight. In both cases, they certainly up your options. If you feel that a laser is an encumbrance in a given circumstance, switch it off or do not put it on to begin with. Virtually all of Crimson Trace Lasergrips have that override feature. There are other manufacturers of laser-type grips, guards, and sights that do not offer this important function. Consider, too, that Crimson Trace Lasergrips have been proven reliable—from the deserts of Iraq to our inner cities.

Another concern when considering laser aids is the cost factor. If weighed strictly in terms of having fun at the range and becoming a better shooter, fine; that is certainly your choice. If weighed in terms of providing home protection for you and your family, I would have to point to that 'penny wise pound foolish' adage. If voted down by a law enforcement's budgetary board as a monetary measure, that in itself would be criminal. In many a documented case, the mere placement of that highly visible dot on a perpetrator's body was enough to quell the situation. If push does come to shove in a shootout, it has been statistically verified that officers' hit ratios went up astronomically in putting down the bad guys when using laser technology, whereas before the figures were nothing short of abysmal.

To quote Sergeant Dave Douglas, a then twenty-nine year veteran of the San Diego Police Department, "Such an expense can easily be justified. Run this cost analysis: one laser sighting system versus one officer-involved shooting. On one hand, you have between $200 and $600 for the [laser] sight. On the other: administrative leave, Internal Affairs investigation, possibly a homicide investigation, crime scene processing, detective call out, critical incident debriefing, weapons lab work from the crime lab, use-of-force review, Officer's Association attorney, psychiatric counseling, officer leave, citizen's review board, and civil litigation lasting years."

Donna and I are merely Jane and Joe civilians, but if we had our druthers, we would make it mandatory for *all* law enforcement agencies throughout the country to purchase and have their personnel utilize laser technology on their primary and/or secondary weapon(s), for there is no question that laser sights can serve as both a lethal and life-saving tool.

Before I received *my* Crimson Trace Lasergrips for *my* particular handgun, Donna clearly had the added edge when employing her .22 Smith & Wesson Model 617 revolver, equipped with Crimson Trace Lasergrips. It is a bit frustrating when the student upstages the teacher because only *she* had the added edge.

Handgun Slings for Hunting

A fantastic aid for hunting with a handgun is a handgun sling, which allows for a solid, steady aim point. It's the next best thing to a benchrest. Preset at the proper length, the extended strap will secure and hold your position so that the desired eye-relief is always maintained, especially when employing optics.

The best single-point handgun sling I found to date is one manufactured by T.C. Handgun Sling Straps (nothing to do with Thompson/Center). R. Wilson offers it through his www.youtube.com site titled *T.C. Handgun Sling Strap*. The sling is actually a standard, wide-web style, nylon camera strap with a sliding clip. A separate attachable/detachable accessory strap (nylon and Velcro with a D-ring) wraps snugly around the butt of the handgun and clips to the sling.

Carefully Choosing Handgun Calibers & Cartridges for Hunting

For deer hunting, I chose the Thompson/Center Encore Pro Hunter .308 caliber pistol for a few reasons. Number one, it is a great all-around caliber for cleanly and humanely dispatching whitetails, elk, and moose from distances near and far. It is by no means considered a *marginal* weapon for whitetails as is deemed the .357 Magnum by a good many hunters. Accuracy at 200 yards is amazing. Actually, in the hands of an expert shooter, 300 yards would be a walk in the park. The .308 caliber handgun was my choice, which will effectively and efficiently drop deer at those greater distances. That is all the gun I need for my purposes at present.

I have an accomplished buddy in the business who wouldn't hesitate to take an elk with a .308 caliber—but with the right cartridge such as a 180-grain Hornady SST® (**S**uper **S**hock **T**ip). For deer hunting with my .308 pistol, I'm using Hornady 150-grain SST loads for superior accuracy. But before I'd move into a more powerful Hornady Superformance® 165-grain cartridge or the 180-grain Hornady SST®, I'd practice, practice, practice—always weighing accuracy from one load to the other for optimum performance.

In addition to Hornady SST® and Superformance® ammunition, you will note other cartridge/bullet designations such as GMX, BTSP BTHP, InterBond®, and InterLock®. What does all that mean, and should you concern yourself with such minutiae? Yes, if you are seeking knowledge in order to gain the best performance from your firearm whether it is a long gun or a handgun. With that said, let's take a quick look at what these specs signify in order to gain a keener understanding:

GMX (Gilding Metal Expanding), BTSP (Boat Tail Soft Point), BTHP (Boat Tail Hollow Point), InterBond® (a proprietary bonding process that holds the core and jacket together), InterLock®, an exclusive Hornady design consisting of a raised ring within the cartridge jacket that is embedded in the bullet's core and keeps both the core and jacket locked together during expansion in order to retain mass and energy for deep penetration.

A term you may see or hear is cannelure, [a channel or grove surrounding the cylinder of a cartridge]. It refers to a crimping process that gives additional 'hold' between the cartridge case and the bullet and may be used to express removing the belly along an otherwise straight-walled casing so as to allow the round to chamber freely. Different crimping pressures greatly affect accuracy.

Knowledge is power, and when it comes to firearms, speed and power are of paramount importance. You don't have to be a rocket scientist to understand the basics of ballistics because the projectiles we'll cover here are—in and of themselves—rockets that have already been put through the science for you. All *you* have to do is select which rocket you wish to launch based on a modicum of education.

For example, in looking for a suitable cartridge (round) for whitetails for my T/C .308 caliber handgun, I simply went online to Hornady and searched .308, then scrolled down the "results page" for any relevant information. I call this the hunt before the hunt. Eventually, I found that the .308 Winchester, 150-grain Interlock® SP American Whitetail® is specifically designed for whitetails; $29.40 per box of 20. I learned that if I desired a more powerful round for bigger game, the .308 165-grain SST® Superformance® would be the ticket. The information was set forth with a brief description of the cartridge, precise pictorial specifications, and a six-minute video. Holding to the KISS principle (Keep It Simple System), this is the way I learn; and it's fun. Of course, one could go ballistic learning ballistics and make things very complicated, which I said we would not do, and we won't.

On the other end of the spectrum, let's take a look at a couple of handgun calibers suited for small game mammals, predators, and vermin—granted that the trio may sometimes overlap and can be argued as to what category each belongs as well as which cartridge is best suited. For the sake of argument, allow me to clarify by way of a definition as it applies to hunting in general: Small *game* mammals are those that are pursued not only for sport but for food. Predators are those animals that prey upon other animals and/or threaten peoples' livelihood, such as folks raising livestock, involved in animal husbandry, farming crops, et cetera. A coyote will kill ranchers' cattle, sheep, et cetera. A fox will kill farmers' chickens and other domesticated animals. Although you can eat virtually anything, we do not as a matter of course eat coyote or fox. The latter reminds me of an Oscar Wilde quote referencing the English and their love of the fox hunt: "Ah, yes," quips Wilde, "the unspeakable in full pursuit of the inedible." ☺

Vermin [noun plural], variant of varmint [chiefly Southern U.S.], are largely lumped into a category of obnoxious and/or simply objectionable animals—animals that many of us would wish to vaporize in a heartbeat. To reiterate, there is an arguable degree of overlap between predator and vermin. Example: a raccoon and crow could be placed in either category. Some would argue that they are simply pests. So be it.

Based on size and weight of the animals that we're likely to encounter in our neck of the woods, let's consider several handgun calibers and cartridges that would positively deal with all three categories: small game mammals, predators, and vermin/pests.

I've broken the above into two groups weighing in at approximately ½ pound to 9 pounds: [weasel (½ pound); squirrel (1½ pounds); rabbits (3 pounds); skunk (7 pounds); opossum (8 pounds); red and gray fox (9 pounds)]. Rimfire cartridges in .17 HRM (Hornady Magnum Rimfire) and .22 Long Rifle Match calibers are fine choices.

For the next group ranging from 10 to 30 pounds—woodchuck (10 pounds); raccoon (15 pounds); and coyote (30 pounds)—a good choice would be calibers like the .204 Ruger and .223 Remington.

Larger calibers such as the .22-250 Remington and the .243 Winchester are also to be considered. However, keep in mind that those higher calibers are just that (meaning sporting bigger bores) and need not be employed unless requiring greater shooting distances for these larger bodied animals.

Carefully weighing in on this information, one might consider a good compromise between these two extremes, leaning to the lighter, left of center caliber; that is, the .223 Remington. Hold in mind, too, that you could kill a deer with a .22 caliber head shot, penetrating the brain. But there is a good reason why it is illegal to hunt deer in many states with such a light load. As bullet placement is the name of the game concerning clean kills, I would veer away from any type of rimfire cartridge, employing centerfire rounds for their accuracy.

Note: As explained in an earlier chapter, light rimfire loads such as the .17 HMR (Hornady Magnum Rimfire) and the .22 LR (Long Rifle) Match rimfire calibers are great for inexpensive target practice and for dispatching small-sized game and varmint (½ pound to 9 pounds). In the right hands, a .22 long-rifle bullet can easily kill a small animal out to 85 yards. In the following chapter, we'll examine a precision .22 caliber air rifle in dealing with vermin.

We pretty much covered the field for small-sized animals, right up to big game like deer and wild boar, drawing a line in the sand at that point. There are, of course, larger calibers in the T/C pistol lineup such as the 6.8 Remington, 7-30 Waters, 7mm-08 Remington, .30-06 Springfield, .44 Remington Magnum, .45/70 Government, .45 Colt/410 bore, and the .460 Smith & Wesson. Note again that this is not rocket science, but it can get rather confusing because of the names attached to these calibers along with measurements—presented in either fractions of an inch or millimeters—applied by whimsical manufacturers. For instance, if I could successfully hand load, tweak, and design a particular bottleneck-type cartridge to leave the muzzle of a certain caliber at 200 feet per second faster than the competition then got an ammunition manufacturer to back me, say Federal Arms Company, Inc. I could and probably would insist that the company include my name—the .308 Banfelder Federal Buster—on each and every box. If they declined and made a *federal* case out of it, I'd give Hornady a shot.☺

In selecting two additional G2 Contender barrels for smaller-sized game, predators, and varmint, I'd choose the .17 HMR 14-inch stainless steel barrel, and the .223 Remington 14-inch stainless steel barrel. With select ammunition, these two lighter additions have proven themselves quite lethal and at varied distances. In selecting one additional Encore Pro Hunter barrel for larger-sized game, predators, and varmint, I chose the .243 Winchester 15-inch fluted stainless steel barrel. Again, with premium ammunition, the .243 is the ticket for dispatching animals exceeding well over 30 pounds; for example, 100 pound-plus wolves to pronghorn—and out to appreciable ranges because of flat trajectory and high impact energy.

If I were being deployed to the Middle East, I'd choose a .243 Winchester caliber in a Kimber tactical rifle for sniper duty. Some would want a .308. Others would insist on a .30-06. Getting the picture? But we'll stay with four-legged animals, drawing the line at the average 170-pound white-tailed deer (200 pounds for a big male).

If and when I reach big game status with a handgun, hunting quarry beyond elk, moose, and *big* bear, I would absolutely opt for a larger caliber and heavier cartridge than my .308 Thompson/Center Encore Pro Hunter handgun. You'll understand better when we enter the bonus feature section of this handbook; that is, hunting the most dangerous big game land animals with rifle and handgun. A bullet's grain weight and design referencing a particular species will best be determined by an ammunition manufacturer's recommendation, followed by practice, practice, practice at the shooting range.

CHAPTER 28

HUNTING VERMIN WITH AN AIR RIFLE

I have owned a few air rifles over the course of many years for the purpose of pest *control*, which has recently turned into the more serious pursuit of vermin *elimination*. A family of raccoons headed the top of the list. Those pesky critters bordered our property, several actually residing under the back deck, creating nightly havoc ranging from ravaging a prized vegetable garden to somehow getting into supposedly critter-proof cans of garbage. The solution was really simple, but it took a while for things to sink into this brain.

Mentioned earlier, I had researched and purchased an outrageously accurate air rifle; namely, the German made RWS Diana 34 T06 .22 caliber Classic. It was a wise choice. With open sights, shooting RWS Superpoint Extra Field-Line lead projectiles, I had sent three 14.5-grain pointed pellets through a paper target in a cloverleaf pattern at 25 yards, then later at 35 yards with the aid of a Bulls Bag Shooting Rest. Although my group was as tight as a swollen tick, I needed to drop down and over to the right several inches in order to put lead through the black bull's-eye. Fingertip adjustments of the elevation knob put the next shot parallel to the edge of the black center. Another fingertip adjustment of the windage knob moved me into the black, but not its very center. A final adjustment put me dead center into the bull's-eye. Happy–happy. Now, could I widen the same hole with two more pellets? I did. As a matter of fact, at first appearance, it seemed as though only two pellets found their mark. However, on careful examination, I could see that all three pellet holes embraced one another, creating a second cloverleaf pattern. Donna was on deck. She is a remarkable target shooter in her own right. At 25 yards, her three-shot group expanded no further than the breadth and height of her pinky nail—all in the black— just slightly left of dead center.

Here is an important tip before choosing an air gun rifle whether for target practice or for varmint hunting. Don't be fooled into making your purchasing decision based solely on muzzle velocity; that is, speed measured in feet per second. Weigh into the equation kinetic energy; that is, force of impact measured in foot-pounds of energy. For example, a .177 caliber RWS Superdome 8.3-grain lead pellet leaves the muzzle of an RWS Diana 34 T06 Classic air rifle at 1000 feet per second while a .22 caliber RWS Superpoint Extra Field-Line lead pellet is traveling at 800 feet per second. However, the heavier .22 caliber pellet is far more accurate. It is also delivering over 20 foot-pounds of energy whereas the .177 pellet is dispensing 18 foot-pounds of energy. This is a negligible difference when considering that it only requires12 foot-pounds of ballistic energy to eliminate a large raccoon.

What this really boils down to is speed versus accuracy. Putting accuracy ahead of speed is a no-brainer so long as the recommended foot-pounds of energy needed to humanely and permanently put down varmints/pests that you're pursuing falls within those parameters. Obviously, you are not going to sacrifice accuracy for speed in this case.

The accuracy of the RWS Diana 34 T06 Classic .22 caliber precision air rifle is mind-blowing. It is how I stepped from the realm of pest *control* into the sphere of varmint *elimination*. Before stepping up in class from shooting mediocre air rifles to entering the world of precision, I had but very little idea of how a high-quality, high-powered break-barrel air gun would perform. Before my purchasing a high-quality air rifle, it was literally a hit-and-miss situation. I'd zero in on a squirrel and receive a score of zero for my efforts. Or I'd hit one solidly, watch it fall from a tree limb to the ground, shake itself off and scurry. No, it wasn't my shooting ability when it came to older model air rifles. It was inferior to mediocre quality—period.

The RWS Diana 34 T06 Classic .22 caliber precision air rifle, known for its legendary craftsmanship, boasts outstanding open sights composed of a shielded full-circular fiber-optic front sight (red) and a rear sight comprising a pair of parallel fiber-optic rods (green) for immediate sight-picture acquisition as well as perfectly positioned windage and elevation knobs, allowing for quick adjustment(s).

The all-new T06 two-stage adjustable trigger design is heralded as one of the best in the industry. Air rifle trigger mechanisms are generally the bane of many air gunners. Not so with the RWS Diana 34 T06. Smooth as silk on the squeeze.

Living in Suffolk County, Long Island, I can neither hunt with a cartridge rifle nor at our son's home in Tompkins County, Upstate New York. That's the law. Hence, a precision pellet air rifle eventually became the answer. Pellet air rifles have, indeed, come a long way since the time I was a kid and even as a young adult. The problem was that I could not justify spending several hundred dollars for an air rifle. I've since learned that you get what you pay for when it comes to high-quality, high-power, and unparalleled accuracy in an air rifle for varmint hunting. When you need dime-size accuracy at unprecedented distances referencing the kill zone of a varmint with an air rifle, and at an affordable price, look no further than the German made RWS Diana 34 T06 Classic .22 caliber precision weapon. With open sights, I have made head, neck, and body shots on Rocky, Rachel, and their distant relatives at 10–35 yards. Those critters did not even take a single step forward or backward when hit; they just folded to the ground, providing me with ample raccoon fly-tying material. I save the tails for fly tying. Deadly in the water column.

Here is how it all unfolded, having taken three raccoons in a single week with my new RWS air rifle. Usually, the culprits were too far away and in low-light or no-light conditions. As dusk was quickly dimming to mark the close of day, from the back deck I had the raucous masked bandit in my sights; just its head. It was at the base of our pier, next to a hanging garden hose loosely draped over a half-moon shaped hose creel. Fat culprit he was. He had been in full view moments before I cocked the gun and placed a pellet in the chamber, slowly and carefully closing the barrel. Twilight was receding rapidly, and I thought about stepping forward for a closer shot, which probably would have been a mistake. His body was now behind the hanging hose—his face in full profile. I guesstimated the range to be thirty yards, knowing that I'd surely hit him, for I had made 25–35yard shots on paper up at our son's upstate home. *Ah, but would the pellet penetrate or hit with enough power to kill the varmint?* I had initially wondered.

Stop thinking and act, I told myself as the fiber-optics framed the center side of the raccoon's head. Yes, surely the one destroying our flower garden (actually, Donna's flower garden) and enjoying our vegetables, too. I released a breath and took up the first-stage slack in the trigger . . . squeezing through the second stage. He immediately dropped from the low-light frame of the red and green fiber-optics—dead as in doornail. The next morning, I measured the distance from our back deck to the hose creel with my Bushnell 1200 Legend Laser Rangefinder. It read 35 yards, the same as one of the distances I had been shooting on paper.

Later in the week, after shooting Rocky Raccoon, I took two more members of the family on the same day and during daylight hours. Pretty unusual to spot a raccoon during the day let alone a pair of bandits. Rachel and her sibling were nibbling on some leftover seed that Donna had put out earlier to feed a pair of mallards. After the ducks flew off, Rachel and her brother (who I posthumously named Roy) stepped out of nowhere, probably from under the deck and were busy eating the seed spread throughout the grass. I went to grab the air rifle, which I fondly refer to as Diana. It was an easy 20-yard neck shot. Rachel was DOA upon delivery of the .22 caliber RWS Superpoint Extra Field-Line lead projectile. Roy disappeared but returned some time later to inspect and feed upon the seed. The seed wasn't something he could quickly grab at and go, not like several ears of corn that had been soaking in a bucket of water to be steamed upon the grill before suddenly disappearing but a month before. We had wondered where the corn had gone before we woke up to the fact that pilferers were on the prowl. I just knew it had to be one of those pesky raccoons.

A 10-yard full-body shot aimed at Roy's vitals immediately ended his repast that late afternoon.

RWS Diana 34 T06 Classic .22 caliber precision air rifle

Scoping Your Air Gun

If you desire a scope for your air gun, seriously consider the EOTech XPS2-RF holographic sight. It is the smallest package offered by the company and is specifically designed for air rifles along with other non-tactical, traditional rimfire platforms. More on EOTech's awesome holographic sights will be covered in the following chapter.

CHAPTER 29

HOLOGRAPHIC SIGHTS FOR HIGH-POWERED RIFLE CARTRIDGES

HANDGUNS TO MUZZLELOADERS

Holographic Optics

Probably pictured in the mind of many folks considering deer hunting with a handgun is the conventional tube-type scope mounted atop a barrel. It was with me. I had begun by researching quality traditional tube-style crosshair and red dot scopes; that is, until I touched base with Jeff Puckett, account executive with Blue Heron Communications, whose client, among others, is Thompson/Center Arms. Jeff recommended the XPS2-0 holographic laser sight for my Thompson/Center Encore Pro Hunter .308 caliber pistol as well as my .50 caliber Thompson/Center Encore 209 x 50 Magnum muzzleloader; two high-power firearms. Of course, I did my due diligence and began researching Jeff's recommendations. The EOTech XPS2-0 holographic laser sight is the perfect optic for my intended purposes of hunting whitetails with a handgun and a muzzleloader. With the right cartridge, the .308 handgun would take down far bigger game such as elk, caribou, and moose. The .50 caliber muzzleloader would, obviously, be equally effective.

I had seen these nonconventional-looking sights but never paid them much mind. Why? Answer: They're expensive. As I began my research, I was wowed! Here is a compact (3.5 x 2.2 x 2.8 inches), lightweight (11.2 ounces) platform, lithium battery-operated [600 hours at nominal setting with a single CR 123 battery] holographic sight that will unquestionably stand up to the rigors of heavy-caliber rifle cartridges.

Target acquisition is immediate and viewed with both eyes open, utilizing a red 65 MOA outer ring while encompassing a 1 (one) MOA center red dot. Employed by both law enforcement and military personnel, these holographic laser sights are battle proven and utilized for up-close and personal engagement as well as for distance.

"At the 2015 Shot Show during media day, folks were consistently dinging a six-inch steel plate at 100 yards with a T/C Encore Pro Hunter pistol chambered in .308 caliber topped with an EOTech sight," said Jeff Puckett. I recently acquired that weapon and sight and can attest to that fact.

The EOTech sight can withstand 150 degree Fahrenheit temperatures down to minus 40 degrees. It is waterproof to a depth of 10 feet; shock proof and fog proof. At

100 yards, the sight displays a 30-yard field of view with unlimited eye relief. No scope rings are needed as the sight is a quick-attach/detach system that locks onto a barrel mount. Warne Manufacturing Company Optics & Mount bases (www.warnescopemounts.com) for EOTech sights come highly recommended. As long as the base mount affixed to a firearm's barrel is the same, you can quickly switch the holographic sight among weapons. For example, the Warne base mount for the barrel of my Thompson/Center .308 handgun takes the same base mount as the barrel of my Thompson/Center Arms Encore 209 x 50 Magnum muzzleloader. Although I dedicate an EOTech XPS2-0 for each firearm, I could switch them out in a heartbeat if I chose to do so. Also, the holographic sight is parallax free, meaning that the visible red dot remains parallel to the firearm bore. With the EOTech XPS2-0 holographic laser sight, all you do is fix the red dot set within the red circle of light (both are highly visible even in bright sunlight) upon your quarry and shoot.

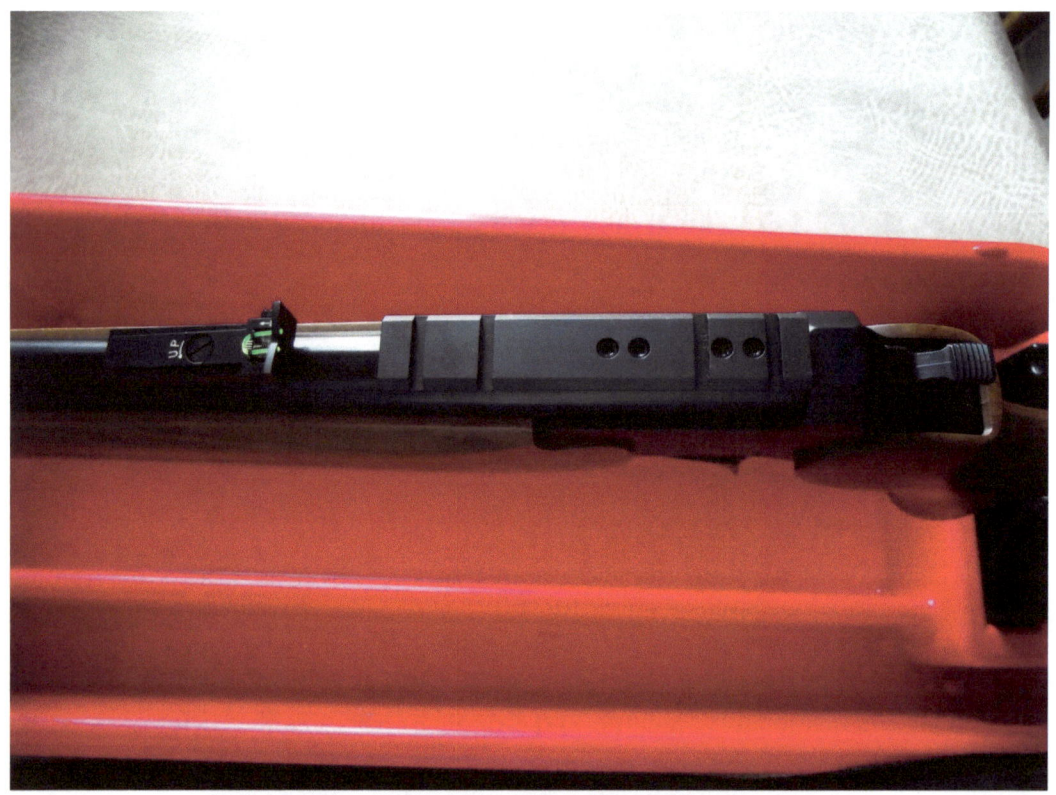

Warne Base Mount on Thompson /Center Arms Encore 209 x 50 Magnum Muzzleloader

EOTech XPS2-0 Holographic Sight

Do not shortchange yourself by falling into the trap of purchasing an EOTech clone. They are out there for a fraction of the cost. However, I would warn against this penny-wise pound-foolish approach, for you generally get what you pay for when it comes to optics. Do it right, and do it once for fast target acquisition and pinpoint accuracy. You won't be sorry in the long run. There are several EOTech holographic laser sights from which to choose for long-range (over 300 yards) shooting. Check out the company's website at www.eotechinc.com.

Additionally, Laser Genetics night vision (green) lights' product line, which can be adapted to mount atop conventional tube-type telescopic sights for long- range nighttime shooting [referencing nuisance permits] are to be considered, too. Check them out at www.lasergenetics.com.

Handguns

When hunting deer with a handgun, I would strongly recommend optics for obvious reasons, for you do not want to wound a deer; you want to execute a clean kill. Optics offers the added edge. Hunting for optics as well as a quality handgun for whitetails is where we enter the arena of choosing a top-notch manufacturer. There are several great handgun companies out there, so it took me a while to make an informed decision. Thompson/Center Arms, titled America's Master Gunmaker [acquired by Smith & Wesson], lives up to that reputation. Bullet accuracy, measured in MOA (Minute Of Angle), is but one of Thompson/Center's hallmark achievements. A basic understanding of MOA will not only help you appreciate firearm accuracy, it will help you in making a final purchasing decision. Refer to Chapter 5 for MOA clarification.

Trying Before Buying

This is admittedly easier said than done. Here are several suggestions: Try calling on knowledgeable friends and acquaintances who may own quality handguns and will be able to help narrow your selection. Search the Internet for related information, but shy away from forums; instead, scour reviews written by professionals. Speak with product specialists at the various gun companies that you are considering. Endeavor to contact gun clubs in your area for assistance. Visit your local gun shop(s) for, hopefully, a hands-on demonstration either at their outdoor or indoor range if available. If not, an over-the-counter inspection may have to suffice. Have a written list of questions ready to ask the shop pro. Do not leave anything to memory, including his or her answers to your questions.

As you home in on your choice of handgun, you have to consider barrel length, which, depending on caliber, generally ranges anywhere between 6 and 15 inches. The handgun I elected to purchase for hunting whitetails is a .308 caliber single-shot break-open type pistol with a 15-inch barrel length. Once you have decided on the right type of hunting handgun in terms of function, finish, and fit (the latter meaning what feels right in your hands), you must decide on handgun grips and forend, for they are certainly an important consideration. In lieu of wood (walnut) grips and forend, I selected rubber (Pachmayr) for superior handling.

After deciding on a firearm manufacturer, you're probably ready to lay your credit card down upon the gun shop's counter. Don't. Not yet. First go home and compare prices with other gun shops in your area. You may be pleasantly surprised. And while you're comparing prices, I'd suggest reviewing every element of the process you've gone through. Too, if you haven't already considered optics for that handgun, now might be the time to do so.

Does the gun manufacturer meet *your* criteria based on *your* extensive homework? Are you settling rather than being completely satisfied with your decision? More than a few guys and gals I know bought impulsively and were dissatisfied. When it comes to handguns and optics for hunting, I more than suggest that you buy the best—not what you think you can afford. It is better that you wait and save up the balance needed than be displeased in the end. For a quality handgun, you will be shelling out quite a few shekels. And that goes for handgun optics as well. I'll discuss optics in a moment.

Thompson/Center Arms (acquired by Smith & Wesson) is a premier gun manufacturer of rifles, muzzleloaders, shotguns, and handguns that meet and exceed most anyone's need(s) for hunting. There are several top-notch companies out there that manufacture fine hunting handguns, too: Freedom Arms, Ruger, and Taurus, to name a few. However, they did not meet my needs referencing one requisite or another. This is by no means a reflection on any of those companies because there are so many variables to consider as already covered.

Down the pike, if you were to require specialized attention to your firearm, such as muzzle breaks or suppressors, or request custom hand-loaded ammunition for your weapon, there is only one company I would absolutely recommend, and that is SSK Industries. Its owner/operator, and president, J.D. Jones—whom I affectionately refer to as the wildcatting wizard—is the man to contact: www.sskindustries.com. J.D. Jones hides behind no curtain; instead, he openly responds to your inquiries with the patience of Job. In point of fact, we had a lengthy correspondence covering a period of weeks. J.D. directed me to the right church and right pew.

J.D. Jones has hunted six continents with a handgun; his custom JDJ cartridges have taken every animal from squirrels to elephants. His custom cartridges for a multitude of firearms (along with custom barrels) are unparalleled in performance as they are expressly designed for hunting. The man's list of credentials is exceptional—from inventor, ballistics magnate, custom quality designer, firearms manufacturer, author, editor—and beyond.

Muzzleloaders

Muzzleloaders give deer hunters two great advantages. One: they offer shooting accuracy at far greater distances than a slug gun, especially with optics as an added feature. Two: they may extend a hunter's deer season in areas that do not allow rifle hunting. For example, during the January 2014 and 2015 Special Firearms Muzzleloader Season here in Suffolk County, Long Island, deer hunters picked up an extra 20 days (weekdays) to pursue white-tailed deer of either sex. As another example, in the southern zone of Central New York State in Tompkins County, the Department of Environmental Conservation (DEC) permitted hunters to employ muzzleloaders and to harvest whitetails of either sex from December 14th to December 22^{th,} 2015. That's an ample nine days in which to score.

These generous allowances via the DEC's Wildlife Management Units (WMU), which can extend your gunning season significantly, coupled with the superior accuracy of a muzzleloader, can put venison on that meat pole. My Thompson/Center Encore 209 x 50 Magnum muzzleloader can easily accomplish what my bow and slug gun would have failed to accomplish, and that is to comfortably cover the distance needed to put down several nice deer. I'll confidently shoot a bow and arrow for a kill shot up to 30 yards without fear of wounding the creature. I'll accomplish the same with my scoped slug gun out to 70 yards with confidence. But what if I need to find a comfortable range for felling deer at 100 to 150 yards in counties that do not allow rifle hunting? A muzzleloader is the answer.

I recently mounted the EOTech XPS2-0 holographic sight on my Thompson/Center Arms, Encore 209 x 50 Magnum muzzleloader—accuracy personified. And yes, the holographic laser sight can take the punishment delivered by a .50 caliber weapon. This was initially a major concern of mine. As mentioned, I did my research. These are quality optics designed for law enforcement and military use and are built to withstand the pressures from powerful rifle cartridges/propellants. I've been using Thompson/Center ShockWave Sabots, 250-grain Spire Point Bullets with Polycarbonate Tips, two Hodgdon Pyrodex Pellets, and .209 Winchester Primers. Good to go.

There are, indeed, newer muzzleloader models available from Thompson/Center Arms. Check them out at www.tcarms.com.

CHAPTER 30

HUNTING SMALL GAME ~ PREDATORS ~ VARMINTS/PESTS

SMALL GAME

Rabbit

Cottontail hunting without a beagle is lot like hunting for your keys in the dark without the advantage of a flashlight. It can be done, but I wouldn't call it a whole lot of fun. In truth, the Eastern cottontails I nailed over the years as a grownup were the by-product of hunting for upland game birds, namely pheasant. I'd be listening and looking up among the cornstalks, when suddenly I'd see something low between the rows. Whereas a good many folks would select number 4 shot for their 12 gauge in bagging pheasant, I prefer discharging number 6 steel shot through a Modified choke tube. It is a good all-around shot size for small game, and in a 3-inch shell, it will handle most upland game birds effectively as well.

It doesn't take a lot of power to dispatch a rabbit. As a matter of fact, you might be surprised to learn that when I was a youngster, I'd take them out with a lever action Daisy Red Ryder BB gun. Most were head shots and at close range. Some were lethally dropped at a distance of about 15 yards if I had to guess. Pretty good for a BB gun that has a velocity of about 350 feet per second. That's when I learned very early on that shot placement was far more important than speed. Think about it; one single BB fired from an air rifle as compared to 317 pellets per ounce of number 6 shot fired from a 12 gauge shotgun. I'd call the latter overkill. Wouldn't you?

Ostensibly, the great irony is that I shot more rabbits as a kid with a BB gun than I did in later years with my 12 gauge Mossberg bolt action. That is, until you stop and realize that I initially hunted (and fished) both before and after school hours, weekends, and holidays, virtually year round, traipsing through the wooded and open areas of a reservoir and golf course, respectively—just a hop, skip, and a jump from my parents' home in Lake Hiawatha, New Jersey. Yes, that was and still is called trespassing . . . but I never shot out any streetlights in my travels with that BB gun. ☺ True.

A quick word about shotgun gauges. A 16 gauge *is* [or *was*] the best all-around shotgun for small game and especially upland bird action—drawing the line at turkeys, where I'd certainly select a 12 gauge with a Full choke and number 4 shot. But the 16 gauge fell into decline early on (specifically1954). Yet, it is a far more sensible selection than a 20 gauge. Why? The answer is simple: A 16 gauge with a one-ounce payload patterns better than a 20 gauge—period. But gun manufacturers at the time aimed for the heavier 1¼-ounce load in the lighter 20 gauge firearm, and the law of supply and demand reared its ugly head. Enough said.

Squirrel

For squirrel hunting, I switch from my 12 gauge to my 20 gauge, using 2¾-inch shells, number 6 shot, and Modified choke. The squirrels that I shoot, I give to my friend to help feed his red-tailed hawk.

Opossum

Opossums are an altogether different species than possums as such, the latter of which are indigenous to areas of Australia, New Zealand, Indonesia, New Guinea, as well as other islands in the southwest Pacific Ocean. Our opossum, properly named the Virginia opossum, are about the size of an average house cat. Opossums are North America's only marsupial, that is, north of Mexico. They range across most of the warmer eastern areas of the United States, and are easily recognized by their triangular head; elongated, narrow muzzled white face; black beady eyes, grizzled-gray to brownish-black upper body; large black, pinkish-white tipped ears; dense guard hairs (long coarse outer *hairs* that cover and protect the soft underfur) are dark gray to black; and a naked, prehensile (meaning adapted for grabbing) buff-colored tail completes the picture.

Although used for garment trimming material, hunting and trapping opossums for their pelts is not a particularly lucrative sport. However, tracking down these creatures for fine fare is another matter, for its meat is praised as a delicacy. I happened to meet a man during the winter of 2014 who had owned a restaurant in Bellport, Long Island for twenty-eight years before selling in 2008; a good year to sell. Real estate was at its peaked before it tanked. We talked guns and hunting.

"As a young man," he related, "an opossum was the first animal I ever shot. You ate what you shot back then as it should be today. It was absolutely delicious," he continued with his story. And, no, I never asked the man if he put mammal on his menu for customer comments.

Most folks are likely to spot an opossum or raccoon as road kill more readily than when we two-legged beings are traipsing through woodland. That is, of course, because those four-legged creatures are normally nocturnal. However, if you were to take up a concealed position in proximity to your garbage can(s) during the wee hours, you would more than likely spy upon these nighttime visitors. But that fails to mark ourselves as hunters because we are not far enough afield. What to do?

A little-known trick for hunting opossum in the daytime, and without a dog, is to beat a stick against trees in an area where you find sign. Their tracks differ from a raccoon's in that the opossum's hind prints exhibit three middle toes spaced closely together while the other two toes are extended further outward. The five-toe fore-print is slightly smaller than the hind print and forms a star-like pattern, unlike that of a raccoon. Compare the paw print information under the Raccoon listing.

Average Weight of North American Animals ~ Small to Large
[Presented in Size/Weight Order Simply for Comparison]

Based on the average weights of the species listed below, ask yourself this question: How much gun do I really need?

Weasel (7 ounces); Squirrel (1½ pounds); Rabbits (3 pounds); Skunk (7 pounds); Opossum (8 pounds); Red and Gray Fox (9 pounds); Woodchuck (10 pounds); Raccoon (15 pounds); Coyote (30 pounds); Wolf (100 pounds); Pronghorn (120 pounds); White-tailed Deer (170 pounds); Black Bear (190 pounds); Big Horn Sheep (190 pounds); Wild Boar [U.S.], including feral hogs and hybrids (250 pounds); Elk (700 pounds); Moose (900 pounds); Brown Bear [Kodiak] (1400 pounds);

Identification and Hunting Strategies

With regard to body color, the identifications presented are general in that variations are subject to seasonal phases. However, distinguishing features are so noted throughout so as to determine closely related species. For example, among a family of foxes (red fox, gray fox, swift fox, kit fox, et cetera), the red fox is differentiated from the gray fox not necessarily by color, but by the former's white-tipped tail.

Depending on any number of circumstances, hunting strategies will, of course, vary considerably. Suggested are methods considered the most common in terms of continued success. Too, the reader may note innovative techniques that also have proven productive. As there is more than one way of skinning a cat, so to speak, certain methods may overlap one another with regard to harvesting the same animal. So rather than present one particular technique, I offer several approaches. Among them are hunting from a treestand and calling with a bird distress call; hunting on the ground and calling with a rabbit distress call, mixing it up vice versa and the reasons why; stalking woodlots, brush, and open fields with a dog, et cetera.

PREDATORS

Red Fox

Red fox are small and doglike in size, yet it is the largest of the family of foxes. Its upper body is rusty-reddish with white underparts: belly, chin, throat, and the front of its ears. The back of its pointed ears are black as are the lower legs and feet. The red fox is distinguishable from other foxes by its long, bushy, white-tipped tail.

A great bird distress call is the Kristoffer Clausen Predatorcall 1. It is an easy-to-use, open-reed call for red fox, coyotes, crows, and other predators. The call comes with an extension for a higher pitched volume and different tone, producing a variety of sounds that will bring predators in for the kill shot. Check out Kristoffer Clausen's other predator calls out at www.kristofferclausen.com.

When hunting on the ground, rather than in a treestand, some folks use a bipod. Keep in mind that fox hunting doesn't have to be a nighttime game, driving around endlessly with bright lights illuminating the world around you. A simple portable ground-blind screen works extremely well during daytime hours.

Gray Fox

The gray fox's upper body is grizzled gray, reddish below as well as atop its head. Unlike the red fox, the gray fox sports a black-tipped tail with a black stripe running along the top middle portion. Too, it does not have the black markings (stockings) on its feet as does the red fox.

Hunting gray fox is much the same as with bobcat or red fox. However, if you have no luck with either a bird or rabbit distress call, try a call designed as a gray fox distress call. One that folks favor is the Fox Pro Griz -N-Grey hand-type distress call. It can be worked with one hand held close to your body by simply pushing one end, eliminating arm movement from mouth back to firearm. A thumb controls the air valve, creating a high- to low-pitch sound. Also, the call will double as a raccoon distress sound made by simply shaking the tube. This is one very cool distress call. Check it out at www.gofoxpro.com.

Bobcat

The bobcat is named for its relatively short, black-tipped [bobbed] tail (approximately 10 inches long). The back of its short black ears encompass distinctive white patches. Depending on its mood at the moment, fringes of flared ruff (tufts), may or may not mark the sides of its face. Dark brown to black stripes, which could include spots, cover parts of the body. The upper part of its body is a reddish-brown; the lower portion is whitish. On average, an adult bobcat, weighing approximately 25 pounds, is about twice the size of a domestic cat. Therefore, a hunter is presented with a relatively small target, allowing for an approximate 3-inch diameter kill-zone shot.

Bobcats are generally hunted with hounds that *tree* the animal or bring it to bay in tight ground-based quarters such as cornering it between rock crevices or other such barriers. Without the benefit of hounds to pick up on a bobcat's fresh tracks, the best way to hunt them is to let the cat come to you through virtual, *incessant* calling.

A trick used to mimic the distress sound of a cottontail (or jackrabbit, if you're hunting out west) is by reversing the Primos Still tube ~ Cottontail Rabbit call (model number 316), then sucking rather than blowing. This produces a raspy sound that should travel well into the next county. Check them out at www.primos.com.

My reasoning for calling repeatedly, rather than every now and again, is that the predator might lose interest if the screeching sounds are suddenly cut short, thinking that its potential prize has been dispatched by perhaps a raptorial creature such as a hawk, eagle, falcon, et cetera . . . for the shrieking has suddenly stopped, replaced by silence filling the void. Ah, but hope springs eternal if the air continuously carries the hope of vulnerable prey. On more than one occasion, I have seen curiosity get the better of the cat.

Bobcats are not only hunted for sport, they are pursued by trappers for the animal's pelt, which brings $50 to $200 per skin. Too, its fur can be dyed to imitate the ocelot pelt, which commands even higher prices. The New York State Department of Conservation's five year Bobcat Management Program was "adopted to increase hunting opportunities for bobcat," hoping to double hunter's/trapper's annual bounty from $500 to $1000. The season for the Harvest Expansion Area opened on October 14th, 2014. There is no question that bobcats have become serious predators in terms of their numbers and the damage they inflict on deer, livestock, poultry, and household pets. Hence, the need for the DEC's new regulations regarding its Bobcat Management Program.

Coyote

Coyotes are generally larger than bobcats. Depending on geographical location, adult male coyotes range between 20 to 40 pounds. Coyotes have doglike appearances, closely resembling a small collie dog. The coyote has erect, pointed ears, a narrow muzzle, long rust- or yellow-colored slender legs, grizzle-gray or reddish-gray body, light gray to a buff-colored belly, and a bushy tail usually held low to the ground.

Calling is your key to success as explained under the bobcat listing. Find areas that have vermin and small game, especially rabbits, and you'll increase your odds. Once again, I suggest hunting above the scent line. Coyotes are very cagy animals, and their sense of smell is uncanny. Too, they have extremely keen eyesight, so be sure to take advantage of good cover, upwind from the direction of your calling. First, settle into your treestand and wait a good half hour before calling. Next, call repeatedly with your cottontail distress cry, keep movement to a minimum, your eyes peeled, and be ready. You may be surprised at what suddenly appears. If nothing happens after an hour or so, I generally set up in a distant area then repeat the process anew.

Raccoon [predator or pest]

A raccoon's dominant feature is its easily recognizable black facial mask that is outlined in white; reddish-brown upper body mixed with black; grayish body below. The raccoon is also distinguishable by a bushy tail marked with four to six alternating black and brown or brownish-gray rings.

The raccoon is a tree-dwelling mammal that is often hunted at night—frequently with dogs and powerful lights. However, it doesn't have to be that involved. First look for their sign along creeks, stream beds, riverbanks, shores, and ponds. The animal's hind print tracks are quite discernible, measuring 3¼–4¼ inches long; much longer than they are wide. Picture a diminutive human footprint with extremely long toes. Their fore-prints are shorter, being almost as wide as they are long. Find their tracks in mud or snow, and you are in raccoon habitat where they feed upon everything, for raccoons are omnivorous, feasting on fish, crayfish, frogs, clams, turtles, turtle eggs; worms, grubs, grasshoppers, crickets, acorns; birds' eggs, voles, squirrels, young muskrats and, yes, virtually anything in your garbage can. Their dexterous fingers can pry off trash can lids, open refrigerators, and turn doorknobs.

Once you have located a raccoon's rec room and feeding area, it's time to plan for a late afternoon/early evening hunt. A method I learned from an ol' coon hunter is to leave the dog home but take along its food; that is, a can of dog food. Also, bring along a couple of nice ripe hot dogs. Twenty to 30 yards from where you're set up, open the can of dog food and empty it on the ground. Set the two hot dogs sticking upright and close together into the small heap—like the exaggerated long ears of some strange animal. Get settled in your treestand or ground blind and wait about fifteen minutes before calling. [Note the highly recommended raccoon call covered under the Gray Fox section]. Be ready for some dusk to dawn action, especially on moonlit, windless nights.

Be sure to check both your state and county hunting guide laws and regulations referencing illuminated sights for nighttime use.

Raccoon meat tastes like (no, not like chicken) something similar to veal. In fact, the first edition of *The Joy of Cooking* had a recipe for raccoon. Also, President Calvin Coolidge had it served at the White House for Thanksgiving. I wonder if any Democrats were invited and would they have accepted had they known what was on the menu. Even today, a good number of raccoons are eaten by hunters and trappers throughout North America. And, no, I'm not including a raccoon recipe in this handbook. ☺

Although not the craze it was among the collegiate of the 1920s, raccoon coats and coonskin caps were a status symbol. Raccoon pelts remained a viable source of revenue until the mid-90s, when the demand plummeted.

VARMINTS/PESTS

Groundhog [aka woodchuck]

You won't have to look far. Under woodpiles, porches, sheds, and stone walls you will find groundhogs. That being the case, I dispatch them with a precision air rifle on and along our property, same as I do raccoon (covered in Chapter 28).

Groundhog taken with RWS Diana 34 T06 Classic .22 Caliber Air Rifle

Skunk

Those who are unfortunate enough to have a skunk problem on their property are better off taking a lung shot (right behind its shoulder) rather than a head shot because the varmint is less likely to spray. That appears to be the general consensus. Personally, I think the whole business stinks. ☹

Weasel

Interestingly, weasels are generally considered more of an asset than a liability, for they feed upon rat and mice populations before they would go after poultry. When it comes to this point, folks usually resort to trapping these critters as opposed to other means.

Crow [varmint or pest]

While growing up in Lake Hiawatha, New Jersey, my childhood chum and I would ride along wooded trails and the periphery of cornfields in an old jalopy with its front passenger side door removed. We'd be on the lookout for crows. You didn't have to drive far to locate them, for they were found virtually everywhere and in great numbers, especially during the fall. One of us would be driving along slowly and steadily; the other would be riding shotgun. Literally. When we spotted those jet-black birds gathered in tall trees, the gunner would quietly roll out of the vehicle and onto the ground. Safety on. Shell in the chamber. The driver would continue ahead nonstop because if he stopped the vehicle for even a second, those birds would suddenly vanish in a heartbeat. The shooter would immediately stand, take the firearm's safety off, aim and shoot. A bird would fall, and the flock would disperse straightaway—but not before one of us took two more on the fly. This is how my buddy and I became pretty good wing shooters.

We didn't shoot skeet in those days, so those crows were our clay pigeons so to speak. With the exception of those prodigious ebony birds (17 inches in length on average), we did not kill anything indiscriminately. Not even squirrels—which the farmer always referred to as ". . . rats with tails." We ate what we shot.

The farmer who allowed two unlicensed youths to borrow his vehicle and remove the damaged passenger side door from the wreck of an automobile (once we had explained our strategy) was happy to have us back again and again, which we did —regularly. There came a point that the happy farmer told us that we needn't bother knocking on the back door when we came by because we came so often.

"The car keys will be on top of the right front tire," he explained. "Take 'er anytime you want. Just don't let me catch you takin' 'er for a spin down that roadway, rural or not. Got it?"

"Yes, sir."

"Yes, sir," echoed my buddy.

"Just keep shooting those dang crows that ruin my crops."

"Yes, sir, and thank you, sir," we said sincerely.

That's how it was back in those days. It's interesting that they call a large group of crows a *murder*. The farmer wanted us to murder them all. All we wanted to do was become proficient wing shooters, and we did.

The following season, we were permitted to hunt the farmer's fields for pheasant. Although we were not too successful, occasionally taking one or two by dumb luck as we didn't have a dog, we were eventually invited to hunt deer on his land that were eating everything in sight. Now, that was something for my buddy and me to crow about, for he had plenty of nice deer on his property. We were in paradise. The farmer's land adjoined my buddy's parents' home, which was right around the block, so we didn't have far to travel. As neither of us were of legal driving age and therefore had no driver's license, we did have our hunting licenses, thank goodness, which were truly more important at the time. The farmer had made sure we were legal in that regard.

My buddy didn't go with me that opening morning of deer season. I went alone and bagged my very first deer, a six point buck, with my new Mossberg bolt action 12 gauge. I had mowed a lot of lawns over that summer and saved up enough money to buy my first, very own, shotgun (having returned the borrowed pump action we had used on crows), a box of double-ought buckshot (one of two shot-loads legal for deer hunting in New Jersey; the other being single-ought buckshot ~ it's still that way today), a real hunting jacket and hat. That news piece was covered earlier at the end of Chapter 9.

A final word on gun safety and gun protection before moving forward: keep those firearms locked up when not in use. Better *safe* than sorry.

CHAPTER 31

GOURMET GAME RECIPES

DELICIOUS, SIMPLE, SAUSAGE MEAT DISH [Serves 4–6]

Before I started making my own venison sausages, I simply used sweet Italian pork sausage with fennel for a recipe that I brought back from Naples, Italy, nearly sixty years ago. I still do today, mixing and varying meats among venison, veal, beef, and pork. Don't be afraid to be creative—experiment. It is so easy to prepare! You and your guests will absolutely flip over this savory, fantastic meal.

INGREDIENTS

2 pounds of venison combo as described above, or simply your favorite sweet Italian pork sausage meat
1 tablespoons fennel
2 cups heavy cream (room temperature)
5 tablespoons flat-leaf Italian parsley, coarsely chopped
1 pound medium-size egg noodles

PROCEDURE

1. Sauté sausage and add fennel, breaking up meat into small pieces until golden brown. Drain fat.
2. Cook noodles according to package directions when sausage is almost completed.
3. In a large serving bowl, place the drained noodles, followed by the sausage.
4. Pour heavy cream over entire noodles and sausage.
5. Add parsley.
6. Fold thoroughly and serve immediately with a salad on the side.

Note: Leftovers are even better; however, there will not be any!

BÉARNAISE VENISON BACKSTRAP OR TENDERLOIN OVER EGG NOODLES [Serves 4]

INGREDIENTS

4 backstraps or tenderloins (referred to as the fillet), approximately 1½ inches thick
½ cup teriyaki sauce
salt
pepper
Béarnaise sauce (recipe follows)
paprika
1 pound wide egg noodles

PROCEDURE

1. Remove the silver skin then Jaccard the backstraps or tenderloins. Although your backstraps and tenderloins are choice cuts and do not necessarily require Jaccarding, the tool will make those cuts of venison even more tender. Employing the tool on other cuts such as roasts, chops, et cetera, will greatly enhance their tenderness.

2. Rub salt and pepper on both sides of venison strips. Place the venison in a shallow dish and cover with teriyaki sauce. Turn the meat over so that all sides are covered with teriyaki sauce. Let the venison marinate overnight, at least 8 hours; 16 hours if not Jaccarded (tenderized).

3. Preheat an outdoor grill to high. Grill the venison to your liking, rare to medium-rare for about 2 to 3 minutes on each side; check for doneness. One minute to a minute-and-a-half on each side if you Jaccarded.

Note: If your preference is medium, medium-well to well done, forget venison. Go to the market and buy yourself a nice steak. Game meat is to be prepared rare to medium-rare, unless we're talking stew meat or anything along those lines.

4. Spoon Béarnaise sauce over meat, and sprinkle with paprika. Serve over egg noodles.

BÉARNAISE SAUCE [4 servings]

INGREDIENTS

¼ cup chopped fresh tarragon leaves
2 medium size shallots, minced
¼ cup apple cider vinegar
¼ cup dry white wine
3 egg yolks
¼ pound melted butter
salt and pepper to taste

PROCEDURE

1. Make the Béarnaise reduction first: In a small saucepan, combine the tarragon, shallots, vinegar, and wine over medium-high heat. Bring to a simmer (do not boil) and cook until reduced by half. Remove from heat and set aside to cool.

2. Once the Béarnaise reduction is cooled, mix yolks and Béarnaise reduction together in a blender. With the blender running, add one third of the butter in a slow steady stream. Once it emulsifies, add the remaining butter. Season with salt and pepper and set aside.

BOBBY B'S GOURMET VENISON CHILI [serves 8]

INGREDIENTS
4 lbs. ground coarsely ground venison
2 lb. package meatloaf mix: pork, beef, veal
3 (28 oz.) cans San Marzano (imported from Italy, not elsewhere) whole peeled plum tomatoes
½ cup red bell pepper coarsely chopped
½ cup green bell pepper coarsely chopped
1 cup Vidalia onion coarsely chopped
½ cup celery coarsely chopped
15 oz. can black beans
16 oz. can dark red kidney beans
½ cup bacon coarsely chopped
½ cup fresh Italian parsley coarsely chopped
7 cloves finely chopped garlic
2 tablespoons oregano
2 tablespoons basil
splash of dry red wine
3 dried red chili peppers
1 teaspoon ground fresh pepper
dash of ground cayenne red pepper (careful)
1 teaspoon cumin
1 bay leaf
¼ teaspoon ground allspice
¼ teaspoon ground coriander

PROCEDURE

1. Brown meat and drain any excess fat.
2. In an 8-quart pot, lightly mash the whole peeled tomatoes.
3. Combine <u>all</u> of the ingredients and simmer for two hours. Stir occasionally. If needed, thin contents with low-salt chicken broth.

Note: [we never use College Inn chicken broth]. When you have time, download my Web site, www.robertbanfelder.com under CONSUMER ADVOCACY ~ Incompetents, Connivers, Con Artists & the Criminally Negligent at the top of the home page as to Donna's and my reasons why.

Preparing Game Birds ~ From Field to Table
Basic Procedures

Before we begin preparing game birds, I'd like you to preview three basic methods. If you ever made a whole chicken or cut chicken cutlets off the breastbone, this is going to be a walk in the park. If you haven't, read these simple instructions and give this a shot. This is not rocket science or brain surgery.

Breasting Out Small and Big Birds
[We'll be cooking goose breasts and goose burgers.]

For smaller birds such as quail, partridge, and grouse, remove the wings with a pair of poultry snippets. Between your thumb and forefinger, pull out the feathers surrounding and covering the breast area. Insert fingers beneath the breast and start separating it from the ribs. Grab the neck muscle in one hand and the body of the bird in the other and pull.

For larger birds such as mallards, pheasants, or geese, you need not remove the wings. However, you will need a sharp paring knife to help separate the flesh from the breastbone. But first, after you expose the breast by plucking that area, split and stretch the skin along the entire breastbone with your fingers by pushing downward and pulling it away. With your paring knife, make two lateral cuts along each side of the breastbone. Peel the breast halves back and continue cutting down and along the ridge of the breastbone, removing one cutlet with its breast tender attached, and then the other.

Rinse under cold water and check for shot. Breasts lend themselves well for roasting, baking, grilling, and sautéing.

Preparing Whole Birds
[We'll be cooking a whole fresh pheasant and several quail]

Pluck, gut, and wash entire bird(s) thoroughly with cold water then pat the outer surface dry with paper towels. Lightly sprinkle the cavity with Kosher salt.

Sautéing
[With recipes other than the one that call for sautéing breasts, use these *savory* ingredients in your own creation(s).]

In a sauté pan, over medium-high heat, melt 3 tablespoons of salted butter. Add 3 tablespoons of extra virgin olive oil, and a splash of Savory & James Deluxe Quality cream sherry. Reduce heat to medium and add 2 thinly sliced cloves of garlic; do not burn. Place marinated breasts in pan, sprinkle lightly with salt and fresh-ground pepper. Turn breasts frequently, and check for doneness.

Spatchcocking ~ Opening the Bird Like a Book
[When you are ready, you'll be creative and prepare your own bird using this method.]

Spatchcocking is simply a method of butterflying whole bigger birds so that they lie flat. This is accomplished by removing the backbone with a pair of kitchen shears then partially splitting the cartilage of the breastbone with a sharp knife. As the bird is now open like a book, you can thoroughly blanket it with your favorite seasonings. Too, the bird will cook evenly and in a far shorter period of time. This method lends itself well for baking, roasting, or grilling.

Handy Tool for Tenderizing

I would like to reintroduce you to an indispensable tenderizing tool covered at the end of Chapter 16, to be used on meat, fowl, or fish. Be reminded that it will cut both your marinating and brining times by fifty and forty percent, respectively. This indispensable tool is the Jaccard, sold as a meat tenderizing machine, although used for tenderizing the flesh of fish and poultry, too. To reiterate, the Jaccard is available in two models: a mini Jaccard with one row of sixteen blades, and the larger model with three rows containing forty-eight blades.

SLOW-COOKED WILD GOOSE BREAST [Serves 4]

This is a recipe that I almost passed up because I argued with a friend, insisting that I had tried many and that they just weren't worth the trouble. Besides which, the breast always came out rather tough. Not with this recipe. As a matter of fact, I always gave away my birds to the fellows with whom I hunted for that very reason. No longer. Thanks, Chris.

INGREDIENTS

½ cup soy sauce
4 teaspoons canola oil
5 teaspoons lemon juice
2 teaspoons Worcestershire sauce
4 cloves garlic, minced
2 lbs. Jaccarded (tenderized) and cubed goose breast
¾ cup all-purpose flour
¼ cup unsalted butter
1 can (10¾ ounces) condensed mushroom soup (undiluted)
2 cups chicken broth
½ envelope onion soup mix
1 pound medium egg noodles

PROCEDURE

1. In a large sealable plastic bag, combine the soy sauce, oil, lemon juice, Worcestershire sauce, and garlic powder; add cubed goose breast. Seal and turn to coat. Refrigerate overnight.

2. Drain and discard marinade. Place flour in another large sealable plastic bag; add goose in batches and shake to coat. In a large skillet over medium heat, brown goose in butter on all sides.

3. Transfer to a slow cooker. Add the condensed mushroom soup, chicken broth, and onion soup mix. Cover and cook on high for 5 hours or until flesh is tender, adding more chicken broth as needed.

4. Serve over cooked noodles.

GOOSE BURGERS [Serves 4]

INGREDIENTS

2-3 skinless goose breast fillets cut into one-inch cubes
¼ pound smoked bacon, diced
1 cup canned diced tomato, drained
1 tablespoon fresh minced garlic
¼ cup minced onion
1 tablespoon Old Bay seasoning
1 egg, slightly beaten
½ cup Italian bread crumbs
½ teaspoon freshly ground black pepper
½ teaspoon salt

PROCEDURE

1. Grind the goose breast cubes in a meat grinder or food processor.

2. In a large bowl, combine the ground goose with the bacon, diced tomato, garlic, onion, Old Bay seasoning, and egg. Mix together well. Add bread crumbs, salt, pepper, and mix until firm enough to hold the patties together. Add more bread crumbs if needed. Form into patties.

3. Place burgers on a medium-hot grill or in a hot skillet and brown evenly on both sides to desired doneness.

4. Serve with your favorite topping(s).

QUAIL SAUTÉED WITH GRAPES [serves 4]

INGREDIENTS
8 fresh quail
6 Tablespoons Kosher salt
1 tablespoon freshly ground pepper
¼ pound clarified sweet butter
2 Tablespoons cognac
1 cup chicken stock
2 pats sweet butter
20 each red and green seedless grapes

PROCEDURE

1. Rinse quail thoroughly inside and out. Pat dry.

2. Split quail from the back side of the bird and remove the bone. Season with salt and pepper mixture.

3. In a large hot skillet (ovenproof), saute quail in the clarified butter. Brown on both sides. They cook fast. Do not overcook.

4. Place quail in oven preheated to 375° F for 4 minutes to finish.

5. Remove the quail from the skillet.

6. Remove the excess fat from the skillet. Deglaze with cognac, chicken stock, whole butter. Add grapes. Sauce should be syrupy.

7. Return the quail to the skillet and coat with sauce.

SLOW-COOKED PHEASANT
[serves 4]

INGREDIENTS
2 fresh sprigs rosemary, leaves stripped and finely chopped
1 tablespoon finely chopped fresh thyme

1 cup olive oil
1 whole pheasant, cleaned thoroughly inside and out and patted dry
4 tablespoons Kosher salt and 1 tablespoon ground black pepper, mixed together

PROCEDURE

1. The day before cooking the bird, stir the chopped rosemary and thyme into the olive oil. Leave unrefrigerated and covered overnight so that the oil becomes infused with the herbs.
2. Preheat an oven to 250 degrees F.
3. Rub the pheasant inside and out with salt and pepper mixture. Place onto a roasting rack grate in a pan. The pan should not be too big for the bird. Pour the herb oil atop the bird.
4. Bake the pheasant for 1 hour, cover with aluminum foil, and continue baking an additional hour, basting the pheasant with the hot oil and juices from the pan every 30 minutes while cooking.
5. Remove the pheasant from the oven, cover with heavy aluminum foil, and allow to rest in a warm area for 10 minutes before slicing.

CHAPTER 32

AFRICA'S LARGEST OF THE SIX MOST DANGEROUS BIG GAME ANIMALS

Over the course of close to sixty years, I have hunted both small and big game, drawing the proverbial line in the sand and ending with Virginia whitetails. For openers, I am going to introduce you to a select group of consummate big game safari hunters who have dispatched Africa's dangerous big game land animals: elephant, rhinoceros, hippopotamus, Cape buffalo, lion, and leopard. Remarkably, several of these animals have been taken down with not only rifles—but handguns! Neither of which is an adventure for the faint of heart. You will meet these men and read their stories in their own words. I ask that you read through the initial information that precedes each of their stories as well as each and every story rather than select a single segment of interest. Absorbing this information concerning *all* six animals will make for a better understanding of the quarry you may seek and helps me present overlapping information succinctly rather than repetitively.

Calibers, Cartridges, Bullet Designs & Firearms

Suffice it to say that many factors come into play in weighing what is and what is not suitable in terms of calibers, cartridges, bullet designs, and firearm selection geared toward a specific quarry.

In determining what might be the best choices, one must consider several variables. What dangerous big game animal will the hunter be pursuing? From what distance(s) will the hunter likely be shooting? What kind of terrain will be traversed? What are the hunter's physical capabilities as well as his or her limitations? Does one have the confidence to make a well-placed *deadly* shot? Does he or she possess the acumen to react to a deadly situation if things turn hairy on the hunt? The honest answer to this last question is that one probably won't know until the moment of truth presents itself, but it *is* something to think about.

The point of addressing all these questions will help direct the hunter along an otherwise confusing path, clear down to caliber and cartridge selection, bullet grain weight, its design, and the type of firearm required to launch that projectile. These elements of consideration are to be weighed most carefully, but can and will narrow the playing field should he or she wish to enter the dangerous world of big game safari hunting—either veritably or vicariously.

Let's aim big and begin with the world's largest living land animal—Africa's elephant.

Elephant

Africa's bush elephant—standing 10 to 13 feet tall and weighing 9000 to 13,000 pounds on average—is the largest living land animal on the face of the planet. The largest elephant on record was felled in 1956, weighing 24,000 pounds, by Jose Fenykovi, et al, in Angola. That's almost twice the weight of your run-of-the-mill pachyderm. You are going to need a very serious weapon in order to deal with these behemoths. Outfitters, guides, and professional hunters strongly recommend a heavy caliber bolt action rifle that will handle powerful magnum loads.

Because you are not permitted to carry an arsenal on safari to Africa, often being restricted to two guns, a compromise should be reached in terms of versatility for hunting the continent's most dangerous six big game animals. For openers, especially elephants, a big bore .400 caliber employing solids (bullets other than standard soft or hollow points) is a fine choice. Shots are generally taken at close range, so open sights or low, fixed power to variable 3–9x scopes are often preferred. Selecting optics are items that you do not want to bargain hunt. Buy quality. The same holds true for binoculars; 7x42 is good glass for the bush.

A thirty-five yard broadside kill shot to the pachyderm's ear for a bullet to enter its brain is ideally the order of the day. Others may aim for the traditional heart/lung shot—the conventional wisdom being that the prodigious animal, to begin with, offers more of a margin for error. Of course, if the behemoth is charging head on, a frontal head or chest cavity shot makes for an even narrower and more challenging target. Lots of luck. A wise hunter will opt for a backup rifle (usually of a different caliber and cartridge) to be quickly handed over by the guide while others in the group stand armed and at the ready, for things could go wrong in a nanosecond. A savvy P.H. (**P**rofessional **H**unter safari guide/outfitter) will have plan B firmly implanted in his client's brain well beforehand should matters take a sudden turn for the worse.

As we continue along this challenging path, you will meet several of these big game safari hunters—armed with either rifles or handguns—who have successfully put down the most dangerous big game land animals across six continents. We'll be reading about their adventures in, of course, Africa, and, perhaps surprisingly, Australia. These adventurous men have generously contributed their stories and photographs for this handbook. Whatever *your* choice of weapon, you will benefit greatly from their extensive experiences and vast knowledge. But for the moment, let's examine closely the primary components of a rifle via a merism found in the early English phrase, lock, stock, and barrel.

When considering the *ultimate* big game bolt [**lock**] action weapon, look no further than SSK Industries (J.D. Jones, owner/operator ~ fabricator ~ wildcat cartridge wizard), working in conjunction with B&M Rifles and Cartridges, creating and customizing serious weapons and ammunition for hunting big game animals. When considering the weapon's custom **stock** for the ultimate big-bore baby, Accurate Innovations is simply the finest in their field. When searching for the *ultimate* big bore weapon, you won't have to look any further than for a true .500 caliber Winchester M70 MDM, with a 20-inch **barrel**; weapon weighing in at 8.5 lbs. The stock has a built-in aluminum framework to absorb recoil and prevent wood from cracking, which could otherwise happen when employing powerful magnum rounds.

When selecting a custom-designed cartridge/ bullet to perform a *perfect* marriage with the Winchester M70 MDM .500, the .550 CEB (Cutting Edge Bullets) #13 profile—leaving the muzzle at a velocity of 2250 feet per second—is the ticket. This proven custom-built package is an *ultimate* weapon for the world's biggest land animal.

William V. **B**ruton and Michael **Mc**Courry's are the first initials of their surnames that form the company's name, B&M Rifles and Cartridges (www.b-mriflesandcartridges.com). Working closely together with SSK Industries, Accurate Innovations, and Cutting Edge Bullets, B&M is the place to go for selecting serious medium- to big-bore rifles for Africa's big game animals, especially the most dangerous six. If it's been drilled into your brain that "You've gotta go to B&H" for your camera equipment because of their catchy, repetitive slogan, then "You've gotta remember to go to B&M for your serious safari Rifles and Cartridges." Got it? Good. Or you just might find yourself crappin' in your pants when a charging pachyderm homes in on *you*. No joke. You want 'drop dead' stopping power.

Whether it's a .416 caliber rifle for Cape buffalo or a .500 caliber rifle for elephant, I'd like for you to weigh in carefully on cartridge/bullet selection. Example: For versatility, a light 250-grain custom CEB Raptor bullet design in a .416 B&M rifle will give you bone-breaking through-and-through penetration for thin-skinned plains animals. Go up in bullet size using the same gun for thick-skinned bull (male) buffalo, and you have an all-around weapon combination for all seasons and reasons. In testing bullet performance, although admittedly not the norm, I've seen cows (female buffalo) shot clean through at 65 yards with the .416 caliber B&M rifle firing a 250-grain bullet. That's really saying something; incredible, in fact, as a 458-grain weight bullet is generally your starting point for buffalo. A 500-grain weight bullet fired from a custom B&M Winchester M70, MDM is your *ultimate* elephant gun. Remember, you've gotta go to B&M.

Are you ready to start meeting these remarkable men and read their extraordinary stories in their own words? Good. Meet Michael McCourry of B&M Rifles and Cartridges.

Elephant Hunt

By Michael McCourry

It was only a few days before my 52nd birthday that I found myself in Zimbabwe. I was there with longtime friend and professional hunter, Andrew Schoeman, and my first time in the Gache Gache Campfire Concession. The owner of the concession, Corris Ferreira and Andrew had been family friends for many years.

Along on this trip was my wife Jaun and daughter Mercedes. Mercedes had just turned eight less than a month before. It was her first trip to Zimbabwe and was proving to be quite an adventure for her. I had a serious agenda planned for this trip, and it involved using the relatively new cutting-edge bullets, Safari Raptors, on Cape buffalo (aka African buffalo).This bullet design is the accumulation of over a year's research, planning, preparation, trial and error. All of which was done at my home range in Conway, South Carolina. The Safari Raptor is a hollow point, solid brass bullet, and is derived from a matching Safari Solid. I was also using a rifle/cartridge of my own design, a Winchester M70 500 MDM. The 500 MDM is a true .500 caliber rifle using a full length Remington Ultra Mag case at 2.8 inches. In addition to the 500 MDM, I had a 458 B&M along with the same purpose in mind, giving the .458 caliber Safari Raptors a workout.

The 500 MDM is the largest cartridge available in the B&M lineup, which consists of thirteen different cartridges in a variety of rifle types specifically for hunting large dangerous game. Five of these cartridges were .500 caliber for different types of rifles, with the 500 MDM being the largest. While the 500 MDM is a large cartridge, the rifle is relatively small for the capabilities of the cartridge, coming in at 8.5 pounds, 41 inches overall length with its standard 20-inch barrel. As a comparison, this is approximately 4 to 5 inches shorter and 2 pounds lighter than anything in its class.

The 458 B&M is even more radical, coming in at 7.5 pounds, 38 inches overall length with an 18-inch barrel and has the same capabilities as a standard 24-inch 458 Winchester.

In 2006, I made the cartridges proprietary to SSK Industries, J.D. Jones and company. Many reasons went into this decision, but the most important one is that these rifles and cartridges had my name on them, and quality and reputation is everything. SSK Industries has the experience and the quality workmanship that I desired for the B&M lineup. I just did not and do not trust anyone else with the B&M line. They are rifles and cartridges built with a significant purpose in mind, and that is, to be used in the field for dangerous game. I am not willing to cut corners when it comes to this kind of fieldwork.

In 2005, I encountered a hippo at very close range in Tanzania. During this engagement, I was using a Winchester M70 458 Lott. A very capable rifle and cartridge, and it ended the affront with success at less than six steps away. During this encounter, I had enough time to think how awkward, bulky, long, and heavy this rifle was for short-range fast work that is sometimes required when hunting dangerous game. There had to be something better.

I found it later that same year using a cut and trimmed RUM case to 2.250 inches, at .500 caliber. The 50 B&M, based on a Winchester M70 WSM Short Action, with standard barrel length of 18 inches is a very handy, fast-working rifle for those close encounters with dangerous game.

From the 50 B&M, the 458, 416, 9.3, and 375 B&Ms were developed in rifles from 18–20 inches depending on caliber. The 500 MDM came later in 2009.

One major problem with any of the .500 caliber rifles was bullet availability. In the beginning, .500 caliber bullets were designed for the 500 S&W handgun, and none of these bullets could withstand the muzzle velocity that the rifle cartridges were capable of delivering. Starting in 2006, I began working with J.D. Jones and Lehigh Bullets to develop bullets that would be suitable for dangerous game. We were very successful and used many of these bullets on Cape buffalo and elephant with *great* success, both in 2007 and later again in 2009 in Australia for water buffalo (aka Asian buffalo). As a point of information, water buffalo can be as dangerous as African Cape buffalo. A mature Asian bull in its prime can be 20% larger than any Cape buffalo.

In 2010, I became acquainted with Dan Smitchko of Cutting Edge Bullets. Dan was eager to begin work with me on what would end up being a great adventure in the discovery of new bullet technology.

We started a very serious study of Solid Bullet Technology here in 2010. Solids are a vital component when hunting large thick-skinned dangerous game: elephant, buffalo, and hippo at the top of the list. It requires deep and straight-line penetration, many times from less than desirable angles, and at times even from the south end of the north-bound animal! Many thousands of man hours and hundreds of designs went into this project to come up with the ultimate solid used today, what we call the BBW #13, and currently in the Cutting Edge Bullet lineup, the Safari Solid. North Fork Technologies, which I had also been working with in addition to Cutting Edge, followed suit with a nose profile very similar to the BBW #13. There is much that could be written here concerning the designs of this bullet. In order of importance, I will merely list below what is called the "8 Factors of Terminal Penetration of Solids" to show you what factors we discovered in this study. Perhaps at a later date and another time, I could go into further detail about how and why these factors are of great importance.

#1 Meplat Percentage of Caliber
#2 Nose Profile
#3 Construction and Material
#4 Nose Projection
#5 Radius Edge of Meplat
(Above factors are in bullet design)
#6 Velocity

#7 Barrel Twist Rate
#8 Sectional Density

Back to Zimbabwe in 2011. The rifles, both the 500 MDM and the 458 B&M had already been successful on buffalo, along with the bullets chosen for the mission. Several days into the hunt, we stopped in the main village of Gache Gache. Corris was speaking with several of the people of the village, including its elders, when they informed him of trouble with elephants coming into the village at night and making pests of themselves, even to the point of literally nosing around the huts during evenings. At times this sort of activity goes well-beyond just being pesky and annoying and can be rather dangerous to the local population; hence, the concern of the people that lived in the village.

After Corris and Andrew had spoken with the people, they had a good idea from where the elephants were coming into the village as well as approximate times. Corris knew the area very well, telling me that it was very, very thick with brush, and that, more than likely, the perpetrators were staying in the brush at the edge of the village then coming out after dusk. Corris and Andrew learned that those nighttime visitors were three medium-sized bulls that were basically behaving like rowdy teenagers. Corris asked if I wanted to take the time to go have a look, possibly harvest one of the elephants, and hopefully scare the others away from the area. Of course I was very interested in the prospect of helping sort out this situation for the local people, and it would also give me a really good opportunity to work with the 500 MDM and these new Safari Solids that we had developed. It was decided that around 4 pm that afternoon, we would make our way over to that brush area to have a look.

The rest of the day was spent in preparation to pursue these elephants. Embarking upon a mission to sort out a few rogue elephants is no small matter and one to be taken most seriously. I checked and then rechecked my rifle, feed and function, and ammunition—specific to their loads. I felt prepared for the mission. These were not the first elephants I had dealt with, but I had not hunted pachyderms since 2007. Still, my confidence in the rifle and bullets was very high, having used them successfully on buffalo. I had selected the 500-grain Safari Solid (a muzzle velocity of 2400 fps) for my .500 MDM rifle. There was no doubt in my mind that this would do the job quite nicely.

Once all preparations were made, we left in time to arrive at the village by 4 pm. We had quite an entourage with us. We had three trackers, myself, Andrew, and Corris as shooters if need be; also, my wife Jaun and daughter Mercedes. We neared the area close to the village where Corris thought these elephants might be found, a place thick with brush and meandering trails made by these huge mammals. We hadn't gone 50 yards when Andrew sighted elephant legs just ahead of us at about 20 to 25 yards. At this point, we all hunkered down on hands and knees to take a closer look. Sure enough, just ahead, we could make out three sets of elephant legs and trunks, standing and lounging around. It was decided that Andrew and I would crawl up to the edge of the brush that they were standing behind to have a closer look. Leaving the trackers,

Corris, and my family behind, Andrew and I made our way very quietly to the edge of some really thick brush. Right behind this spot stood the three troublemakers. The wind was in our favor, so they did not have any clue we were around.

Time slows down to a crawl, literally, when one finds himself in such a situation. I don't have any idea how long we studied these elephants, but it seemed like hours. They were close; between 7 to 12 yards. There was a small gap in the brush, maybe a foot wide, that we could see through. Most of the time, however, it was not possible to see the entire elephant; they were just too close. Finally, one moved into that small opening. Andrew whispered in my ear to take this one. I lined up for what was going to be the perfect brain-side shot and was ready to squeeze the trigger, when the elephant suddenly turned his head away from me. Taking that shot was out of the equation. As he started to turn, I dropped immediately down to what I thought was a perfect heart shot and turned loose one of those 500 Safari Solids. At that point, all hell broke loose. The other two elephants turned and ran to our left. The elephant I had just shot ran a few steps to our right then turned to follow the other two. As he passed the opening in the brush, I had already reloaded and fired a quick shot. That shot was too far back, and I was sure it missed any vitals.

After the mayhem settled, we started tracking, which was easy. There was an extreme amount of blood along the trail and no doubt as to my first shot being a good one. Andrew took the lead, I was second, followed by Corris and one of the trackers. The girls brought up the rear along with the two other trackers, whose job it was to look after the girls should a problem arise. We all fell into our respective duties without a word being said.

The brush was thick, the trail meandering back and forth. Figuring a straight line, we hadn't gone more than 100 yards when Andrew spotted the legs and trunk of our elephant standing ahead of us. Andrew and I continued cautiously. Again, Corris and the other tracker fell in behind while Jaun, Mercedes, and the other two trackers took up the rear about 10 to 15 yards behind us.

Rifles were at the ready.

Andrew and I made it right up to the edge of another brush thicket. The elephant had backed himself up into a small opening, about 10 yards wide, on the other side. He was facing us. He was also waiting for us, knowing we would be closing in. There was no shot from a standing position. All we could see was the bottom of his front legs and his trunk swaying slightly back and forth. Just off to my right, flat upon the ground, was a small opening. I went down on my hands and knees in an attempt to reach that spot to get an upward shot up through that bantam breach. It was but a step away to my right.

As I was down on my hands and knees, the elephant caught my movement and charged full-out, hard as he could come. I took a quick snapshot from a very poor position upon my knees. The shot hit the elephant mid-body and had no effect at all. My poor balance resulted in my falling backward. I had reloaded, and as I continued to fall backward, I accidentally fired the second round into the sky. As I reloaded my third and final round, now lying on my back, the elephant hit the extremely thick brush in front of me, just to my left. At the charge, Andrew had backed up a couple of steps and was waiting for the elephant to come through the brush; he had no shot. Corris had stepped off to the left of the brush through which the elephant was about to crash. Corris, too, had no shot. Just a couple of steps in front of me, I was now staring up into the elephant's chest. Time seemed to stop. The beast was pushing through the brush in its attempt to get at me. I could not get the rifle to my shoulder, so I pushed the weapon with both hands upward toward its chest, firing my last and final round directly into him. At the shot, he turned sharply to my right, then straight ahead in an attempt to run but fell over on the spot.

I recovered, reloaded the 500 MDM then put in a couple of insurance shots. It was over at that point. I had been very lucky on several counts, as had the entire group. Had things worked any differently, it could have been disastrous for any one of us, and I was first in line. We experienced here a situation that is somewhat like "what comes first, the chicken or the egg?" Had that extremely heavy, thick brush not been in between me and the elephant, I would not have gotten off that third shot! Then again, had that brush not been there, I would not have been on my hands and knees to begin with and would have had ample opportunity to sort matters out. As it turned out, everything just happened to work perfectly. Had Andrew or Corris been able to shoot the elephant while in the brush in front of me, it very likely would have dropped straight down on top of me. Had I been able to fire a brain-side shot, the same thing could have happened. In the end, any small change of our circumstance might have resulted in a completely different outcome.

Michael McCourry and daughter, Mercedes, with bull elephant

In retrospect, we learned that the first round fired, which I thought should have been a heart shot, actually took out only one lung because of the angle. I could not see through the gap in the brush clearly. While this would have been a fatal shot, it was not fatal in the time frame we were working. The 500 MDM and the 500 Safari Solid proved to be an incredible stopper. With the very last shot while on my back upon the ground, the bullet had hit with such force, at a full 2400 fps impact; it did tremendous damage, causing a lot of trauma to the heart. So much so, this elephant wanted no more trouble at all and turned away. It had stopped the charge completely, taking all the malice out of this elephant's intent, and that is the purpose of a rifle and cartridge for dangerous big game. But one should always remember and take into account that no rifle or cartridge can do it separately. The bullet does the heavy lifting in these situations, and having a bullet that is properly designed is imperative to say the least. Any rifle and cartridge is enhanced by having specially designed bullets that are capable of completing the mission upon which you—in terms of hunting dangerous big game—stake your life! Had I chosen a lesser bullet, this situation would most likely have turned ugly.

Big game hunting can, indeed, be quite dangerous. One needs to be prepared for many scenarios in which folks might find themselves. The choice of tools is the first step in that direction and of paramount importance and, therefore, should always be taken quite seriously!

By the time we had the elephant situation sorted out, and a few photos taken, it was approaching dark. It was decided that we would leave the elephant overnight and return first thing in the morning to begin the process of recovery.

There was much discussion about the affair that night, along with much celebration. Not so much the celebration of taking the elephant, but rather a celebration of life itself—a celebration of survival, of adventure, and of being in such a wonderful place in time and history—a celebration of great experiences, which most folks only dream or read about. It became a time to reflect back on the day's activities, of what each individual experienced during those moments—a time to remember and store away those memories for the future—to realize how we had helped the local people, not only to remove a present danger from their lives, but, in fact, to provide much needed nourishment and protein for those villagers, which is almost always in short supply. One of the most asked questions that night was "Where were you?" when this event was taking place. Each person gave a detailed description of where they were and what action they had taken at that moment. Yes, there was much to ponder that evening back at the camp, and much to be thankful for!

One of the things I thought most about was "What could we have done differently?" As I considered all possibilities, there is no doubt that this elephant projected its intentions. He had backed himself up into the brush as far as he could. This gave him room to maneuver and evaluate our approach. He knew he was being trailed and was on very high alert. Knowing from what direction we would be coming, he had turned to face us. All these things were taken into account and put into perspective, but I had become complacent and overconfident. A serious mistake on my part. While I had not lost my respect for the elephant, knowing just how dangerous it can be, I was lax in my ability to handle the situation.

In the end, a lesson was well-learned; or should I say, relearned. For there wasn't anything one could change given that exact scenario. The only thing that I might have done differently is to allow the very first bullet that raked the single lung more time to do its job. While we did not rush into the situation, we did not allow time to lapse either. With dangerous game, we always wish to finish the dance we start in a quick and efficient manner; however, in some rare situations, one might allow *time* to work in one's favor. Regardless, it is what it is because the past cannot change present circumstances. Hopefully, we learn from those experiences.

The very next morning, while on our way to recover the elephant, I found myself in a battle with a Cape buffalo, which turned into a close range encounter of another kind. Ah, but that's a story for perhaps another day.

CHAPTER 33

AFRICA'S SECOND LARGEST OF THE SIX MOST DANGEROUS BIG GAME ANIMALS

Rhinoceros

The white rhinoceros is the larger of Africa's two species, topping the Toledo at 4000 to 6000 pounds. Although the animal's sense of hearing and smell are keen, its eyesight is poor, making it a relatively easy game to stalk from a downwind position. The name of this game is to approach this big boy slowly and very quietly while grazing. Whereas the smaller 2000 pound black rhino (presently protected by the South African government) is the more aggressive of the two species and can charge without provocation, the white rhino is comparatively docile—except when (like many animals) protecting its young or mating. As the white rhino mates throughout the year as opposed to a mating season, this should tell you something. No? Apparently an easier target than Africa's five other big game animals, the white rhinoceros is still *dangerous*. A charging 5000 pound bull rhino, with its two massive in-line horns aiming for an approximately 180-pound body . . . well, I think you get the picture.

Much like the hide of an elephant and Cape buffalo, the thick-skinned rhinoceros is best handled with a big bullet that will penetrate deeply and shatter bone. A large caliber and heavy cartridge are therefore the key to quickly dispatching a trophy white rhino bull. The .458 Winchester Magnum and the more powerful .458 Lott are powerful cartridges to deal with this thick-skinned mammal. Chambered in a .458 caliber bolt action rifle, this combination is a mighty tool. Keep firmly in mind that calibers and cartridges should be your first considerations in matching these elements to the game you seek. After that, the list of fine firearm companies from which you will select must (not should) be determined by how much gun you can comfortably handle (meaning mainly recoil) as well as how comfortable it is to hold, aim, and shoot. In other words, try (as best you can) before you buy.

You are about to embark on quite an adventure with consummate safari hunter Leon Munyan and his family.

THE ARNOLD SCHWARZENEGGER RHINO

By Leon Munyan

My wife, daughter and I had been on a two-week safari, traveling to various ranches and lodges in search of trophy species. As usual, we had some good luck and some bad luck. After hunting lion unsuccessfully for forty-two days on previous trips, I did manage to take a full-mane lion. We were on the second to the last day of the safari, and it was time to pursue rhino.

This hunt, with TAM Safaris, was for the final animal I needed to complete the Big 5 Slam of African species: lion, buffalo, elephant, leopard, and rhino. As with most very large game hunts, planning for this one had been ongoing for the past two years. The first choice I had to make when I started the process was to decide whether to *shoot* a white rhino or to *dart* a white rhino. To tell you the truth, I had never considered darting an animal. The decision was made easier because shooting a real trophy rhino cost in the range of $100,000, while TAM Safaris had made me an attractive offer to dart what they hoped would be the SCI #1 white rhino—and for far less cost. This particular rhino had never been darted because of the fear of harming it, thus losing a very expensive future trophy. My timing was perfect because the rhino had grown to a size they wanted, needing to have it on the ground to certify its measurements for a safari *shooting* hunt. TAM Safaris allowed me the opportunity to hunt and dart this rhino because I only use a handgun, and there were no handgun darted rhino in the record book. I had waited until the end of this hunt because I thought to myself *how hard could it be to take a rhino?* Little did I know!

We started scouting at very first light with the assistance of several trackers on horses and on foot, scouring the area for this particular rhino. It only took a few hours to locate the bull and start our stalk. That's when I discovered the major problem: rhino are not necessarily afraid of humans; they can run like sprinters and attack. It turns out that the average dart gun *rifle* is capable of tranquilizing a rhino at approximately 45 yards. I had found a gunsmith in Johannesburg who was willing to build me a *dart* handgun. When we tested the gun on the day before the hunt, we soon discovered that the dart's effectiveness was only good out to 18 yards! So much for an easy hunt.

We went into "full stalking" mode and actually came within 30 yards of the rhino before his younger partner, which had wandered downwind, scented us, both of them blowing out of the area. In spite of my preconceived notions, when you're hiding behind a small bush and a 5000 pound animal shakes the ground as it runs past, you know you are hunting Africa's "dangerous game." My wife, who had been along with us, decided, wisely, to keep a safer distance back (that is, 45–50 yards) on the next stalk!

Another surprise for me was the condition of these rhino. These were not the flabby rhino I have seen in various zoos around the world. These guys had to haul their bulk all day over rough terrain in order to sustain themselves; they were buffed out. I called them the "Arnold Schwarzenegger" of rhino.

Now that we knew this was "hunting," not just shooting, we decided the only way to get within 18 yards of this rhino was to wait in ambush. Rhino do not necessarily graze in a straight pattern. After two hours, the rhino finally lowered his guard and grazed leisurely. We tried several attempts to determine his pattern and set up an ambush. Finally, we got lucky (sort of) because it fed straight to us. Sounds like a perfect situation, unless you're the guy with the dart handgun sitting behind another small bush when the beast comes straight at you then veers around the bush at the last moment. As the rhino's shoulder cleared the bush at less than 5 yards away, I squeezed the trigger. POOF! That didn't sound good. I asked my PH (Professional Hunter), who was standing behind me with the cameraman, "Did I hit him?" The cameraman took his camera and focused it 3 feet in front of me to show the dart lying on the ground! (Thanks; great video!) We then discovered problem number two: The dart gun would not hold the pressure of the compressed air for more than a few minutes. So, now I would have to get within 18 yards of the rhino, undetected, and *then* load the gun—lovely! The next stalk didn't work either because I made too much of a commotion in trying to load that unfamiliar contraption.

Another two-hour wait, and there was only time for one more attempt before we had to quit for the evening. By now this otherwise docile animal was on full alert. After being chased for eight hours, he was as keen as a whitetail. We found the bull and made it to within 45 yards. As he was, indeed, wary at this point, he would not leave the open plains, so there was ostensibly no concealment. I thought we were through, but the PH came up with a game plan—not necessarily a plan I would've come up with, but when in Africa . . . .

Other than putting me at considerable risk, the plan was relatively simple: There was a very shallow drainage channel (about 1-foot deep) in front of us that had been eroded from the recent rains. This channel eventually wandered to within about 18 yards of the rhino. Our plan (the PH's plan!) was to lie flat in this channel and inch our way forward to the rhino. I had no idea what we would do or what would happen when we got there—other than get trampled—but there was no other choice. To compound matters, the rhino had seen us and was glaring in our direction, all the while, during the following scenario:

The PH got into the ditch and slithered along the muddy bottom by using only his feet to push himself forward (no hand or body motion to disturb the rhino). Too, I slithered into the ditch with my head at his feet. As I saw his feet move to push himself forward, I followed suit, never looking up to see where the rhino was [hopefully, not on top of us]. Forty-five minutes later, after slithering and sliding, the PH slowly motioned with his fingers for me to slide up beside him. I did, and he proceeded to explain that the rhino was 19 yards away, looking straight at us, with a bush in front of him. He explained that I would have to jump up and instantly shoot over the top of the bush; the rhino would whirl, and I would have a broadside or a rump shot, either one of which would get the job done, tranquilizing the animal.

When I jumped up, not knowing whether the rhino would charge or run, I discovered the bush was taller than we had anticipated. I could barely see the rhino's backbone above the bush. The rhino instantly whirled, and I had a split-second decision. My thought was that since the dart from this handgun would drop about 6 inches at 18 yards, I could aim at his backbone and the dart would zero in perfectly. NOT! With the naked eye, it appeared that the dart bounced off the top of the backbone and did not tranquilize the rhino. Fortunately, TAM Safaris had hired a professional videographer to accompany us on the hunt, so they could certify the rhino's size and measurements. We reviewed the videographer's footage and saw that the dart flew straight as a bullet, with no drop, and went through the rhino's backbone. About that time, the trackers who had been pursuing the rhino radioed us that the animal was semi-tranquilized and crashing through trees and bushes. This was a major problem because a rhino's horn is a growth of hair that detaches from the skull if it suffers enough blunt trauma! Hence, the rhino would not be offered up for another hunt.

We covered a one-mile trek to the rhino in a time that would make any Olympic runner smile! The rhino was stumbling around and crashing trees and the PH was shouting, "Shoot, shoot him anywhere you can hit him." After another dart, the rhino was finally down for the count! Then the excitement really began because the rhino had one and a half doses of tranquilizer in him, and they were worried that he would expire before they could administer the antidote (adrenaline).

We quickly took pictures and certified the SCI measurements on the horn size, and the attending veterinarian did shots, blood tests, eye drops, and inserted an identifier chip (up the butt; the only place a needle would penetrate!). As I was standing alone next to the rhino, with a hand on its shoulder, Peter Tam told me he had administered the antidote. Everyone else in the hunting party, including my wife (whew), was a hundred yards away at the hunting vehicle. I thought the rhino would take fifteen minutes to slowly wake up and stagger around for a while. Wrong! When the adrenaline hit his system, the rhino jumped up, whirled around and gave me a "you must die" glare. I screamed like a little girl and started running. Two problems: The nearest tree was more than 50 yards, and the Arnold Schwarzenegger of rhinos could run a helluva lot faster than I could! The ground was shaking as the rhino ran after me, and I swear I could feel his breath down my neck when Peter Tam (the PH of TAM Safaris) ran between the rhino and me. Peter, 30 years my junior, had assisted and guided many rhino hunts. From his experience, he, of course, knew that a rhino could easily run down a person, but that they could not maneuver in tight circles after being tranquilized. Peter had the red rag that we had placed over the rhino's eyes in order to keep him calm while we took pictures. So, while moving in tight circles, Peter waved that red rag in front of the rhino's face in order to distract it, taking the attention off of me. After a couple revolutions, the rhino wandered off into the brush. Somehow, my pants were still dry!

Leon Munyan and Darted Rhinoceros

Leon Munyan and his team quickly taking photos and specs of darted rhinoceros

The Tam family really knows how to throw a celebration party. They had invited fifty of their friends and neighboring landowners to the fest that evening. Wearing colorful costumes, the local natives put on an authentic African dance exhibition. The highlight was when I was put on a large "king's seat" and paraded around on the shoulders of the trackers. There were five huge barbecue pits for cooking more food than we could all possibly eat. After a day of adrenaline rushes and several Sundowner cocktails, that evening is still somewhat fuzzy. That celebration surpassed others put on for me by the natives in other countries, as when I shot a leopard, a lion, and a giant Lord Derby eland—and those were all *grand* parties.

What I thought would be a simple point-and-shoot hunt turned out to be one of the most memorable hunts of my life—and I have taken 113 species of animals in Africa with a handgun.

****

Let's meet Mark Hampton, consummate, six-continent safari rifle and handgun hunter, magazine writer (Handgun Hunter Magazine), and recipient of the Handgun Hunter of the Year Award. Mark also has a white rhino story for you.

WHITE RHINO

By Mark Hampton

After elephant, the white rhinoceros is the largest land mammal, with big males tipping the scales at over three tons. The rhino appears to be a relic from the past – prehistoric so to speak. It's an impressive-looking beast, massive in size–intimidating in appearance.

An impressive looking relic from the past

Why would anyone want to hunt rhino? Good question. The plain and simple truth—without the financial resource that hunting provides, the rhino would be doomed. In other words, hunting is conservation. Granted, this is a concept not clearly understood by a lot of folks, but it is the brutal reality. Rhinos have come under intense pressure from well-funded, well-organized poaching rings in recent years. Their horn is highly sought by some Orientals as an aphrodisiac. In Yemen, the horn is used to make dagger handles (jambiya) and highly regarded as a prized gift. In both cases, the demand for this horn commands such a hefty price that it's difficult to fathom. The poachers use advanced technology in the form of night vision optics along with other methods, including the use of helicopters to achieve their goal. Basically, it is war. If you have rhino on your property, you better have 24/7 patrols guarding these animals. The amount of revenue it takes to protect rhino—having to pay for all this protection—is substantial to say the least. It's a shame. So, the bottom line is that without hunting, conservation does not exist.

I was lucky to have hunted rhino back in 1985 when prices were somewhat sane and populations were healthy. The weather was hot in November as I loaded my Thompson/Center Contender .375 JDJ. My good friend J.D. Jones built this gun, and it is a serious hunting tool. A .375 is the minimum caliber for an animal of this size. Heavy, solid bullets capable of penetrating thick hide, strong muscles, and large bones are highly recommended. As with any other dangerous game, shot placement is crucial. For a number of days, we had been looking for rhino tracks on a huge concession (property area). It was no drive-out-and-shoot-one type of hunt. On the fourth day, we found tracks indicating two bulls. The trackers followed spoors (tracks/trails) for a few hours. Late in the afternoon we finally came upon the rhino. I loaded the .375 JDJ with 300-grain Hornady Solids. We worked our way to within 60 yards or so and tried to get set up for a shot. I was nervous, trying to steady the crosshairs of the Leupold scope. Every time the big bull would present a shot, the smaller of the two got in the way. Rhino do not have keen eyesight but do rely on their hearing and sense of smell. When a broadside shot eventually materialized, I squeezed off a round. The big slug penetrated its thick hide and passed through the lungs. As the rhino quickly ran out of sight, I wasn't sure I hit him! Heck, he hardly flinched at the shot. After a follow-up, we found the bull down within a few hundred yards. It was a hunt I'll never forget—and an experience to last a lifetime! This will be the only rhino I will ever hunt, and I am most grateful for having had the opportunity. I just hope this great creature will be around for a long time. Hopefully, with revenue generated from serious hunters, the conservation efforts will succeed. Only hunters and concerted conservation projects will save the rhino.

CHAPTER 34

AFRICA'S THIRD LARGEST OF THE SIX MOST DANGEROUS BIG GAME ANIMALS

Hippopotamus

Weighing in at 3300 to 4000 pounds for a male adult, the hippopotamus is a highly aggressive, unpredictable, semiaquatic sub-Saharan African powerhouse. Arguably accounting for more human deaths than Africa's five other most dangerous big game animals when pursued, this basically herbivorous mammal is certainly a formidable challenge. Meet the man who met that call: a world-renowned ballistics wizard, book author, editor, and accomplished safari hunter himself—J.D. Jones. J.D. is owner/operator, and president of SSK Industries—having invented JDJ cartridges used worldwide.

HIPPO

By J.D. JONES

Just take a look at him. In the water, mainly you just see a huge head often with great jaws open as if to yawn. On land—a huge, short legged, slick skinned stupid looking guy almost too big to move.

WRONG on both counts. In the water he isn't a ballerina. He is more of a fast pocket battleship when aroused. His cannons are those huge jaws and teeth, capable of ripping a modern boat to pieces. His armor is the water that protects him until he is right upon you. On land he is faster than any human, and although usually slow to anger, when angry, a terrible opponent. His speed, size (second only to an elephant), determination, those jaws and huge teeth turn him into one of the most dangerous animals on earth. He can take a hell of a lot of lead and keep on coming!

Think for a moment. There are many survivors of elephant, Cape buffalo and rhino attacks who tell terrible tales of injuries suffered in those encounters. I've never heard of a human survivor of a hippo attack. That is because there aren't any survivors. Professional hunters give him a great deal of respect. Certainly, as an animal to be hunted, he isn't tough. There is no "walk a hundred miles" for a hippo as there is a bull elephant. Nope—no close contact in the heavy bush so often encountered in hunting Cape buff either. He isn't spooky. That is because he is BOSS of his domain. Not afraid of anything. The lakes and streams are his habitat. He spends most of his days in the water feeding and loafing with his buddies and lady friends; simply a nice easygoing life. He seems to like fighting with his mates over the affections of the ladies as demonstrated by all his scars. He likes to get out on dry land and, at night, feed on whatever vegetation is handy. This makes hunting him a relatively easy job.

Depending on a lot of things, the cartridge for the job may need to be a laser or cannon. If a laser, it needs a lot of penetration and placed with precision. If a cannon, it must also be placed with precision in the right spot to put him down right *now*. Normally, a brain shot is most desirable.

Is hunting him a challenge? Sometimes it's easy, sometimes not—just like any other type of hunting. Like last week my buddy Lou dropped a deer that scored 187 within 10 minutes of the start of his hunt. Other times it may well be quite dangerous and a time-consuming pursuit on water or dry land.

I've been fortunate enough to have had a few encounters with hippo, and hopefully you will enjoy reading about some of them.

When the TCR (**T**hompson **C**enter **R**ifle) 83 was still a bit on the experimental side, Kenny French asked if I would like to take one along to Africa and give it a workout. Normally, I'm a handgun hunter, but that was too good an opportunity to miss. The TCR was a single shot, break-open barrel with a double-set trigger. That means two triggers. The rear trigger is a normal trigger until the front trigger is pulled to "set" the rear trigger, which is usually adjusted to be around 12–16 ounce let off. It allows for really accurate offhand shooting. I chose a 24 inch barreled lightweight .30-06. Ammo was loaded with 180-grain Nosler Partitions and 220-grain Hornady round nose "solids"—full metal jacketed bullets. Kinda light for Africa?? Sure, for some things, but the 180-grain bullet made the .30-06's reputation, and a 220 Solid is a marvelous penetrator.

The first day was to be a multiple hippo day. Finding and obtaining a boat and operator was tough. The boat was to be solely operated by the owner's son who was about 14 years old and didn't know squat about running a boat. If possible, the shooting was to be done from land so as to have a stable shooting position. In the beginning, the hippos didn't care a bit about those funny two legged creatures walking around on the bank; after all, they usually scattered when a hippo got out of the water.

Hippo were plentiful. There were around twenty in a small local area of a river. They were simply feeding, relaxing, and talking to each other. Close by, several were submerging and rising to breathe. This was a slow movement with a slight hesitation between going up and going down. I sat on the riverbank with an empty rifle and practiced sighting on several until I got the cadence. Swing on him, align the crosshairs, and pull the less than a pound trigger. Practice makes perfect, so I finally loaded the .30-06 and waited. He broke water right in front of the sight, the crosshairs aligned on the correct spot on the side of his head for a brain shot, and I fired. Quite a large water spout rose on the far side of the hippo. Both the boy and the native trackers put up a howl that I missed. The PH (Professional Hunter) seemed to think it was a miss, too. Actually, no one thought the 30-06 was much of a hippo gun and that I should really be using the PH's .458.

I assured them the hippo was dead. They assured me the 06 couldn't penetrate the head of the hippo and exit. I assured them it did—I saw it! No one seemed to want me to shoot another with the little rifle. Okay, now it was a "wait and see game" as the usual wait allows the gasses in the hippo to accumulate and cause the body to float so it can be recovered using the boat. Time varies depending on hippo and water temperature. Full belly and warm water is fastest. This water was cold. No one seemed happy about the situation, so I decided to take a walk.

While I was standing on the bank looking at glass-calm water, the head of a large Python slowly broke water 15 feet in front of me; its head and about six inches of neck came up—rotated left—then right, and submerged with scarcely a ripple while I thought . . . did I really see that?

I took my SSK 45-70 Contender pistol—loaded with a 500-grain Hornady Solid (velocity of 1500 fps)—from its 14 inch barrel with me on my walk. Walking back up the riverbank, another hippo broke water in a perfect spot, maybe 15 yards from me. He was facing directly away from me, and I hit him in the back of the head with one of those great 500 grainers. That brought everyone running.

"What in the bloody hell have you done now???"

"Shot another hippo," I answered.

"You can't kill a hippo with a bloody 45-70 pistol," came the next remark.

Well, without dwelling on how unhappy the PH and the "boys" were with me, we went back to the scene of the first supposed *screw-up* and waited. And waited. And I listened to the grumbling. Suddenly, their mood changed when the wet gray back of the first hippo broke water. WOW—everybody was happy. I was no longer a bloody dirty bastard!

"WE EAT TONIGHT!" was everyone's jubilant refrain.

Then the work begins. I was advised that if other hippos got pissed about the death of their buddy and presented a problem, to shoot into the water when they submerged and that would drive them off. Good plan, but the kid with the boat had been told by his dad, "No guns in the boat." Okay, the boat was small—only room for two. I said I'd go rope the body, and if the other hippos come, I'd thrash hell out of the water with a paddle, imitating gunshots.

The rest of the hippo group didn't like these happenings at all. Lots of roaring, demonstrations, and drama ensued. It was a very small motor, and slow-going towing the beast's body. Actually, I wasn't scared—I was terrified but found the show they put on intensely interesting while wondering if I was going to suddenly die. Then it happened again when the hippo that couldn't be killed with a 45-70 floated to the surface, too. We finally got the job finished after dark.

Another time in Zimbabwe, shortly after the war, my PH was going to take me to a friend's farm at night to shoot a hippo on land. Lights were still on in the house as we passed it. The PH had not intended to stop. I told him I would be more comfortable if we stopped to let him know we were going to shoot a hippo on his property. While having tea and cookies, our host advised it wouldn't be a good idea to hunt that night as a squad of soldiers was guarding the bridge a couple hundred yards from the house and about 400 from the field the hippo hunt was going to take place. He said they had a heavy machine gun set up, were drinking, and if a shot was fired, they were sure to open up in that direction with everything they had. This ranks high in the number of close calls I've had hunting.

While hunting with a gentleman [I'll call Doc] on his farm near Krueger Park, he asked if I would like to take a hippo, no charge. He explained he farmed tomatoes, and every night the hippo raided the tomatoes, eating/ruining a hectare or so. As this was a cash crop for him, he could ill afford it. It was the dark of the moon. The plan was to wait until around midnight then walk into the field and up close to the hippo—on one side or the other. I loaded the 375 JDJ SSK Contender, cocked it, and put it on safe. Not something I recommend doing except in such an occasion as this. A hundred yards or so into the field we could hear it and were soon able to make out a huge black blob. Plan A: get close and broadside. When Doc saw me raise the gun, he would turn on the flashlight, and I would quickly put a 300-grain Solid through her brain. The hungry hippo contentedly munched tomatoes and paid no attention to us. At about 25 feet I got ready to shoot. Doc lit her up! She was pregnant; her belly just about dragging on the ground. She paid no attention to us. I looked at Doc. He looked at me—hesitated—whispered, "Screw the tomatoes. Let her have them."

Probably one of my best hunts ever.

CHAPTER 35

AFRICA'S FOURTH LARGEST OF THE SIX MOST DANGEROUS BIG GAME ANIMALS

Cape buffalo

Of Africa's six most dangerous big game animals, the Cape buffalo is certainly among them, arguably the most dangerous . . . *arguably* being the operative word. The five men featured throughout have successfully hunted and dispatched the Cape buffalo. I've reached a conclusion (as you may well) that all six of Africa's most dangerous big game animals are quite lethal in their own right. As to which animal is *the* most dangerous, I believe is a matter of perspective, based predominantly on one's experience. Wait till we shift the scene from Africa to Australia. Surprises may surely await you.

Anyhow, I know of instances where the hunter instantly became the hunted. Picture an average size 1000-plus pound Cape buffalo, with its helmet-like horn structure formed above its forehead, suddenly charging you. Game over if not fully prepared. Imagine someone hunting this bull on foot instead of being protected within the body of a vehicle. This could prove to be more than a bit challenging. A female buffalo (cow) could easily stomp a body to death upon the ground.

The .375 Remington Ultra Magnum (aka RUM) is a suitable medium-bore rifle caliber to handle such smaller, lighter female beasts as is the widely used .375 H&H Magnum (Holland & Holland) caliber. But a big bull (male) can weigh between 1400 and 1750 pounds, reach heights of 6 feet and lengths of 5½ feet. In Africa, the Cape buffalo is often referred to as Black Death and vies with the hippo for the record of killing more big game hunters than any other animal. As Police Chief Martin Brody said to seafaring Captain Quint in the movie *Jaws*, "You're gonna need a bigger boat." When hunting Cape buffalo, you just *might* need a bigger bore. Calibers and cartridges become very important elements when hunting the most dangerous six big game animals.

The .416 Ruger M77 Hawkeye "Alaskan" bolt action rifle is a light (7 lb. 15 oz.), compact package in a big-bore alternative. Chambered with either a 400-grain DGS (Dangerous Game Solid) or DGX (Dangerous Game eXpanding) bullet, this combo could be your ticket; three cartridge magazine; one round in the chamber; 20-inch barrel. Hornady's 416 Ruger cartridges are good for CXP4 game; meaning, the four thick-skinned big game animals: elephant, rhinoceros, hippopotamus, and Cape buffalo. CXP is a rating system of hunting cartridges, which stands for **C**ontrolled e**X**pansion **P**erformance. Stopping power (also called knockdown power)—meaning, deep, penetrating bullet expansion—is the name of the game. You want a cartridge/bullet that will *stop* or at the very least *turn* a dangerous big game animal in its tracks.

The .416 Ruger No. 1-H Tropical bolt action rifle is also chambered for the 416 Ruger cartridge. Bolt action rifles are considered the conventional big game gun; double barrel rifles are referred to as the more traditional type.

Now, imagine pursuing Cape buffalo with a handgun—a muzzleloader pistol, no less. A quick reminder that you met ballistics wizard in the previous chapter referencing hippo.

Cape buffalo

By J.D. Jones

As a little kid growing up on a farm, I learned the hazards of most everything connected with farm life. At the age of three, I was old enough to wander the barnyard alone and get into trouble—trouble with geese and turkeys. Those geese were almost as tall as I and could run a lot faster. Ever been bitten by a goose? They leave a hell of a mark and bruise. Turkeys peck, and once in a while try to spur you. Goose bites and being spurred by a turkey hurt. One of my chores was gathering eggs. Some of those old biddy hens didn't like that, but at least I could hold my own with them. Constantly being goose bitten and turkey pecked, my young mind figured out that I needed a weapon to even things up and maybe tip the scale in my favor. It worked, and I never forgot that lesson.

Pigs are mean; they bite. Stay away from them. Sheep, especially rams, butt hard. In later years, I had to work with them, and I got knocked on my ass a lot. Bulls; stay away from them as you may not get up if a big one nails you. Cows are dumb as rocks but big. They can, by accident, squash you against something solid. And they can kick! I saw one kick my uncle in the right thigh and knock his backside through the side of the barn. Horses kick, bite, and buck. They got me all three ways. Never liked or trusted them and haven't changed my mind to this day. Remember: WEAPON.

After Dad died when I was about twelve, we quit actual farming and rented out the land. One guy put some young bulls into the pasture around the house when I was fifteen or sixteen. They were mean. I convinced my mom to stay away from them. I had an old Savage .22 pump, and while groundhog hunting, three of the bulls decided they wanted to play. Suited me fine. A few .22s (as one shot wouldn't do it) into the base of their horns taught those three a little respect. A .22 is a fine weapon. Before I got around to teaching the rest, several of them got out of the pasture. OK—I opened the gate by the creek, and all but one returned peacefully. The bad guy went in the other direction. I tried to run him into the barnyard and through a gate that my mother had opened. That didn't suit him, and he charged at me. I ducked, but his horn took off the top of my thumb knuckle before hitting my bicep. Spinning to come at me again, he slipped and fell on the oil-top road, giving me time to collect myself. A road crew had been clearing, and I found a club about the size of the business end of a baseball bat. I grabbed it. WEAPON—not scared—pissed. Too dumb to be scared, I ran at him. He headed into the barnyard but wouldn't go through the gate. He came at me fast. I stepped aside and let him have it with the club, just below the eyes. If you have ever shot a running rabbit and seen it roll, that's just what the bull did, and it was a hell of a lot more satisfying than rolling a rabbit. I could still feel that mighty satisfying jolt all through my arms and shoulders. He got up but was in bad shape. I went for the .22, but Mom talked me out of it, thinking we would have to pay for the bull. Didn't matter. He was dead in a few minutes anyway. His owner screamed and yelled threats at Mom. Being kind of pumped up anyway, I told him to get out. A skinny kid of about sixteen was no match against a big older guy; no match at all . . . except I had that bloody club in hand. WEAPON—always remember.

I've always liked to hunt, and the bigger the animal the better. I like rifles, but on my 13th birthday I got a 6-inch Hi Standard Sport King pistol along with a brick of ammo and a warning that I better learn how to shoot it and not get into trouble with it. I guess the club was my first puppy love, but the Sport King was the real thing. Pistols have been a lifelong love affair that I'm not yet willing to end. The guns got bigger, and the animals did, too.

My first really big bugger was a Bison bull taken at Custer State Park in the Black Hills of southwestern South Dakota. Each year they have offered hunts for surplus animals. I got lucky and drew a permit. First day a Ranger took us for a ride and spotted an old herd bull. He said we would look for him the next day. Auto Mags were pretty popular, and Lee Jurras made the finest custom rigs in existence. Lee met me in Custer and brought a fancy .44 loaded with 265 Hornady soft points. He and I were always able to use each other's sight settings, so after trying the trigger a few times, I was ready to go. But—no bull. Apparently, a fight had occurred and the old guy lost. Found him a couple miles away. Hurt and mad. Caught up with him in a couple more miles and got to within 50 yards, broadside. Hit him with a center double-lung shot. He ran. Hit him twice more in the same spot—later found all three shots could be covered with the palm of my hand. He painted the snow with red, six feet on both sides, blowing out a chunk of lung about 10 inches long, another about 6 inches before he turned in a half circle to come back; not charging. Broadside to me, I shoulder–spined him for an instant crash. Found he had a hole in his side about 6 inches in diameter as a result of his fight. The Ranger claimed he was 2200 pounds, and as there was no scale, I accepted it. It was a real lesson on how much fatal damage a big animal can take and keep on going. I learned a lot from that rodeo, walking the blood trail and checking bullet damage. Use a good weapon; there is no such thing as 'too much gun' unless you cannot handle it. Animals don't die until the brain runs out of oxygen. It sometimes takes a while.

Next came the Big Bad Cape buffalo. Hell—this guy's reputation alone scares me. No doubt he can be a really bad nightmare under the wrong circumstances. That includes it being hurt in some way or just a coincidental meeting with a human. Under those circumstances, Elgin Gates (world-renowned sporting hunter) got treed, and the bad guy wouldn't leave. Elgin was carrying a 4-inch Smith & Wesson .357 Magnum revolver with the right bullet, braining him with a single shot. WEAPON— does you no good if you don't have it on you or the skill and mental ability to use it correctly. In my limited experience with these animals, they like to travel in herds and are really spooky. In herds, there are lots of eyes and noses to find you. If you're found, all that will remain, ostensibly, is a dust cloud upon the group leaving. It often makes sense to hunt 'Dugga Boys,' old bulls kicked out of the herd by younger, stronger bulls. Often found in twos or threes, they are easier to hunt but usually take a lot of tracking and walking. I watched Mark Hampton (consummate handgun hunter) drop one with a shoulder shot, using a .375 JDJ and incorporating 300-grain solids.

The bull's buddy was startled at the shot and ran a few steps, realized his buddy was down and came back to him. I expected him to attack the downed animal, but he just stood there looking at it. The PH (Professional Hunter) urged me to shoot him, but I didn't. It would have been like shooting a bull in a pen. It didn't want to leave. Again, the PH urged me to shoot. Instead, I hit it with a few rocks, and he left peacefully. After several days of tracking, I wished I had shot that bull. However, I would have missed a neat experience. I feel this was simply accidental. Others credit the bull for setting up an ambush. Either the bull we were tracking or another stuck his head out of some foliage directly in front of me at maybe 15 to 20 yards. His left horn looked good; most of the right wasn't visible. At 20 yards facing me, literally anything could happen and happen quickly. I shot him in the forehead with a .375 JDJ SSK 12-inch barreled Thompson/Center Contender loaded with a 300-grain Hornady Solid. Instant death. No drama at all. Wound examination revealed that the bullet entered its head, traveled down the neck, breaking a few vertebrae on the way. We found the bullet slightly beat up inside the heart but probably still usable (for reloading). The right horn was badly blunted, which makes the story even better. The skull with the bullet hole slightly off center resides in my office to this day . . . reminding me of WEAPON.

In retrospect, under the circumstance cited, I feel if that buff had reacted instantly, as I had, and came at me straightaway, it would be highly likely I could have been dead in the dust instead of him. They can move very, very fast, and a brain shot in close-up quarters following a surprise attack would prove quite difficult. I guess long-range shots at buff in the open do happen, but I've never had that opportunity. I feel there is a heck of a lot of hype about hunting dangerous game. After having done a bit of it, I think some individuals feel the need to justify the death of the animal as a "him or me" type situation and *"the reason why I shot him."* I recall reading one incident where our hero killed his charging Cape buff at a range of 200 yards with his new whizz-bang rifle. Frankly, if hunting dangerous game was as dangerous as it is portrayed, and an even-steven situation existed, damn few guys would be risking their lives doing it. Remember—WEAPON makes us the big bad guy. Nobody goes after game without a weapon of some sort or another. Don't get me wrong—dangerous animals can certainly kill you, but generally if you really screw things up in the first place.

My last encounter with a Cape buffalo was while hunting with Doc (mentioned earlier in my hippo article). I was using a Thompson/Center Scout muzzleloader pistol. Actually, we were not hunting buff. It was dark. Doc was behind-beside me. I saw a black blob right in front of me. I held the trigger back and cocked the gun, not making any *'clicks'*. Doc lit it up. Standing at no more than 15 feet in front of me was a huge Cape bull contentedly chewing his cud, perfectly posed for a back-of-the-ear into-the-brain shot. Thoughts raced through my mind: *Hey, kinda neat. Bet no one has done this in a long time with a single-shot muzzle-loading pistol. $7,500 trophy fee or downstroke on a new Porsche? This is too easy—any ten-year-old kid could* *make this shot.* As it turned out, the Porsche was a blue convertible with white leather interior. Jane and I enjoyed it for many years.

****

Later, in another story and on another continent (Australia), J.D. Jones may surprise you with another bad-to-the-bone member of the buffalo family that dwarfs the Cape buffalo in terms of size, weight, and deadliness. Still, there is no question that Africa's Cape buffalo is a formidable adversary.

CHAPTER 36

AFRICA'S FIFTH LARGEST OF THE SIX MOST DANGEROUS BIG GAME BIG GAME ANIMALS

Lion

Again, arguably, some consider the lion Africa's most dangerous big game animal. Place it where you will on your most dangerous list. Keep in mind that it takes a pack of lions to tackle and kill a Cape buffalo. Nevertheless, picture 330 to 400-plus pounds charging toward *you* at 35 to 40 miles per hour; that's around the average weight and speed of a male lion. The largest on record topped the Toledo at over 800 pounds.

Let's consider a cartridge that is specifically designed for lion hunting. Namely, the A-Square Lion Load for .33 and larger calibers; that is, bullets designed for big cats. As a lion is all muscle, deep penetration and expansion is *all* important. Therefore, a 400-grain bullet in a .416 caliber (as mentioned for Cape buffalo) would be a wise selection. Bullet placement (your point of aim) should be placed on a par with caliber selection. Going up in caliber to compensate for poor bullet placement is not the way to determine decision making. Realize, too, that the issue of a larger, heavier caliber than a .416 is compounded by extreme recoil. If you're not confident in delivering deadly bullet placement, or can't handle a heavier weight weapon and excessive recoil, don't put yourself in harm's way by hunting dangerous big game animals. Know your limitations.

Taking a step back from a big-bore caliber cannon, consider the medium-bore Browning BAR (**B**rowning **A**utomatic **R**ifle) Mark II Safari grade rifle for hunting lion. It is a superior autoloader (semiautomatic) that is chambered to handle the more powerful magnum loads. Virtually all other autoloaders are *not* chambered for those more powerful magnum class cartridges. You want a rifle and cartridge that are capable of stopping or turning a charging, dangerous big game member of the cat class. Take a pass on the .300 Winchester Magnum caliber, and select the .338 Winchester Magnum caliber. The Browning BAR Mark II Safari grade .338 Winchester Magnum is up to the task. With a 24-inch barrel and weighing in at only 8 pounds, 6 ounces, it is possibly the closest precision weapon in terms of versatility. Let's examine why.

First off, we've just eliminated all other action-type rifles from the decision-making process: single-shot bolt actions, contemporary repeating bolt actions, traditional double rifles (meaning two barrels as the side-by-side or the over-and-under styles), pump, and lever-actions. As we are discussing Africa's six most dangerous big game animals, firepower coupled to stopping power should be foremost in your mind. Let's break these rifle types/styles down one by one.

A single-shot rifle gives you very little time to reload for a follow-up shot. It is definitely not a wise choice for hunting the most dangerous six. Repeating-type bolt action rifles are slower to re-chamber a second round than those mentioned. Although double-barreled rifles are obviously faster in getting off a second round, they are not as accurate because of their configuration. Additionally, they are extremely if not prohibitively expensive. Hardly the point when it comes to saving your life but still worth mentioning when weighed against the downside of diminished accuracy. Finally, both the pump and lever-action rifles for hunting Africa's dangerous big game animals can be ruled out because of continued debate concerning their reliability, especially in terms of weather conditions.

The autoloader, too, may have fallen into this category some years ago. Today, however, one weapon in particular has received safari-grade status and kudos concerning reliability and firepower coupled to stopping power by utilizing powerful magnum cartridges. Seriously consider the Browning Mark II Safari grade hunting rifle in .338 Winchester Magnum caliber.

Before we continue, I'd be remiss if I didn't point out one of the most important features often overlooked by hunters selecting a rifle, any rifle, in fact; especially, a hunting rifle for dangerous big game. And that is the firearm's stock. Is the rifle or your arms too long or too short for a comfortable fit? Can the issue be remedied with spacers added forward of the butt plate or recoil pad? Is the comb (the top section of the stock) too high or too low for your cheek? Is it adjustable? Or can it be altered via a kit, or tooled (shaved) to perfection? If not, you would want to select another gun. You could own one of the finest rifles in the world, but if it doesn't fit your shoulder, arms, and cheek comfortably, the weapon is, therefore, useless to you. The firearm would be better off in a collection rather than risk taking it afield.

Are you ready to meet the handgun lion king?

HANDGUN LION

By Larry C. Rogers, M.D.

Just repeating the title aloud gets most anyone's attention. Thinking about hunting a lion with a handgun, no less, sends chills up the spine. When I was a little boy, I dreamed of going to Africa to just *see* a lion. Maybe fate was listening, but not so carefully.

Years ago I was the first gunshot victim of the West Virginia deer season. The shooter said I looked just like a buck (an orange one?). He had shot across my chest, missing my heart by two inches, and destroying half of my left bicep. After that event, a monetary settlement was reached. I thought I'd better do something that I could not have done otherwise. So, initially, I went hunting for lion, Cape buffalo, and leopard —three of Africa's most dangerous big game animals; the others being elephant and rhinoceros.

I take my hunting seriously. I prepared for months, selecting clothes, equipment, guns, and developing specialized loads. Guns and load considerations are, of course, of paramount importance and the fun part of planning. But what guns? Well, it was going to be a handgun as I haven't hunted with a rifle since 1978. I'm 100% handgun hooked.

Lions are big and nasty. I needed a big, nasty gun. My friend, J.D. Jones of SSK Industries, has been building my handguns for many years. I had some reasonably large calibers in mind that initially satisfied expectations as well as past hunts, but I needed more gun. I had two weapons in mind.

First, a Remington XP-100 single shot in .375/.284; that is, a .284 Winchester case necked up to .375 caliber. It uses the same bullets as the .375 H&H rifles, shooting at a muzzle velocity of 2400 fps. It's good for big animals, but it is a bolt action and is therefore difficult to use for fast follow-up shots. Most every big game hunter knows that you can't kill a lion with one shot.

Choice two seemed a little more practical. It was a single shot Thompson Encore in .416 Taylor. That's an old African caliber made by necking a full-length .458 Winchester Magnum to .416. It shoots 350–400 gr. (grains) bullets from 1900 to 2200 fps out of a 12-inch barrel. Now, that's a handful! J.D. helped tame the monster by putting a large Fish-Gill muzzle brake on it. It's still a handful, kicks like two mules, but is manageable with a *lot* of practice. I like big. This is my big gun.

What bullet? Most .416 bullets are heavy and minimally expanding, made by Nosler, Hornady, Swift, and Woodleigh. Their bullets have taken lions, but I needed an edge with my handgun. I wanted something big enough to get into a lion's body, but fragile enough to ruin its insides. Sort of like a big Nosler Ballistic Tip or Accubond.

I stumbled on a custom bullet maker in New Jersey, Northern Precision. I told them what I wanted. After thinking it out, I got a 350 gr. bullet that was bonded in the lower two-thirds like a Nosler Partition, but had a soft, large nose that would expand rapidly after entering the lion. I shot a few groundhogs with the bullet and even a cinder block. It was accurate and had violent expansion.

My arrival in Africa had everyone buzzing. My friend and I were the PH's (Professional Hunter) first handgun hunters. I was after three dangerous game: lion, Cape buffalo, and leopard. The leopard was taken with bait on the second night with my .375/.284 XP and a 220 gr. Hornady FP. My PH was concerned about the lion.

We took the .416 on a warm-up trial before the lion hunt. I took a #3 handgun roan (antelope) with one shot at 120 yards. The PH looked a little more relaxed.

The day of the lion hunt was like no other day of hunting I had ever experienced. I was going to hunt an animal that could kill me. A little fear. A lot of excitement.

What a day!

This was to be a spot-and-stalk hunt. Soon after we started out, about a half mile away, we saw the lion. It ran from us after the spotting. A little later we jumped him off a warthog kill. The lion growled as he ran. He wasn't happy.

We jumped him several more times. He growled and ran each time. We trailed him into a dry river bottom with steep sides. There were five of us in single file: the PH, me, two backup rifle guys, and a cameraman. The PH still wasn't so sure about my performance; hence, the backup guys.

The tracks led up the steep bank and headed in the direction from where we had come. There was an area in the sand where the lion had bedded on the bank and watched us pass. The cameraman had about lost it, since lions are known to jump on the last man in line in a situation like that!

We kept tracking and jumping him. It was getting hot; about 95 degrees Fahrenheit. I kept wondering why the lion wasn't running any farther away. Later, my PH told me lions do not dissipate heat by panting like a cat, but rather by lying down and losing heat through the pads of its paws. We were making him run in the hot sand, and he was getting irritated.

We came to a brushy area with many small shrub-like bushes about three feet tall. I guess the lion had all he could take. He jumped up, let out a gigantic roar, and started running at us. The scattered shrubs were preventing him from running in a straight line. He was weaving back and forth between them.

My 2–7X Simmons scope was on 2X. Much past practice allowed me to track him reasonably well. That memory is embedded in my mind. He came to a large bush and had to turn broadside to get around it. That exposed his shoulder to me. The crosshairs were fixed. I fired. He turned in a tight circle several times, growling even louder. Wow! What a rush! He dropped and lay still. We slowly worked our way to him and confirmed that he was dead. The distance? 23 yards! Double wow!!

Larry Rogers with his male lion.

What a lion: 475 pounds; 9 feet 9 inches long; 4-inch canine teeth. Ultimately, he scored #4 SCI (Safari Club International) Handgun Lion. While it was being attended to, my PH turned to the two rifle guys and told them he wouldn't need them anymore. The next day my PH and I took a charging 40-inch Cape buffalo (outside horn spread) at 32 yards with a single shot.

Impressive size lion's paw

The Northern Precision bullet did what I wanted. It entered the center of the shoulder, destroyed the lungs and top of the heart, and stayed inside the lion. Damage was massive and impressive.

That was beyond exciting, but I wanted more. And I did get what I wanted. All told: Cape buffalo, leopard, rhinoceros, elephant, hippopotamus, crocodile—all with handguns. I still had the desire to get another lion, but with a little bit more of a challenge—if that was possible. My big male lion scored #4 SCI Handgun, so I didn't need to try to best that. I just wanted additional excitement. My PH for hippo and croc had access to a lot of land in famed lion country; that is, the Kalahari Desert of northern South Africa. He recommended chasing a lioness. They were less expensive to hunt and, actually, a little more hyper than their male counterparts.

To make this more of a challenge, I would use my 7½-inch Freedom Arms .475 Linebaugh revolver. Not enough power, you're thinking? It worked on my 5000 pound rhino. A 350 pound lion should not be a big problem . . . I hoped.

I wanted no scopes on my guns this time around. I had a little trouble keeping my moving male lion in the 2X scope last time. My FA .475 wears open Express sights: a rear V, and a front fiber optic bead. I used it the entire spring before my hunt on local groundhogs. That got a rise out of the country boys around my town, but I already had a reputation of being a little radical in my hunting.

The bullet? Again, I wanted something that would open up, create a lot of penetration and damage. That's a tall order for a revolver bullet. But I'm a constant bullet tester, and I already had the answer. Most hunters know that Barnes Bullets Inc. makes the great X Bullet for rifles, but not too many of those hunters realize that Barnes makes them for handguns, too. It is a solid, one piece, all-copper bullet that has grooves cut into the sides of its nose to reduce pressure and aid in expansion and accuracy. It has a large hollow cavity and weighs 275 grains. I put it over 30.0 gr. WW (powder) 296 for around 1400 fps. It creates massive holes in groundhogs and deer. Case in point: Last year, I dropped a black bear—with which I had issues—on the spot at 10 feet!

The Kalahari is a special place. There are very few people. Trees are rare. Even the bushes present are not plentiful. And, of course, sand is everywhere. It is heavy sand that doesn't create massive amounts of dust.

Desert days are predictable. In July (winter in Africa) it is in the high 30s during the morning and high 70s throughout most of the day. Clouds are rare. The sun is bright and burns you easily. The day I hunted proved no different.

Since the country is so vast, the way lions are hunted is by driving around and looking for tracks in the sandy soil. When a fresh track is found, your legs do the hunting.

And away we went. Two trackers rode on seats upon the hood of the Land Cruiser. They found a track. They led the way. My PH and a local PH were next. I followed them. Another PH followed me with a .505 Gibbs, because the "crazy client" was using a revolver! While the sand is cool in early morning, the cats wander around looking for food. We were tracking a male and female traveling together. We came upon the carcass of a very large rabbit (yes, they're in Africa) they'd killed and eaten recently.

A little later the two separated, and we stayed on the female's track. She was wandering erratically. As the sand heats up, lions look for shady places to rest. They don't like hot feet.

Finally, one of the trackers spotted her under a rare 10-foot shady tree. She was resting and not fully awake, allowing us to get close. Both the PH and the lioness decided 22 yards was close enough. Good idea! She was on full alert. Our movement caught her attention.

I'd been told early on to put the shot at either the back edge of, or directly into, her shoulder. I did. She growled and dropped. A few seconds later she got up! I put another Barnes X in her shoulder. She dropped again. We could see her breathing, but she was lying quite still. My PH said wait and let her die. No argument from me.

About thirty seconds later, she got up and started running! As she turned to get by the tree, I put another X in her shoulder. She ran. We saw the brush shake but couldn't see her. We all got shoulder to shoulder and S-L-O-W-L-Y walked toward the bush that had shook. A snail's pace of movement, and we finally found her—dead.

Did screwed up shots cause this ruckus? No, they hadn't. The three shots were all placed in the shoulder. Two had completely penetrated. One was recovered just off-shoulder, expanded with 100% weight retention.

Larry Rogers with a lioness taken with Freedom Arms .475 Linebaugh revolver

This was a very big lioness, approximated at around 325 pounds by the PHs. Her paws and claws were very impressive. She had a strong will to survive all those well-placed shots from the big revolver.

Lion hunting is quite habit-forming. Am I finished? Probably. Well . . . maybe.

CHAPTER 37

AFRICA'S SMALLEST OF THE SIX MOST DANGEROUS BIG GAME ANIMALS

Leopard

The next and last animal on the list of Africa's six most dangerous big game animals is the leopard. But don't be fooled that just because it's the smallest of the six that it's the easiest or least dangerous to hunt. *Au contraire.*

Though considerably smaller in size and weighing significantly less than Africa's six most dangerous big game animals, make no mistake that the leopard is in any way a pushover pussycat. A leopard's eyes and ears miss nothing; its graceful body is built for speed and power. At 130 pounds on average, these cats are stealth personified, seemingly shrinking within their own skin when stalking prey—suddenly pouncing upon their meal of the moment. They are powerful climbers, quite capable of carrying off a freshly killed impala or duiker (small- to medium-sized antelope) high into the treetops for an uninterrupted repast from the local competition; namely, hyenas.

Leopards are secretive, elusive, highly intelligent creatures, so hunting them with hounds is often the name of the game. Hold firmly in mind that a charging leopard presents a smaller target than the other five of Africa's most dangerous game. I have seen a wounded leopard maul a hunter badly before the PH (Professional Hunter/guide) could safely get off a kill shot. A client's *well-placed* initial shot helps ensure a successful hunt so that hunter, guide, personnel, and dogs can all return home safely to hunt another day.

Of Africa's coveted dangerous big six, fledgling hunters sometimes mistakenly assume that because of the leopard's size and weight, in comparison to the other five, that it is the easiest to hunt. In fact, the leopard is considered by many professionals to be the most difficult to hunt. So what we have here is a paradox of sorts: *dangerous* versus *difficult*, leading us into discussions, if not inviting downright arguments, such as most dangerous versus least dangerous; most difficult versus least difficult. Answering these questions is tantamount to my pinpointing out specifically what the *best choice* of weapon is for *you*. Too many variables prevail, but I trust that, together, we have covered most of them. That is why I had asked you at the beginning of these related chapters to read through the information as a whole rather than select a single segment of interest.

Leopards are predominately nocturnal. As such, hunting them is usually a nighttime adventure. Hence, high-quality, light-gathering optics is a must. Also, you want optics that can withstand powerful shock from recoil. I've covered holographic sights in an earlier chapter. Regarding traditional telescopic sights, Swarovski and Leupold are both excellent choices. A variable 2-7x40 rifle scope is a good choice. This will give you the versatility of taking close to longer range shots. Your average shot will probably be from 50 to 70 yards. Hunting with hounds or over bait from a stand will generally be the determining factor.

Again, rather than suggest a specific gun manufacturer for reasons already mentioned under the rhinoceros section, we'll home in on caliber. We are dealing with a thin-skinned cat (like the lion) as opposed to the thick skin of say a pachyderm (elephant). Therefore, you do not need a monikered .50 caliber *elephant gun* chambered with a 500-grain weight bullet.

In fact, a .30-06 caliber rifle chambered with a 180-grain bullet suitable for deer hunting would be the ticket for leopard. However, the law in some African jurisdictions decree the .375 (and larger) caliber as the minimum weapon requirement for leopards as well as other big game. If it's the government's official edict, you could stop at that caliber in dealing with this cat because raw power becomes secondary to initial shot placement. Accuracy, as with all six of Africa's most dangerous big game species, is the name of the game. A wounded leopard is a very dangerous animal. Bullet expansion referencing that first and hopefully only shot is of paramount importance.

As versatile as the .30-06 is for most of North America's big game animals, so too is the medium-bore .375 for many of Africa's thin-skinned bush and plains animals. For the thick-skinned group, the big bore .416 is hard to beat for all-around merit.

You have already met Mark Hampton earlier referencing his White Rhino story, consummate, six-continent safari handgun and rifle hunter, magazine writer (Handgun Hunter Magazine), and recipient of the Handgun Hunter of the Year Award. Here's another of his stories.

LEOPARD

By Mark Hampton

The leopard is Africa's most efficient predator. It is the smallest of Africa's Big Five, but that doesn't make this cat any less desirable. The leopard is sleek, fast, cunning, smart, and if wounded, one of the most dangerous animals you will encounter. A big male leopard is an impressive animal – providing a real challenge for adventurous hunters.

There are basically three methods hunters employ when hunting leopard, with baiting being the most common practice. By far the majority of leopards taken in the past have succumbed to this method. Hanging bait, checking bait, building blinds, sitting and waiting for a leopard to jump into the tree are just part of the routine. If you have hunted leopard before, you know the story. I'm sure you've heard of someone sitting in a blind the first night of their hunt and whacking a cat before they recovered from jet lag. How wonderful. Unfortunately not everyone experiences this kind of fortune, and I am one of those hunters who fall on the flip side of that coin. After spending over fifty nights in a blind, I have become familiar with this procedure. I know very little about killing leopard, but I certainly possess more than a basic understanding of hunting these solitary creatures. Some of many evenings in a blind have lasted several hours, sneaking into the blind around four in the afternoon then climbing out by nine or ten o'clock and heading back to camp. There were other times that found us in the blind all night, waiting for "ol' spots" to show up in the wee hours of the morning. No talking, not making any noise, just sitting there and being quiet. By the time daylight arrived, I would be so stiff I could barely crawl out of the little hut. Boy, was that fun! These uneventful scenarios went on for days and nights. Several hunts with different outfitters in different countries produced little results. It seemed like I was jinxed!

Another way to put your cat in the salt is by good fortune. You could get extremely lucky and take a leopard by bumping into one accidentally, a chance encounter, while hunting for other game. This happens very rarely in broad daylight, but it has happened. I missed two opportunities such as this in less than twenty-four hours. That's right; twice I have seen leopard in broad daylight and missed both cats. Neither shot was particularly difficult. I got nervous and excited and, to be perfectly honest, simply blew both opportunities. One came in the evening, the other early the next morning. Pretty amazing, isn't it? I had nightmares about those encounters for months afterward. While I haven't labored on the subject as it is too psychologically painful, it's plain to see my luck with leopard is dismal. Somehow I did finally manage to take a leopard, but it never did satisfy my cat-hunting endeavor.

Another way to take a feline is with the use of a well-trained pack of hounds. This is basically the same method we use to hunt mountain lions here in North America. At one time, hound hunts were popular—especially for hunters with track records like mine. This is not a new way to hunt leopard. Cats have been pursued with hounds for decades in Africa. Long before this method became popular with itinerant sportsmen, leopards were pursued with dogs on what was earlier in time referred to as the Dark Continent. There are a few outfitters with well-trained hounds that provide today's leopard hunter with an exciting option, much different from the traditional blind-hunting method. I can only assume there are hunters like myself that don't "jump for joy" when they think about sitting endlessly in a leopard blind. After hunting bear, mountain lion, and other game with man's best friend, I thoroughly enjoy watching and listening to a pack of well-trained hounds in hot pursuit. I was more than ready to experience this type of hunt. Granted, there are a few critics of dog hunts. However, one could argue that while hunting a cat over bait with a light may be traditional, it is not exactly purism by any definition.

It was late June when my wife, Karen, and I flew to Namibia for a ten-day hunt.

At that time, hunting leopards with hounds was perfectly legal. Since this hunt, Namibia no longer allows leopard hunting with dogs. Namibia is a beautiful country with diverse habitat including deserts, mountains, rolling savannah (grasslands and scattered thornbushes). Its scenic beauty and abundance of game makes for an ideal safari experience. Some of Africa's best gemsboks thrive here, along with some monster kudu. Compared to many parts of Africa, the cost of a hunting safari provides a real value-for-money bargain. This country is big geographically but sparsely populated by humans. Namibia has a stable population of big game including leopard. At that time, the country issued two hundred fifty permits annually. Many of those leopards thrived in ranch country, and their presence was not welcome. The cats are decimated by employing poison, rifle, trap, and any other way imaginable. Some of the ranches have breeding herds of black-faced impala as well as roan, not to mention other plains game. An efficient predator like the leopard is not well thought of when they decimate a rancher's game. This is not much different than any other ranch country regardless of its border. It doesn't take long for these elusive cats to become well-educated. This could be one reason why success rates are relatively low when baiting. Over the years these leopards have learned that when they encounter a free meal in the form of bait, they encounter a problem. This is another reason I wanted to increase my odds by using hounds. Lord knows I needed all the help possible.

John, our dog handler, has been hunting with hounds most of his adult life. I had been talking with him for several years about doing a hound hunt. John likes hunting leopard in Namibia, coordinating his efforts with other Namibian professional hunters and landowners. That year, Karen and I decided we were going to quit talking about a hound hunt and go experience the chase. After clearing customs in Windhoek, our PH (professional hunter) drove us four hours north near Outjo. Baits had been hung previously, hoping some big cat would make a mistake, plus we would not only spend time looking for tracks around those baits, but along riverbeds, roads, and wherever else we could search. This can be time-consuming but all part of the game.

We hit the ground running the first morning, and I was anxious to start looking for tracks. Ideally, once tracks have been located, you determine if they are fresh enough, or large enough to turn the dogs loose. Hopefully, they can sort out the tracks, and a chase pursues. This could happen the first day or may take several days to find suitable tracks. I told John previously not to turn the dogs loose until a big track, indicating a large male, was found. I didn't care if that took two days or ten.

At first we checked some bait sites. Nothing left tracks except for a few small varmints. Then we began searching around waterholes. Only spoors (tracks) of many species of antelope were found visiting the water. Several outstanding gemsbok bulls along with plentiful herds of beautiful springbok were encountered frequently. Some of the trackers wanted to walk down a dry riverbed in hopes of locating signs of leopard activity. After walking up and down the riverbed for a few hours without finding any leopard sign, I was beginning to think my leopard jinx was still in place.

We were hunting an area with a decent population of leopard. As our PH had a ton of experience with cats, you put in your time . . . and eventually the odds swing.

Later in the hunt, when we finally did find a large set of tracks crossing the road—definitely made by a big tom—John turned four of his hounds out of the truck to see if they could get something going. The dogs worked the track methodically. They eventually became more excited, sorting out the tracks, then took off. Our PH dropped the tailgate and let the rest of the pack join in. The hounds consisted of various breeds of fox hounds, Walkers, and bluetick. When the barking became more intense, I knew we were in for a chase. I was armed with a Thompson/Center .308 Encore rifle and Winchester's newest XP3 cartridge offering. Keeping up with the dogs was impossible. I took off running as fast as I could, which is pretty slow, trying to stay at least in hearing distance. When I first heard the dogs baying, it gave me a boost of energy, motivating me to pick up the pace as fast as possible. But that didn't last very long, and you could tell the dogs were off and running again.

Apparently the cat had jumped from the tree and took off. The chase lasted longer than I anticipated. When the dogs finally barked and bayed the second time, Mr. Spots was in the top of a huge thorn tree. Some of the dogs managed to *climb half way up the tree* in all the excitement. If I hadn't seen this with my own eyes, I wouldn't have believed it, either. The Namibian PH and dog handler both told me this cat was getting nervous and wasn't going to stay around long. The dogs were barking frantically. I tried to find the feline, but the leaves were so thick it was difficult to see. As I worked my way around the tree slowly, Karen kept asking, "Do you see it, do you see it?" When I did get in a position to see a part of the body, John informed me it was a big male—and not to take all day for a shot. After getting in position to determine the best possible view, we were somewhere around fifty yards away. It was impossible to see any more than his block-shaped head and thick neck. I thought to myself, *if ever you need a good shot, now would be a wonderful time*. The last thing any of us wanted was to see is a wounded leopard hitting the ground. I quickly placed the crosshairs in the middle of the base of its neck and dropped the hammer on the T/C Encore .308. As the Winchester 150-grain XP3 bullet struck home, the cat slumped and went limp, never knowing what hit him. Instead of falling to the ground, he became entangled in all the thorns and hung there in the tree as the dogs continued barking enthusiastically. At this time, I don't know who was happier, me or the hounds. All of us were surprised and pleased that the cat was stone dead on a single shot as the Winchester factory load performed flawlessly. One of the trackers had to climb the tree and shake the cat loose. I didn't envy his job, what with all the thorns he endured. When the 150-pound cat hit the ground, my leopard hunting quest had been fulfilled. It was a rewarding moment thanks to the hard work of the well-trained hounds. Karen couldn't wait to hold the leopard; I couldn't wait to take her picture. It was an exciting hunt, and I'm thrilled my wife could experience the chase and extreme adrenaline rush.

Mark and dog handlers with big male leopard

Hound hunts are currently available in certain regions of Zimbabwe and Mozambique. After hunting bear, mountain lion, boar, and other game with dogs, I personally enjoy the action and watching the dogs work. There are some that frown on these hunts. Others may get the idea that when you use hounds, the hunt is 100% successful. I can assure you this is not the case. You may want to experience it for yourself before you rush to judgment.

Mark and Karen enjoyed the leopard hunt in Namibia

Every hunter, at some time or another, faces an adversary that presents challenges and difficulties. If that hasn't happened to you, it will if you hunt long enough. I know that my initial, dismal track record concerning leopard caused me psychological trauma and many sleepless nights. But today, this big tom leopard is just a few feet away from the computer in my office. Every day I look at him and remember those sleepless nights in a leopard blind. I remember the chase and thrill of the hunt—providing everlasting memories.

With my previous track record on leopards, it would be difficult to give anyone advice. I would recommend booking your cat hunt in an area yielding a strong population. Plus, hiring an experienced PH with lots of cat hunts under his belt will only stack the odds in your favor.

Firearms ideally suited for leopard do not necessarily have to be big-bore calibers. Heck, a big male leopard will top the scales at 150 pounds. These thin-skinned cats are of small bone structure and, therefore, do not require the same treatment as Cape buffalo or elephant. However, I cannot overemphasize the importance of shot placement. There is nobody on this planet with an IQ of over 75 who will enjoy following-up on a wounded leopard. The shot is usually not a difficult one, and the distance is rarely over 75 yards. Nevertheless, you may not believe how challenging such a shot can be when your heart feels like it's beating out of your chest. A well-placed shot from your favorite firearm—be it handgun or rifle [as is the latter in this case]—will be cherished, providing a lifetime of fond memories.

Note: Although Mark Hampton is predominantly the consummate handgun guy, having taken over 190 species on six continents with a handgun, no less, it is illegal to take a leopard with a handgun in Namibia.

CHAPTER 38

AUSTRALIA'S BAD-TO-THE-BONE BOVINES

In terms of hunting the world's most dangerous big game land animals, one would certainly envision Africa, picturing at least some of the six we encountered in the bonus section of this handbook thus far. But how would certain members of the Down Under cattle family stack up against Africa's deadliest? Well, before J.D. Jones introduced me to two such animals through his exciting prose, I initially and ignorantly thought of them as beasts of burden. I truly hadn't a clue. You met the man in Chapters 34 and 35 narrating his hippo and Cape buffalo stories. Let's see how these seemingly placid Australian brutes measure up against Africa's most lethal. You may be quite surprised. But first, a brief description:

Banteng

Australian banteng, a bovine species, are hunted on the Corbourg Peninsula in the Northern Territory. A trophy bull can top the Toledo at 1300 pounds, with horns measuring 24 to 30 inches long. Banteng can certainly present a challenge to the safari hunter in that the animal is intelligent, elusive, and highly alert. It is interesting to note that Australia has the only legal hunting population of banteng in the world! A .375 caliber rifle is your standard weapon of choice; a .338 Magnum being the smallest caliber you would want.

Water buffalo

Australia's premier big game guy is the water buffalo. A smarter choice of weapon would be a .375 caliber rifle over the .338 Magnum. A trophy bull weighing in at 2400 pounds is going to prove a handful. The Australian water buffalo is every bit as challenging and dangerous to hunt as Africa's Cape buffalo, and many would say even more so. The water buffalo is not an easy animal to put down, and may require several shots, at which point you could expect a charge. The horns of a mature bull could span anywhere between 38 and 60 inches, with an average length of each horn measuring between 27 and 36 inches. The diameter at the base of a horn varies between 16 and 19 inches. The weight of an average bull runs between 1500 and

1700 pounds.

Now that you have something of an idea referencing these potentially dangerous creatures, let's see what J.D. Jones has to say. Another reminder that J.D. is owner/operator and president of SSK Industries—having invented JDJ cartridges used worldwide. The man is a world-renowned ballistics wizard, book author, editor, and accomplished safari hunter.

THOSE BIG BAD BOVINE TYPE BUGGERS (Part I)

By J.D. JONES

Water buffalo

Really big guys abound in Australia. The Asian Buff (aptly called water buffalo) has often been viewed as being anything but a dangerous animal. Water buff may bring to mind an image of some poor soul toiling behind the beast in a rice paddy, working his ass of for a starving family. After work, it doubles as the family pet. That may be true in Asia but not Australia, because they are not domesticated. First, an adult male is far larger than a Cape buff—up to twice the body weight! Secondly, in places such as Arnhem Land (located in the northeastern corner of the Northern Territory), where they have never seen a human being, they are the king of that region. There are no predators to fear, and most of them are not afraid of you. Some may resent your puny-appearing presence and will take offense to it. That can mean an aggressive act toward you. When I was hunting them, I was testing the larger JDJ handgun calibers. The Australian government had an eradication program in progress. Wow! Shoot all you can, and thank you, Mate. Come back and do it again.

The best hunt was to helicopter half a fuel load into Arnhem Land, find a lot of buff, put down a camp, and move in two or three days. I found the reaction of those animals quite interesting. Walking in knee-high grass, often a bull would get up 20 to 30 yards ahead of me, give me a look, then trot toward me—nose-level. Obviously, they had no intention of stopping. Generally, I would drop to one knee, bringing the gun to about heart level, then simply heart-shoot him. Each one turned to his left in a "J" hook and went down at the point of the "J". What would have happened if I didn't shoot or screwed up the shot? Barry, my PH, said they were charging. Initially, I felt it was more of a curiosity thing on their behalf. Barry explained that in close quarters the head goes down and the horns get ready for work. Standing and shooting for the brain wasn't really an option as the nose would have been the target, which presents an up-down-sideways moving target with a LOT of mass behind it for a bullet to travel through on its way to the brain. Guess I'll never really know as I felt 10 yards was close enough. Eventually, I did get the feeling that they didn't want to make a new friend. The 'charge or no charge' question got interesting, but Barry really didn't care much if one handed me my ass. That led to trying to get them to charge.

My hunting partner put a 500-grain Solid through the shoulders of an old bull below the spine and above the heart. It just stood there. Barry said he missed as he saw dust kick up behind him. Looking through binoculars, I clearly saw the hit. I could see that it looked like he wanted to move and couldn't. I took the Super

Redhawk .44 Mag loaded with 320-grain JDJ cast bullets and went around in front of him, carefully approaching. He appeared to be getting excited. At 6 to 8 yards, he attempted to lunge at me, but his broken shoulders collapsed—he went down with a bellow. As soon as he tried to move, the broken shoulders failed him. I believe it to have been a true attempt to charge.

In another incident, an old swaybacked bull slowly walked past at 30 yards. I rested my forearm against a tree and put a 550-grain .475 JD cast bullet dead center through both lungs. He instantly became a mad bull. The swayback walked away, straightened out, slashed his tail violently then swung his head around looking for what stung him. As he breathed, clearly visible vapor came out of the entrance hole. I handed Barry the .475 and stepped out beside the tree so the bull could see me. No hesitation; he came at me as fast as he could and lowered his nose to get the horns in attack position. The first 320-grain .44 at 1500 fps went high—into its neck, penetrating only the skin until the bullet stopped. The second 320 went through its head, under the brain. No reaction. I finally got it right and brained him with the third shot.

Maybe I better even up the score a bit. My hunting partner dropped a bull on his chest with a 500-grain .45-70. It didn't even roll over. I went after his buddy and dropped him in a few minutes. While taking a few photos, Barry told me of the other bull. Said he had been fighting, and his boss (the continuous bone shield of their horns) was all beat up and full of maggots. Wow—he was right. I quickly changed to a macro lens and knelt in front of him to get close-up photos, so he jumped up and ran over me. Luckily I was just bowled over as he left the scene. Then comes the 'run for a while, shoot 'im in the ass for a while,' continuing a couple more times to get him down. This type of shooting on very large animals is how we learned that a 500-grain 458 FMJ from a .45-70 at 1500 fps will penetrate up to about seven feet of animal. In this case, the first shot was a bit high and struck the spinal process at the base, breaking the vertebrae and either paralyzing or knocking him out. It didn't seem to bother him much when he got his dander up.

While walking on an eighteen-inch wide dirt strip between water on both sides of me, suddenly a buff erupted out of the water like an atomic submarine at max surface speed, right beside me. I had a .375 in my hand, and by the time his hips broke water, I had snapped a shot into his spine just ahead of the pelvis, which promptly paralyzed his backside. Another shot to the head ended it. I know it doesn't sound like much, but to me it ranks right up there in fun with a real charge.

On another trip, I got involved with three other Australian mates (mate: a friend who may be really crazy) with a rented Toyota pick-up and a trailer-full of gear. We struck out into the wilderness. What a misadventure! But what fun. I was in the cab when we drove into what was apparently a large herd of buff sleeping. The buff jumped and ran. The truck stopped. The two guys in the bed let loose with everything they had. When it got quiet, I yelled, "Everybody empty?" and was answered in the affirmative. I jumped out with the .44 and ran after the herd. In a short while, as I ran, a buff jumped up in front of me and, obviously surprised, went up on his back legs, moving its head to my left to avoid collision. I raised my left arm, jabbed the .44 at his head, and yanked one off double-action, bumped him slightly, and kept on running. I recall one badly hit buff wanting to come at me but was just too far gone. After the rodeo, I checked the one I bumped into. The 320 grainer went into his throat and exited out the top of the boss—instant dead brain shot. The muzzle blast blew quite a lot of hair off, and I'm guessing it was less than a foot from contact. The next issue of *Water Buff News* was headlined, "Family Member Charged and Killed by Crazed Human!" Ha, ha.

There were a lot more fun incidents, and I'm sure this sounds like a lot of shooting. Correct; in the good old days it was a varmint hunt—donkeys-horses- buff- and an occasional camel. My normal ammo load for a trip was 2500 rounds, and I never brought a live round back.

Well, I've got to stop here before these pages become a book instead of a chapter. So, as an aside, getting away from the exciting incidents referencing Australia's water buffalo, let's tame it down a bit and taper off with a brief banteng hunt.

THOSE BIG BAD BOVINE TYPE BUGGERS (Part II)

By J.D. JONES

Banteng

Its reputation is mixed. Spooky and smart, it is not afraid of anything when wounded. They live on the north coast of Australia near the equator in what I call jungle forest. It is fly-in country inhabited by a few Abos (Aboriginal), government employees, and saltwater crocodiles that are truly dangerous. Shortly before I went, two friends each spent three miserable weeks there without firing a shot. Both urged me to forget it. Barry had a camp there and suggested we spend a few days looking around and radio for a plane to get us whenever we felt liked leaving. There were a few vehicles around, and Barry rented one. We opened camp; it was HOT and HUMID—exactly the kind of weather I hate. Barry suggested a ride to cool off. Ten minutes from camp we entered an area where there had been a recent fire. Everything was black, except where bright sunlight penetrated the trees. There were huge anthills, and Barry wanted to tell me about them. We walked about 50 yards from the truck, and a herd of about twenty banteng slowly walked past us. Dragging up the rear was the herd bull. Barry said, "He's good—it isn't much of a hunt—but . . . . " I raised the .416 JDJ loaded with a 400-grain Woodleigh soft point and, before I could shoot, he laid down. The ashes from the fire were black. He was black. The light was really poor, quite contrasting. I could just make out a big black lump through that miserable 2X scope. Barry looked through the binoculars, asking if I could see the green weed. I nodded a yes. He said, "Shoot it." It was about a 40-yard shot. The weed got cut off, and the banteng never got up. Yeah, I'll take an easy one whenever I can get it. Barry radioed for a plane, and we left for more misadventures in the casino nightlife of Darwin, which I am absolutely NEVER going to write about.

****

www.ingramcontent.com/pod-product-compliance
Lightning Source LLC
Chambersburg PA
CBHW041402020526
44115CB00036B/4